P9-CBS-633

JAN 1 4 2020

796.0284
Metzl. B

Praise for Brian Metzler and *Kicksology*

"No one alive knows more than Brian Metzler about that great modern indulgence: the running shoe. *Kicksology* captures the science, the sagas, and the surprisingly tantalizing backstories surrounding a subject that's as personal and passionate to true believers as any religion. If you've ever laced rubber to your feet for a run, you'll be captivated by this delightfully probing book."

CHRISTOPHER MCDOUGALL
author of *Born to Run*

"If there's a such thing as a living encyclopedia of running shoes, it's Brian Metzler. Not only does he own more shoes than anyone I know, he knows more about them than anyone I know. His passion for running shoes, their history, evolution, and application is unmatched and speaks to my sole."

MARIO FRAIOLI
The Morning Shakeout

"It takes a true running shoe geek to write an informative and entertaining book about running shoes. That's who Brian Metzler is, and that's what he gives us with *Kicksology*. Like the proverbial kid in a candy store, Metzler samples each new shoe—minimalist, maximalist, zero-drop, VaporFly, and so on—with unabated enthusiasm. He also interviews the researchers and designers behind each shoe to provide crazy stories and new insights we haven't heard before."

AMBY BURFOOT
1968 Boston Marathon winner,
Runner's World editor at large

"*Kicksology* is a great survey of the modern history of running shoes. A must-read for anyone in the sneaker game."

MATT POWELL
sports industry analyst

"I loved reading *Kicksology* and recommend it a must-read for anyone who runs. Brian Metzler has been one of the country's top running writers for a long time because he asks the right questions and delivers smart, thought-provoking answers with exceptional storytelling. He presents the untold stories of running shoes: where we are, how we got here, and what the future holds for your feet." **JAY DICHARRY, MPT**
leading biomechanist, running gait expert,
and author of *Running Rewired*

"No one has more knowledge and passion about running shoes and the industry than Brian Metzler. With *Kicksology*, he delivers a compelling and engaging read." **LISA JHUNG**
author of *Trailhead* and
Running That Doesn't Suck

"In *Kicksology*, we too can run in Metzler's shoes and gain access to his hard-earned insights. The result is a fascinating journey." **LAURA CLARK**
American Trail
Running Association

"*Kicksology* is a personal tour of running shoe history, design, and business that only Brian Metzler could write. He has the uncanny ability to be near the center of every new trend and takes the reader on an informative journey through the many interesting characters, stories, and ideas that make running shoes fascinating." **JONATHAN BEVERLY**
Editor, *PodiumRunner*

KICKSOLOGY

THE HYPE, SCIENCE, CULTURE & COOL OF RUNNING SHOES

BRIAN METZLER

Boulder, Colorado

Copyright © 2019 by Brian Metzler

All rights reserved. Printed in the United States of America.

No part of this book may be reproduced, stored in a retrieval system, or transmitted, in any form or by any means, electronic or photocopy or otherwise, without the prior written permission of the publisher except in the case of brief quotations within critical articles and reviews.

4745 Walnut Street, Unit A
Boulder, CO 80301-2587 USA

VeloPress is the leading publisher of books on endurance sports and is a division of Pocket Outdoor Media. Focused on cycling, triathlon, running, swimming, and nutrition/diet, VeloPress books help athletes achieve their goals of going faster and farther. Preview books and contact us at velopress.com.

Distributed in the United States and Canada by Ingram Publisher Services

Library of Congress Cataloging-in-Publication Data

Names: Metzler, Brian, author.
Title: Kicksology: the hype, science, culture & cool of running shoes / Brian Metzler.
Description: Boulder, Colorado: VeloPress, [2019] | Includes index. |
Identifiers: LCCN 2019025044 (print) | LCCN 2019025045 (ebook) |
   ISBN 9781937715915 (paperback) | ISBN 9781948006088 (ebook) |
Subjects: LCSH: Running shoes. | Sporting goods industry.
Classification: LCC GV1061.6 .M48 2019 (print) | LCC GV1061.6 (ebook) |
   DDC 796.028/4—dc23
LC record available at https://lccn.loc.gov/2019025044
LC ebook record available at https://lccn.loc.gov/2019025045

This paper meets the requirements of ANSI/NISO Z39.48-1992 (Permanence of Paper).

Art direction by Vicki Hopewell
Cover photo by D. Scott Clark
Cover and interior design by Karen Matthes and Beth Skelley
Composition by Beth Skelley
Interior photographs by Brian Metzler except photo insert page 1 (bottom), page 2 (top and bottom), page 3 (top and bottom), page 4 (top), page 5 (top), Scott Draper/*Competitor*; page 6 (top), courtesy of Hoka One One; page 7 (bottom), courtesy of University of Colorado; page 8 (bottom), courtesy of Saucony.

19   20   21 / 10   9   8   7   6   5   4   3   2   1

CONTENTS

Preface

I vividly remember the day I got my first pair of kicks. They were cherry red, and they made me feel really fast.

I was 5 years old and had envied the sneakers my older brother had gotten the previous year while I was still stuck wearing a pair of little boy's saddle shoes. When it was time for me to get new shoes the next spring, my mom took me to the Shoe Tree store in our suburban Chicago town. The salesman measured my foot in one of those metal devices and then disappeared into the back. I remember him coming out of the back room with a red-white-and-blue box and kneeling down in front of me. I was smiling from ear to ear, feeling like my chest would burst open with excitement, when he fit them to my feet. Even as I write this, more than 40 years later, I can still feel that pure joy.

Once I got those sneakers, I started running everywhere. Places you might normally walk—to the bus stop, in the grocery store, across the playground—I ran instead. It was as if the shoes had helped me discover a new part of myself—a yet untapped inner athlete—and gave me license to dart around with short, sharp bursts of speed wherever I went.

Back then, I certainly wasn't what you'd call a runner. Like most kids, I just enjoyed the sheer thrill of racing around at recess, with neighborhood friends, and with my brother. I wouldn't join a cross-country team for another six years, in middle school. Yet early on, there were inklings. I vividly recall first grade "field day," when, wearing a pair of sharp blue-and-white sneakers, I ran my guts out in the 50-yard dash and finished second to a girl in my class, Lori Habbegar. This was hard to swallow because I had already beaten all the boys and was certain I would wind up with the fastest time of the day. A humbling blow, but inspiring nonetheless.

I'm not sure what it was about sneakers—and eventually running shoes—that moved me so powerfully. I know I liked the feeling of running fast, the cool sensation of tearing around under my own power, and I'm sure I correlated those positive feelings early on with the shoes I was wearing. I didn't have a profound Forrest Gump moment, but wearing sneakers just made me want to run.

That first pair of red kicks was likely a pair of Pro-Keds, a popular brand for kids growing up in the '70s. And so were most of the other pairs I wore through elementary school. For me back then, sneakers were just sneakers. I had no idea about the first running boom that was rising up around me, making everyone want to join the jogging craze. I wasn't aware that a nascent company called Nike was starting to make waves as a running shoe brand or that long-standing companies such as New Balance, Brooks, and Adidas, along with upstarts Saucony, Pony, and Etonic, were all part of a mushrooming industry that was growing by leaps and bounds year after year.

Even when I joined the cross-country team in 1980 as a sixth grader, I didn't know anything about shoes. I ran in the same sneakers that I wore to school and everywhere else except church. But I was a typical adolescent, so before long the brand and style of my sneakers started to matter. Some of the older kids I admired on the cross-country team bragged about their shoes—mostly Nike and Adidas—and some of my sixth-grade friends mimicked their chatter.

Just before the start of seventh grade, I informed my parents that I had saved enough money from my paper route to buy a pair of Adidas Oregon running shoes. They had a light gray nylon upper with maroon stripes, but it was the mesh netting around the midsole that drew me in. I had learned from Adidas advertisements that this mesh was known as the "Dellinger Web" and had been codeveloped by University of Oregon track coach Bill Dellinger as a way to harness Newton's third law of motion. The netting was said to disperse the shock of heel-strike impacts through the entire sole, ultimately reducing leg fatigue. I didn't know what most of that meant, but it sounded like exactly what I needed.

Although those ads seem entirely gimmicky to me now when I spot them on Pinterest, they sure grabbed my attention back then. I dragged my mom to a running specialty store, the Competitive Foot, in a nearby town to see this shoe for myself. Holding it was the clincher. These were by far the lightest shoes I'd ever held, and they just *looked* fast. Cool, too, which was as important as anything else to my seventh-grade sensibilities.

I didn't know anything about the long history of running and shoes connected to the University of Oregon; I would learn about Steve Prefontaine, Bill Bowerman, Phil Knight, and the rise of Nike only after reading a *Sports Illustrated* article a few years later, when I was in high school. But in my estimation, those Oregons were worth every penny of the $41.95 suggested retail price. Although I was disappointed when the high-tech webbing wore out after a few months of training, the shoes inspired me to run more and took me to new heights as a runner. Even when the season ended, I wore them every day because I was sure they were supercharged with an intangible vibe that just made me better.

That was my first real touchpoint to a product and an industry to which I would be intimately connected later in life. I made a personal connection to the sport through that shoe, maybe because of my modest running success that season or maybe because I was plenty gullible and intrigued by the seductive marketing that had become pervasive among running shoe brands. Probably some of both. Years later, my heart still races when I see a new shoe model for the first time.

After the Oregon, there were new obsessions: a pair of New Balance 894s that propelled me to a fourth-place finish in the middle school cross-country championships and a pair of Nike Yankee lightweight trainers that helped me set some sprinting records during track season the following spring. And on it went. For every highlight I had in my early running, there was a shoe to go with it.

By the time I went to college, running and a fascination with running shoes were in my blood. As a track athlete in college, I envied my elite-level teammates who received free training shoes and spikes as part of their scholarship deals. When my shoes wore out during my freshman year, I sheepishly asked my coach if a lower-level walk-on runner like me could get new shoes, as my All-American teammates did. He pulled a paper voucher out of his desk, scribbled his signature, and told me to go get some new shoes.

I visited the Body 'n' Sole running specialty store in Champaign, Illinois, where I felt the comforting and stirring vibes I'd always felt at the Competitive Foot near my hometown. They sized me up for a pair of white-gray-and-black Converse shoes with a cool black star logo on each side, which many of my teammates were wearing at the time. It's hard to describe the pride and joy I felt when they sent me out the door without having to pay for them, but it closely resembled the exhilaration I'd experienced years before with those red Keds at the Shoe Tree.

My college running career didn't evolve the way I had hoped, but I was a convert now, a lifelong runner and shoe geek. After college, I left the track behind for 5K road races. While working my first newspaper jobs around the Chicago area, I would visit every running store I came across and stay up-to-date with new shoes through ads and reviews in *Runner's World* and *Track & Field News*. If I ever felt as if I was starting to get burned out with running, I would visit a running shop or sign up for a race. Sometimes just seeing new shoe models was enough to inspire me anew, and actually buying a new pair was the unfailing catalyst to reinvigorate my training.

When I started visiting running stores in the 1990s, however, it was clear that running and shoes were changing dramatically and rapidly. Light and fast models were being replaced, largely by shoes that were bigger and significantly built up, with more girth, more height, more weight. Many included flashy plastic, metallic, and see-through elements.

I could see that these models weren't for me. I reverted to wearing lightweight, low-to-the-ground racing flats. I wasn't doing much fast racing by then, but I appreciated the proprioceptive feel those shoes provided that was missing in the padded, clunky shoes on the shelves. Still, I was perplexed and intrigued by the evolution I was seeing—why were running shoes evolving like this?

Within a few years, I started writing for a few sports magazines. One day my editor, who knew I was an avid trail runner, asked me to review trail running shoes for a spring issue. I jumped at the chance and began contacting all of the major running shoe brands for wear-test samples. I was impressed with some and disappointed with others. Trail running as a sport was new on the scene, and two types of companies were competing for the trail running shoe business: hiking boot brands and running shoe brands.

The running shoe brands were producing models that were similar to their road shoes, only with a more traction-oriented outsole. The hiking boot brands were producing rugged and durable shoes that were heavy, rigid, and not very nimble or runnable, even if they did offer loads of protection.

That article and its examination of a nascent trail running and running shoe trend was part of the impetus that led me to found *Trail Runner* magazine. As the fledgling magazine's editor-in-chief, I was suddenly no longer just a fan and attentive observer on the outer edge. Rather, I was thrust deep into the running shoe industry itself, meeting with brand representatives at trade shows and race expos, connecting with marketing and PR directors, and getting my first glimpses of how this growing industry really worked.

I had a behind-the-curtain view into an enormous business that was becoming more powerful every year, with sales of more than $2 billion by the late '90s. It was fascinating, but I started to become both more curious and more skeptical about how running shoes were conceived, designed, built, and marketed. As a longtime sports journalist and devoted runner who had competed in everything from short sprints to ultramarathons, I had what I'd consider a fairly encyclopedic knowledge of shoes, yet even I couldn't understand how certain shoes ever made it to market.

Furthermore, the industry's seeming obsession with limiting the movement of the foot to control pronation and supination had me stumped. I had long preferred to run in lightweight, neutral shoes and in doing so had remained entirely injury-free, yet once I started wear-testing the popular stability and motion-control shoes, I found myself getting injured often.

And it wasn't just me. Injury rates were on the rise, a subject that I was reading and writing about and being asked about constantly. None of this was adding up for me. What was really going on?

Finally, there was a growing chasm between runners. With performance-oriented competitors wanting light, agile shoes for training and racing and an increasing number of recreational participants seeking cushioning, comfort, and casual style, the industry was receiving and delivering seriously mixed signals.

With all of that muddying the waters of shoe design, development, marketing, and sales, how could I—or anyone—find an optimal shoe amid the cluster of conflicting aims and variables?

In more than 20 years of work with the leading running and outdoor media outlets, I have had the opportunity to explore nearly every corner of this wide, ever-morphing world of running shoes. I've wear-tested, analyzed, and reviewed more than 1,200 pairs of shoes from nearly every major and minor brand. I have conducted magazine wear-tests with input from recreational and elite runners, written countless shoe reviews, visited shoe factories, sat in on the design process with brands, analyzed shoe trends on National Public Radio, and helped a new running retail store get off the ground. Along the way, I've interviewed hundreds of shoe designers, biomechanists, marketing executives, physical therapists, podiatrists, retailers, top athletes, running form gurus, coaches, and business leaders. And I've personally run more than 75,000 miles in my life.

Yet with all the miles I have run, all of the shoes I have tested, and all that I've learned about the industry, I still have questions. Why are shoes constantly changing yet still not making a dent in the injury rate? Can a shoe really make you more efficient, faster, and healthier? Why have the prices of running shoes more than doubled in the past 30 years? Why do some shoes thrive, whereas others just don't cut it? Why are most runners getting slower, while a select few are running unfathomably fast times? Can specialty shops, long the go-to source of not just running shoe knowledge but also running culture, inspiration, and community, survive in the digital era?

The journey of writing this book has helped me answer some of those questions. It dives deep into the powerful industry of running and also marks the continuation of my own quest to find the best next pair of shoes for me, even as the business constantly morphs and changes at the mercy and behest of new fashion, new online sales mechanisms, new science and research, and, new runners who view the act of running—and running shoes—differently.

At its core, this book celebrates a fascination with and curiosity about running shoes—what is real, what is hype, what has advanced running, what has advanced fashion, and what's next—that I suspect many runners share through our common joy of lacing up a pair of shoes and heading out for a run.

1
THERE'S NO BIZ LIKE SHOE BIZ

You cannot put the same shoe on every foot.
PUBLILIUS SYRUS

It's a humid Saturday morning in mid-August in Naperville, Illinois, and this picturesque suburb of Chicago is just starting to wake up. I'm up and out early, hoping to beat the coming heat. Just before 7:30 a.m., I lace up a pair of New Balance 1080s and head to the Naperville Riverwalk for an easy-paced out-and-back along the concrete paths that follow the West Branch of the DuPage River as it meanders through town.

The route is virtually empty when I begin the 9-mile jaunt, save for an elderly man out for an early walk with his dog. But after I turn around at my halfway point in the heavily wooded forest preserve northwest of town and start to head back, I'm met by a continual stream of runners, cyclists, and walkers, all apparently eager to meet the day before summer temperatures start to rise.

As I pass an empty playground, two women jog by in the opposite direction, their animated conversation about their kids' sporting activities fading in and then out as we pass. I note a vague blur of brightly colored tops and swinging ponytails, but what stands out in crystal-clear detail are their shoes. One sports a pair of black-teal-and-magenta neutral Brooks Ghosts, while the other has on royal-blue-and-pink ASICS GEL-Kayano stability trainers. Stability makes sense, I think, given the second runner's wide-swinging elbow and slightly off-kilter gait.

In the next mile, an older man in a shapeless gray T-shirt and black shorts ambles toward me with a staccato shuffle. He nods, which in the universal language of running is a gesture of greeting, acceptance, and best wishes for a good run. I've already taken in his blue-and-white New Balance trainers, which look like they've covered quite a few miles. I nod back and raise my hand in a congenial wave. *He probably bought those shoes at Dick's,* I muse, knowing that that midlevel pair was never sold at specialty running stores. Given how beat-up the shoes look and how dead the midsole foam must surely be, I wonder what kind of chronic running ailments he suffers from.

I slow to a jog as I approach Naperville Riverwalk Park, where I parked my rental car. A runner is stretching beside the path. His Cubs hat, perched jauntily backward on his head, catches my eye first, as I'm an avid Cubs fan myself. But my gaze quickly sweeps down to his royal-blue Hoka Bondi 5s, shoes so cushioned and high off the ground that they look almost cartoonish. He's a tall guy with a big frame; no doubt he appreciates that particular shoe's extra cushioning, I think.

I'm not judging these runners. I'm honestly just a running shoe geek, and this is a guessing game I enjoy playing. Truth is, I can't help but check out what kicks the people around me are wearing.

I flew to Chicago from Boulder to visit old friends, but I'm here in Naperville this morning on a different kind of mission: to meet with Kris Hartner, founder and owner of the Naperville Running Company (NRC), to discuss the state of the retail running shoe business and to experience a day in the life of his store.

Hartner opened NRC in 2000 in a trendy downtown section of Naperville, and it has since earned a reputation as one of the most successful running shops in the United States, including Running Store of the Year honors in 2009 and 2013—the only store in the country to earn that distinction more than once since the trade magazine *Running Insight* started the award program in 2006. I want to know what NRC is doing so right in a climate where so many other retail stores are struggling.

After a light stretch, I head back to my car for a quick change of clothes, ditching my sweat-soaked running gear for shorts and flip-flops. In need of caffeine and postrun nourishment, I pull out my phone and consult Yelp for a nearby coffee shop. The app comes back with an assortment of national chains in a six-block radius, including two Starbucks, a DAVIDsTEA, an Einstein Bros. Bagels, and a Le Pain Quotidien café, and I'm disappointed that there isn't a truly local shop in the bunch.

As I reluctantly head toward a Starbucks a block away, a tight pack of wiry 20-somethings zips by, running at a fast clip along the river path. I surmise from their red-and-white gear that they're from nearby North Central College, which I know has a standout cross-country team. Most, but not all, are wearing Nikes, I note, but as fast as they are running, I can make out only a few swoosh logos, not the specific models.

I queue at Starbucks to order a skinny vanilla latte and an egg sandwich, scanning my phone for sports scores and catching up on e-mails as I wait. One e-mail is from LeftLane Sports, a discount running site that is currently advertising hot deals on running shoes for as low as $29.95. When I tap on the e-mail and open the newsletter, I notice that last year's version of the New Balance 1080—the shoes I wore on my morning run— is on sale for $79.99. I paid $140 for that very shoe less than 10 months ago. The reason it's so cheap, I know, is that a new edition has come out, devaluing the previous version.

Located about 30 miles west of Chicago, Naperville is the quintessential modern Midwestern town. It began as a mill site and farming town in the 1830s and got a boost when an east-west rail line connected it to Chicago in 1864. The town began really growing after World War II amid the area's suburban boom and never stopped. By the late 1990s, it was the third-largest city in Illinois, and thanks in part to large tracts of rural land continually being developed into residential property, it had mushroomed to a population of 148,000 by 2018.

You'd never know it's that big, though, because amid the massive growth, Naperville has held on to its small-town charm. Unlike some suburban municipalities whose vibrant downtown business districts give way to more profitable but decidedly placeless strip malls adjacent to busy roads on the outskirts of town, Naperville has avoided the boom-and-bust flow by preserving and promoting its historic city center, including creating the riverwalk in 1981 to commemorate the city's 150th anniversary. It also proactively attracted high-tech companies to some of those large parcels of rural land, creating a sustainable microeconomy within the city limits and bringing in a well-heeled population in the process.

Some of those factors certainly figure into why Naperville is also at the epicenter of the modern American running boom and a hot spot in the running shoe retail business.

To understand Naperville's catbird seat in the boom and business of running, we'll need to take a step back and look at running's own story. As the initial generation of American runners who took on the unique challenge of running a marathon in the 1970s, '80s, and '90s grew older, new runners emerged with less lofty goals in the early 2000s.

While some purists scowl at that development, it turns out that the "slowing down" of American running has not just been good for the running industry and the shoe business but just might have saved them, too. While the first running boom was primarily about people becoming empowered to run a marathon, the group was limited, and running 26.2 miles wasn't for everyone. Many of those who reached the finish line and accomplished that bucket-list goal vowed never to do it again, and some even gave up running altogether.

The running boom of the early 21st century has been more of a "you do you" approach, to use the modern lexicon. Running today is multifaceted; it is whatever an individual wants it to be. Spurred on by the intel and unlimited inspiration offered by the Internet along with the frenetic pace of life in the burgeoning digital age, everyone is to some degree "on the run." And as new digital devices and forms of communication extend our 9-to-5 workday to something more like 24/7, fewer people have the time to truly train for a race as long and arduous as a marathon. So while there are still plenty of people training for races, over the past 15 years, the trend has shifted toward shorter distances, with the 5K, 10K, and half-marathon the races of choice for American runners. Naperville is home to several such races every year.

Population shifts across the United States have affected the face of running, too. The echo boom that produced a huge number of millennial offspring also led to a surge in high school cross-country and track participation numbers starting in the early 2000s. This surge is writ large at Naperville's three public high schools, all of which have won numerous cross-country and track state championships. At the same time, the busy parents of those kids, along with the many dual-income, no-kids professional couples living in Naperville, were turning to running with what little free time they had in order to get exercise, reduce stress, lose weight, or carve out some much-needed "me" time.

For the past 20 years, that's been Naperville in a nutshell. With a median household income above $116,000—48 percent higher than the U.S. average and the 12th highest of any U.S. city in 2018, according to U.S. Census Bureau figures—and a string of national accolades that tout Naperville as one of the best places to live, best places to raise a family, and best places to retire, life is good here.

So perhaps it should come as no surprise that Naperville has such a high per capita population of recreational runners. The suburb also has some of the best high school cross-country and track programs in Illinois, one of the best NCAA Division III running programs in the United States at North Central College, and—not coincidentally—one of the most successful running retail stores in the country.

NRC's clientele reflects the world outside its doors. Whereas running was once about hard-core athletes training to run fast races, today, a far wider slice of the U.S. population is wearing running shoes not just for running but also for a wide variety of fitness activities. While there are plenty of new runners chasing fast race goals, the massive growth of running since 2000, when Hartner's store opened, has meant an influx of more casual runners with myriad running and fitness goals.

"The big difference over the past 20 years is that running has gotten so much bigger," Hartner tells me as customers start streaming through the door moments after the store opens. "There are more people running, especially more women. There are more brands and more stores and more *kinds* of stores that sell running shoes."

While he's realistic about the competition he faces, thanks to a tidal wave of alternative outlets selling shoes, he says he thinks his business is actually invigorated by it. "It puts us in position to do everything we do even better. We know shoes, we know running, and we also know that our customers could go somewhere else to buy their shoes."

Hartner, 52, wanted to get into the running business since he was a kid growing up in Minnesota. When he was tasked with creating a business-card prototype in an eighth-grade printing class, he created one for himself as the owner of a running store called "The Complete Runner."

Two years later, when he turned 16, he landed a summer job at the Garry Bjorklund Sports (GBS) store in his hometown of Minnetonka. "It was my dream job," recalls Hartner, who would go on to work at GBS for the better part of the next eight years. "Most of the people who worked there were running 120 miles a week and sleeping on cots in the back in the afternoon. I was so inspired, and the whole experience stuck with me."

He kept his running store dreams alive even while earning degrees in biology, exercise science, and biomechanics. Once out of school, he worked for Reebok, Adidas, and Stride Rite in various capacities, including product management, research and development, and sales and marketing. But he never forgot about that business card, and after 10 years on the supplier side of the business, he took a leap into retail. Opening the store was a risk—after all, he was a rising talent on the lucrative corporate side of the business—but he was ready to stop working for the man and sensed that Naperville was a community ripe for such a business. He couldn't have been more right.

=====

Saturdays tend to be the busiest day of the week at running stores across the United States, and this appears to be especially true at NRC on this Saturday in mid-August. With summer vacation winding down, people are out shopping: parents buying back-to-school shoes for their kids, cross-country runners getting shod with training shoes and spikes, and recreational runners prepping for upcoming fall races, including the nearby iconic Chicago Marathon.

It's an animated scene, and all hands are on deck, Hartner included. In the hours before a postlunchtime lull, the vibe hovers between a slow-churning frenzy and a brightly colored tornado, with customers coming in and out the door at a nonstop pace. Standing on the sidelines sipping a still-warm latte, I enjoy watching it unfold around me.

When runners come in, they immediately migrate to the massive shoe wall and its rainbow palette—more than 140 men's and women's models from a wide range of brands. High schoolers head right to the Nikes, though a few gravitate to Hoka, Saucony, and New Balance models. Most shoppers take a shoe off the shelf, heft it, bend it this way and that, and turn it over to check the price. Some customers appear a little intimidated by the variety of choices and stand back from the wall, waiting for a staff member to help them navigate.

Energy swirls around the store. At any given time, there are a half-dozen customers sitting on long wooden benches having their feet measured and examined, or trying on a pair with the help of a shoe fitter. Some are tapping at their phones, but I can't tell whether they're doing price comparisons or getting some wear-test feedback. Others are jogging in place in front of a staff member or mimicking a running motion on the two-lane rubber track inlaid in the wooden floor. Staffers walk in and out of the back room with stacks of shoeboxes, and customers disappear into dressing rooms with shorts, shirts, and sports bras.

It's lively and a little chaotic, but Hartner assures me that there is a structured process guiding each shoe-fitting session. It starts with finding out what kind of running a customer does, he says. Does she run every day or just a few times a week? Does she regularly log long runs? Focus on racing? Does she prefer shorter distances that complement other workouts, such as CrossFit®, Orangetheory, or Zumba? What are her current running shoes? What are his unique biomechanical and anatomical needs? What is his injury history? What does he like to feel underfoot when running: cushy softness or no-frills firmness? Answers to those questions and others inform the shoe fitter's choice of which models from the back room to show the customer.

While the questions may be one size fits all, the answers decidedly are not. And that's a challenge faced not only by every runner but also by the entire industry. Like snowflakes, no two runners are alike. Foot size, shape, and volume, along with anatomical anomalies and injury history, are uniquely our own, as is how we move and run. All of those variables combine to make the quest for the "perfect" running shoe for any given runner almost impossible. And while there are conflicting studies and opinions about whether long-distance running is good or bad for you, one thing is indisputable: It's a high-impact sport with a high injury rate. Studies have shown that between 50 and 60 percent of recreational runners are sidelined with an injury every year. Whether a shoe helps or hurts will be explored later in the book, but suffice it to say, finding the right shoe matters to most runners.

However, finding the right shoe is no easy task, even for trained fitters. If considered as a math problem, they are tasked with considering hundreds of permutations of runner variables and then funneling those through 25–50 models of shoes (depending on the store size) to come up with a select few for the try-on.

I watch this problem play out over and over as shoe fitters collect the information from customers that they need to select the best options. Some customers struggle to answer the questions; they don't really know how to describe how they run. Most don't know how their feet are unique or different than anyone else's.

To get some more objective data, the fitters sometimes put subjects on a treadmill to watch them run and then view a slow-motion video replay. It's not the scientific gait analysis you'd get from a high-tech kinesiology lab, but it is another tool in the shoe fitter's toolbox and an opportunity to see the key idiosyncrasies of a runner's mechanics in action.

The goal is to get every runner into shoes that optimally fit their feet, meld with their running style, and allow them to run as efficiently and comfortably as possible, Hartner says. But he admits that it's a fluid craft, complicated by individual variables and preferences, new research, and ever-changing shoe models, paradigms, and design philosophies.

To make it even trickier, it's not as if once you find a shoe that works for you, you are set forever. Not only do shoe models change every year, but we change too, as does what we want and what works for us.

For years, I ran in lightweight, neutral cushioned models without issues. But as my speed waned and my fitness ebbed in my late 30s, things changed. I suffered many injuries—some major, some minor, some lingering—and that, combined with some extra pounds, changed my gait and with it the range of shoes that worked well for me. What I personally want and like in shoes has also changed through the years. That's human nature.

Nonetheless, Hartner insists that finding an ideal shoe isn't rocket science: "The process shouldn't be hit or miss. With experienced staff and the right shoes from the best brands, it's a targeted and curated process."

He makes it sound so easy. But is it?

I eavesdrop on conversations at the store, listening for how a shoe fitter describes the various shoes and what questions customers ask. What quickly becomes apparent is how little most runners know about shoes or their own running gait and how much they rely on the store's expertise and fitting service.

Some are familiar with brands and even specific models and know a fair bit about their running style and needs; however, most seem happy to lean heavily on the staff's know-how. I watch the shoe fitters bring out models—usually three or four—from the back for the try-on. Before putting them on, customers tend to handle a shoe, wave it in the air to see how light it feels, and squish the midsole to see how soft or firm it is. It reminds me a little of shaking, squeezing, and smelling cantaloupes in a grocery store's produce department.

Almost every runner—from middle schoolers to high-school harriers to masters-level marathoners—cares about color, many asking if there are other options for a particular model. When one teenager finds a Nike Pegasus on his phone that matches his red-and-white high school colors, the shoe fitter tells him he can special-order that color in his size and have it at the store in a few days.

A young mom with a toddler in tow is training for a fall half-marathon and buys the Saucony Freedom ISO, while a tall, middle-aged man who is just getting back into running after an injury leaves with a pair of cushy Hoka One One Clifton 5s. Three high schoolers go out the door with the latest model of the Pegasus, and two new runners—both deemed to have severe overpronation following their fittings—go home with the newest version of the Brooks Adrenaline GTS stability shoes.

Despite differences in age and running experience, what almost every customer has in common is that they leave smiling. I find I'm smiling, too. From what I can observe, the synergy seems to be just right, with a runner's particular needs and desires matched with a promising shoe. It leads me to wonder where that leaves runners who shop elsewhere. What about those who get their kicks at big-box retailers or a mall store? Those stores don't tend to carry the top-tier performance-oriented shoes or have the level of know-how and analysis available at a specialty shop. So how do those runners go about finding an optimal shoe? If it's mostly a guessing game for them, what does that mean for healthy running, good performance, and potential for injury? Or does it really matter? If it doesn't matter, how sustainable is this model of doing business?

As I leave the store to meet a former high school cross-country teammate for lunch, I have a few more questions than answers about the business of selling shoes.

The friend I meet for lunch lives less than 3 miles from NRC, and he tells me—a little bashfully—that he shops for shoes elsewhere, namely, at discount sporting goods shops or online. We were high school cross-country teammates for four years, a bond that has led to a long friendship even though he hasn't gone for a run since he was in college. He appreciates my enduring fascination with running and shoes, and although he doesn't run, he owns several pairs of running shoes, as most Americans do. He says it's because they're comfortable and cool.

Our chat over lunch runs the gamut from my recent trip to run an ultradistance race in the Alps to his son, Jack's, excitement over his upcoming cross-country season. I gave Jack some shoe recommendations a few weeks ago in a late-night text exchange and told him to visit NRC and to let Kris Hartner know that we're friends.

"We never had time to get to the store, but I found some good deals online," my friend confesses. "He only wanted Nikes, and I found a pair that he liked for 75 bucks. Click. Click. Done."

The shoes arrived two days later, he said; they fit perfectly, and Jack loved the blue-and-white color motif.

"I totally get it," I say, if a little ruefully. "Running shoes are expensive."

"I never expected to get rich selling running shoes . . . and I didn't," laughs Carl Brandt, who cofounded Movin Shoes in San Diego in 1977 and operated it for more than 35 years before selling it in 2013. "For me, selling running shoes has always been a labor of love."

That labor of love, shared by roughly 800 privately owned shops across the United States, has been around since the mid-1970s, when the first running boom led to the advent of running specialty stores. These shops have long been more than just an outlet to buy shoes; they have been the lifeblood of the running industry and the sport itself, providing community and spreading knowledge and passion to runners. While some of those stores have perhaps had more passion than they've had merchandising, marketing, or business sense, they are how the culture of running has thrived for decades.

But as a sport and as a recreational activity, running has changed and grown considerably since the 1970s, with shoes the brightest and biggest star. What started as a small-change niche product has ballooned to seriously big business in the decades since.

In the early 1980s, roughly $100 million in running shoes were sold annually, a huge increase from the 1970s. But that's a drop in the bucket compared to today. Annual sales of running shoes increased from $2.32 billion in 2010 to $3.09 billion in 2018, according to the National Sporting Goods Association. More than 48 million pairs of running shoes were sold in 2018, up from 37.1 million in 2010 and a mere 1.5 million in the late 1970s.

Sounds like a golden dream for running specialty store owners. And so it was for many years. But as much as it may be fulfilling to live your passion every day, going it alone as a mom-and-pop store has become increasingly more difficult. With the pie so much bigger, some locally owned running stores are thriving, seeing annual sales double or even triple over the past 10 to 15 years. But like sharks on a school of fish, that appealing pie has also attracted large chains and online retailers, all aggressively grabbing for a larger slice.

For example, between 2011 and 2015, Finish Line gobbled up more than 70 of the top independent running specialty stores in the United States. The Indianapolis-based retailer group was trying to garner business in the specialty arena to match its massive group of mall-based general athletic footwear stores. It rebranded many of the stores under the JackRabbit name with the goal of centralizing buying and warehousing, boosting online sales, and developing economies of scale while also taking best practices from its higher-performing stores and thereby bolstering its entire chain.

The model made sense on paper, but in their haste to make changes, the parent company replaced many longtime managers and employees and, as a result, wound up severing connections with the local communities. A few years into the venture, Finish Line sold the entire operation to a new investment group at a fire-sale price. That new group has since righted the ship by returning to an emphasis on local communities with in-store events, training groups, and product curation tied to each store's needs.

Meanwhile, Fleet Feet Sports operates a network of about 180 specialty running stores, of which about 140 are owned by independent franchisees and the rest by the corporate mother ship.

Both retail chains have gained footholds with national branding and marketing, online sales, and the ability to effectively consolidate and close out the previous year's unsold models without impacting the overall business in the same way that such practices affect a privately owned running specialty store.

It's all part of the bigger picture of a retail business in flux. Running specialty stores dominated the industry in the 1980s and 1990s. But by 2017, just 12 percent of running shoe sales came from specialty shops, down from 18 percent in 2012 and 19.6 percent in 2011. At the same time, online sales increased from 12.2 percent in 2010 to 26.8 percent in 2017. Still, as of 2018, specialty running stores were selling more than 6 million pairs of shoes per year.

Privately owned brick-and-mortar running stores such as NRC had always been challenged by large sporting goods stores and catalog sales, but today, online running stores like JackRabbit.com and

DEENA KASTOR ‖ ASICS DS Trainer

Three-time U.S. Olympian, American record holder in the marathon

A couple years into being a professional runner, I finally earned myself a contract from a shoe brand. I had paid my dues, working as a waitress and winning races, until finally, I won a national championship that landed me a $12,000-per-year deal with a brand, allowing me to quit my job serving weak coffee, mile-high cinnamon rolls, and breakfast burritos smothered in green chili so I could focus solely on training.

I was grateful—up until a cold winter day when Andrew and I were visiting his parents in Ohio. The towpath was icy, and I was slipping with every step. Frustrated, I said, "If I'm going to spend 10 days here, I need shoes that grip better." I visited Second Sole running store, where a patient employee brought out several shoes for me to try on. I had a Cinderella moment when he slid my foot into an ASICS DS Trainer. The shoe fit perfectly. It was as if the heavens shone a light down on me, or maybe the shoes themselves said, "Oh, yes! We're going places together!"

I bought them immediately, and when we got in the car, I called my agent and told him I was in love with the shoes. I asked if he could get me a contract with ASICS even if it was less than what I was already getting, and I have been running in ASICS ever since. I alternate shoes throughout the week to give my feet different workouts, but the DS Trainer remains my true love and a reminder of finding my place in this sport.

RunningWarehouse.com, along with major online shoe retailers such as Zappos.com, have gained a growing slice of the sales pie and have contributed to a reduction in walk-in traffic at specialty shops.

How people shop has changed considerably since those original running stores opened in the 1970s. Even as recently as the early 2000s, few running shoes were sold online. The prevailing attitude had always been that you had to try on a shoe and run around in it a bit before you knew whether it was right for you. Fit and feel were the deciding factors. But undeniably, price, convenience, and free shipping have strong appeal for just about any consumer product, and today, these appear to have started winning over the hands-on analysis and customer service of the specialty stores.

For some shops, this shift is painfully obvious. Although running participation is still trending upward, shoe, apparel, and accessory sales are sharply on the decline in those stores, a sign that customers are likely shopping elsewhere. Some customers still prioritize fit and feel; however, they seek out cheaper prices online even as they're being fitted for a shoe in a running store, ordering off their phones as they're walking out the door.

It doesn't help the brick-and-mortar businesses that all shoe and apparel brands now sell directly from their own websites; in fact, it creates an unusual economic situation in which specialty retailers are competing with the same brands they're selling in their stores. But the most unsettling competition by far for most shop owners is that Amazon.com, the world's largest and most successful online retailer, has locked its sights on running and made a big push into running shoe sales in recent years.

While Amazon typically honors a brand's suggested retail prices in the same way that local retail stores do when a product is first released, the free shipping, discounts, and ability to display dozens of closeouts on the same page—not to mention its brand power and ubiquitousness—

give the behemoth the power to beat the price in a local store with next-day shipping.

Finally, there is the cottage industry of venues selling outdated models. The rock-bottom prices on last year's shoes at online closeout stores such as LeftLane Sports and The Clymb, in addition to those offered by FleetFeet.com, JackRabbit.com, and RunningWarehouse.com, are deals that are nearly impossible for specialty shops to beat.

In the past, the specialty shops themselves would offer past-season models on a sales table or during a special once-a-season tent sale. This was a predictable way to sell off inventory, improve cash flow, recoup a bit more than the wholesale cost of old models, and at the same time get customers in front of new models on the shoe wall along with new apparel and accessories.

The strategy worked well when those shops were the most likely place for runners to buy new shoes for the upcoming season. But as running has exploded in popularity, many runners care less about "latest and greatest" and more about getting shoes at a cheap price. And heck, if their favorite models from last year worked well, why wouldn't they buy those shoes again at a discount if they can find them?

Sale shoes are all over the Internet, partially because many shoe brands are dumping their own unsold models onto discount sites online. The Internet's back room is one giant sale table if you have the inclination to click around in it. And it doesn't take much time or effort, given how search engine optimization drives those deals directly to your Facebook, Google, and Yahoo feeds.

At NRC, I think back to earlier in the day, at Starbucks, when I was a click away from buying the exact shoes I had just worn on my run for $60 less than I had paid for them. Had I been a typical running consumer— i.e., a cost-conscious shopper rather than a wear-tester who gets a lot of free shoes—I might well have purchased them and gone on my way without setting foot inside the store. The thought depresses me. Although it was a financial win for me, it feels a lot like a loss. I wonder if the days of locally owned, service-oriented retail stores—whether selling coffee, running shoes, or books—are on the wane forever.

A few weeks later, I hear that the Movin Shoes chain, where Brandt toiled in a labor of love for 35 years, is shutting down because of declining sales. The new ownership group didn't adjust to the modern trends and lacked the tireless service that Brandt and his partners provided for so long.

"It's a different world," Brandt says. "I miss helping to inspire runners, but I don't miss the decline in sales or the concern that people are price-checking shoes on their phones while they're in the store."

At NRC, however, there are few signs of this struggle. The flow of customers ebbs and flows throughout the afternoon, dwindling to a few final stragglers before the doors close at 5 p.m. The day turns out to be one of the store's highest-grossing days of the year, with more than $22,000 of goods sold, including more than 130 pairs of running shoes.

Hartner is clearly a savvy businessman who is doing something right to counter the changes that he faces. At a time when there are huge challenges to brick-and-mortar retail businesses—shoe and otherwise— Hartner has found a formula for success. While many shops have been sold to chains or gone out of business, NRC has thrived, opening a second store on the south end of Naperville and a third in the bordering town of Wheaton in 2018.

Although Wheaton has a demographic base similar to that of Naperville, it has seen three running stores come and go in its historic downtown over the past two decades. To ensure a strong foothold, Hartner's staffers there have been intentional about immersing themselves in the community. It helps that one of the managers grew up nearby, ran track and cross-country in high school, and knows the coaches in the area. Having two thriving NRC stores nearby has also enabled the company to spread some of the fixed costs over the entire business. That has allowed the new store to be stocked conservatively because additional shoes and gear can be delivered from one of the other locations with just a few hours' notice.

"We didn't do things that much differently with this store; we just dug in," Hartner says.

As for the ongoing appeal of digital purchases, Hartner isn't letting online closeout businesses steal his customers, either. In a bold move, he's opened a retail shop a few doors down from the original NRC called The Annex, which sells the previous season's unsold shoes and apparel from the NRC stores at a discount.

While acknowledging the pressures and challenges in today's retail climate, Hartner says he doesn't dwell on those problems, instead focusing on making his business the best that it can be. "If we put our energy into our connection to our community and focus on running a smart business, I think we can all coexist," he says.

He credits his staff's shoe knowledge, running know-how, and care for customers as the crucial criteria that have enabled NRC to thrive. Therefore, he says, he compensates employees well with competitive pay and good benefits, including health insurance and a liberal maternity leave policy, so he can retain them. His managers even earn equity in the business.

But with tight margins and competition from every corner, it's also about running the business shrewdly and making everyone accountable for its success. Running and the industry have changed, he admits, and brands have more leverage with shoe vendors when it comes to pricing, inventory, and sales resources, not to mention access to a much wider customer base online.

Ultimately, though, Hartner believes there will always be a space for exceptional running shops. The strong will survive, and today, being strong means that those shops have to know as much about marketing, merchandising, digital audience acquisition, and business ops as they do about running shoes and marathon training.

"It's an awesome business to be in because you're improving people's lives," he says. "And it's pretty much recession-proof in a lot of ways because running is a gateway for someone to do something better for themselves; it's an investment in their health."

———

Late that afternoon, I submit to a shoe fitting myself, curious to see what shoes the analysis will suggest for me. I acknowledge up front that my slightly lopsided gait from a leg-length imbalance is currently controlled by an 8mm heel lift that has allowed me to continue running with a neutral gait, which the store's shoe fitter confirms by watching me run on the treadmill. Taking into account my narrow foot shape, high arch, and preference for a lighter shoe, he has me try the Hoka Clifton 5, Saucony Ride 10, and Brooks Launch 5.

Do I need to buy a pair of shoes from NRC today? Decidedly not. Given all of the wear-test models I receive on a regular basis, I have more than 20 go-to pairs in my active "quiver" (aka my garage) back in Boulder and at least another 20 that I wear occasionally. Heck, I packed three pairs just for this four-day trip to Chicago.

But there is something inspiring about being at one of the best running shops in the country and watching customer after customer leave satisfied and smiling. I want to be part of that. The Brooks Launch fit well and feel great when I try them on, so I pony up $100, buy them on the spot, and leave the store smiling.

It reminds me of what I've been telling people for years: Happiness really *is* a new pair of running shoes.

2 KICKIN' IT OLD-SCHOOL

We are not makers of history; we are made by history.
MARTIN LUTHER KING JR.

Beverly, Massachusetts, about 15 miles north of Boston, is a densely populated resort and manufacturing suburb that lays claim to being the birthplace of the U.S. Navy. As I inch along in heavy traffic on Route 1, sports talk radio personalities are jabbering about the evening's Red Sox game, but my head is deep in thoughts of evolution—of running shoes, that is. Beverly and the greater New England area in which it sits are one of the world's meccas for athletic footwear development—specifically running shoes—and I've spent key moments of my career here, reporting on new models, visiting development laboratories, and becoming saturated with the many nuances of my running shoe fascination.

Embedded in New England are countless connections to running and shoes, not least among them the historic Boston Marathon. There are also several running retail shops (including the now-defunct shops once owned by running legend Bill Rodgers); numerous researchers at Harvard and MIT who have contributed much to the science of the human running gait; one of the original Nike shoe factories in Exeter, New Hampshire; and brands such as New Balance, Saucony, Puma, Reebok, Inov-8, and ASICS, which have set up their headquarters here to tap into the rich talent pool of shoe designers, manufacturing know-how, and running prowess.

But none of that is the reason I'm heading to Beverly. I'm here because an abridged version of that rich history can be found tucked away in a gray-and-white two-story colonial on Clifton Avenue. The well-kept and nicely landscaped property is the home of Dave Kayser, a retired museum curator who, years ago, found his personal and professional passions increasingly overlapping. A longtime runner with more than 50 marathons under his belt, he developed an affinity for running shoes in his mid-20s and started what has grown into a museum-worthy collection of kicks.

I'm eager for a look at the assortment, anticipating a step back in time that will allow me not just to reconnect with forgotten shoes of my youth but also to see and touch a bit of history through his vintage models. My inner shoe geek wants to fill in some blanks in my running shoe erudition as well by seeing how rare or ballyhooed models of the 1960s and 1970s fit into the evolution of kicks through the years.

Over the past 40 years, Kayser has collected more than 120 models, ranging from his earliest—1930s handmade leather track spikes—to the first mass-produced training shoes of the 1960s all the way to the flashy, technologically enhanced models of the 1990s and 2000s.

Some of the shoes are his own, models he bought or prototypes he received in the 1970s and 1980s when he was a wear-tester for Nike's erstwhile research and development division in Exeter. He's added to his collection by acquiring old shoes from friends or friends of friends who donated them when they were cleaning out a garage, attic, or basement. He's also sifted through his share of thrift shops and estate sales and purchased some shoes on eBay, becoming a discriminating and meticulous shopper at the world's largest online auction-based garage sale.

Despite a professional predilection for history and preservation, Kayser didn't really start his personal collection on purpose. Like many longtime runners, he just wound up with a lot of shoes that he was attached to and didn't want to toss in the trash. Some were sentimental favorites because of the good race results they helped him produce. Some he was fond of because of how comfortably they fit. Others were about the color, style, materials, or some transcendent appeal that had nothing to do with running.

"Being a curator, I was always interested in stuff," he said over the phone the week before my trip to Beverly. "I had saved some shoes because of the pleasant memories attached to them, but they just sort of hung around. I wasn't thinking about being a collector."

Kayser got the itch to collect shoes more formally after discovering that Ed Ayres, a good friend and the founding editor of *Running Times* magazine, had grown his own running shoe collection to 150 pairs by the early 1990s. Kayser had helped Ayres organize the shoes, and when Ayres was ready to sell his collection, he pulled out a few key pairs and gave them to Kayser.

"That's when I decided I wanted to start collecting them," Kayser recalls. "I liked it and thought it was fun, but I knew it was going to get harder. Some of the good stuff from the 1960s and 1970s was already disappearing."

Indeed, before we even break into his massive treasure trove of shoes, tucked into a spare bedroom on his second floor, Kayser tells me about a shoe that got away: a pair handcrafted by Ron Daws. The 1968 Olympic marathoner from Minneapolis was notorious for cutting shoes apart and rebuilding them as he saw fit. When distance standout Steve Hoag finished second to Bill Rodgers in the Boston Marathon in 1975, he was wearing a pair of Daws's modified shoes, Kayser tells me. "Hoag really paid the price for wearing those that day. His feet turned to hamburger, but, man, I lusted after those and kept asking him about them."

But he never saw the shoes again. "A few years ago, Hoag told me they were in his garage somewhere and that he'd dig them out and give them to me, but then, sadly, he passed away in 2017, and they're long gone now."

＝＝

As he prepares to show me his collection, Kayser is as giddy as a teen at a school dance. He keeps the shoes in stacks of off-white, acid-free preservation boxes that sit behind a four-panel room divider, creating an aura of something cherished and protected but rarely shared. The shades are pulled, and the room is dark to keep the temperature from getting too high in the summer.

I interviewed him a few times over the past several years for articles in *Running Times* and *Competitor* and even sent a photographer to shoot photos of him with his stash, but I have never actually seen the collection in person. I admit, I am equally giddy.

"Here they are," he says proudly, pulling back the divider to expose the stacked boxes. "I'm really glad you came out to see them. I never look at these unless someone is interested in them." He pauses. "And there really aren't many people interested in them."

The cardboard boxes are uniform, about 3 feet long, 2.5 feet wide, and 6 inches deep. He hands me two that fill my arms and grabs two more himself. As we head back down a narrow wooden staircase to the living room, I try to keep my balance on the creaking steps.

We stack the boxes carefully on the floor, and I reach over to open one. As I slide the top off, I feel as though I'm immediately swept back in time. Inside are a dozen pairs of shoes in two tight rows of six, packed laces to laces and puzzle-pieced so that they neatly fill every square inch of the box's interior. Some are well worn and dingy; others look like they've barely been worn at all. One thing is for sure: It's a boxful of pure

Americana, not only harkening back to the original running boom of the 1970s but bringing back a rush of my personal memories as well. I feel my eyes well up as I glance at the shoes. It's an unexpectedly emotional response that I can only explain along the lines of how a longtime baseball fan might react to handling a 1950s New York Yankees jersey or how a classic car fanatic might tear up to see the colorful vintage American vehicles in modern-day Cuba.

Kayser gives me license to dive in, and I eagerly oblige. The first pair I pull out are ASICS Gel-Lyte III trainers from 1993 with fluorescent yellow laces. I remember the shoe well and ran a lot of miles in the original model that came out several years prior to this one, in 1987.

Despite the name "Lyte," the shoe feels far heavier than some of today's high-mileage trainers. I recall the original model as fairly light, but the reasons for the '93 model's additional heft are obvious: more stitched-on suede overlays and technological features such as a sturdier plastic heel counter; a firmer, thicker midsole; a unique split tongue; and a window in the rear of the foot that showed off the brand's GEL cushioning system. Looking at the shoe, I'm reminded of how clunky and overbuilt shoes became in the 1990s and yet how acceptable—desirable, even—that kind of design was. The shoe was a huge hit at the time, and these bells and whistles were a big part of the draw.

"They weren't light, especially compared to now, but they sure were hot stuff," Kayser says, echoing my thoughts and beginning what will be an ongoing commentary on every shoe in the collection. His memory is sharp as a tack, though he also keeps a tidy spreadsheet close by that categorizes all of his shoes for the rare moment when he can't recall a model name. Sometimes the shoes conjure up memories of how Kayser acquired them; other times he offers brief historical soundbites that provide context for a shoe in terms of the shoes that preceded and followed it.

I pull out a Mizuno Wave Rider 2—a 1999 model that updated the brand's energetic Wave spring technology in the midsole and helped make the Rider franchise Mizuno's best-selling shoe of all time. "Those aren't as old as some of them, but they look pretty dated compared to today's shoes," Kayser says, referring to the shoe's color scheme—primarily white save for a few bright, gaudy highlights, a popular look for shoes in the '90s that appears old-fashioned 20 years later.

I spy a familiar model, 1984 Nike Terra Trainers, a pale-blue-and-white shoe with a maroon swoosh that I wore in high school. Lightweight and stable, it used a newfangled material called Phylon, a compression-molded foam compound injected with tiny air bubbles, for the midsole. The Terra Trainer was one of the models that helped make Nike the dominant running brand of the 1980s, and seeing these shoes stirs me, remembering all of the miles I ran in them as a sophomore en route to earning my first varsity letter in cross-country.

I root around and am surprised by a rare treat: a pair of late-1970s Nike Axis, which Kayser tells me was a shoe originally developed as a prototype for marathon great Joan Benoit Samuelson, although Nike never actually made it in a women's model.

When I come across a pair of 1982 New Balance 420 racing flats, it's Kayser's turn to get a little emotional. This was the shoe that he wore in one of his fastest marathons, he says with pride. Although now 66 and retired from running, Kayser was a consummate amateur runner from the 1970s to the 1990s. Lanky, lean, and always determined to get faster, he tells me he typically ran two to four marathons every year but never quite reached his ultimate goal of breaking 2:30. "I ran right around 2:30 many times but could never get under it," Kayser recalls. "I just wanted to go 2:29:59 once, and I would have been happy."

His best shot, he tells me, was at the 1982 Boston Marathon—a race in searing weather made famous by the book *Duel in the Sun*. As Alberto

Salazar, wearing Nike American Eagle racers, famously finished in 2:08:52 and narrowly outran Dick Beardsley, shod in a pair of custom-made New Balance 250 racing flats, on the homestretch along Boylston Street, Kayser, wearing a pair of New Balance 420s, ran 2:30 and change for the fourth or fifth time.

He doesn't blame the shoe for his shortcomings that day. "I really liked the shoe," he recalls. "It was light and energetic, it fit well, and the foam was soft and comfortable. It was much better for running a marathon than some of the earlier shoes I wore."

The 420s may have been his fastest pair, but a beat-up pair of vintage yellow-and-navy-blue Onitsuka Tiger Jayhawks is his favorite, he says. It was the shoe he wore for his first marathon, in 1975, so it has both senti-mental and performance-oriented connections.

Minimally designed with just a little cushioning, it had a lightweight (and not very durable) nylon upper and a gum-rubber outsole that pro-vided great traction on wet and dry roads. The Jayhawk was emblematic of the shift that occurred in running shoes in the mid-1970s as midsole cushioning started to become a focus.

As the jogging craze grew and more recreational runners joined the fad, cushioning and comfort became key design criteria among running shoe manufacturers. "The midsole was thin in the Jayhawks, but it was very responsive compared to a lot of other shoes that I had run in prior to that," Kayser says. "The nylon upper was soft and snug, and racing in them was a delight."

Another highlight in the box is an exotic-looking pair of EB Lydiard Marathon shoes, a circa 1970 kangaroo-leather shoe with laces offset slightly to the left of center. Developed by renowned New Zealand coach Arthur Lydiard and Germany's EB Brütting company, it had a wider toe box than most of its contemporaries and was one of the first to include a heel counter—a built-in heel cup to keep the rear of the shoe from slipping. With a $32 price tag (which also covered mail-order shipping charges), the shoe was more than twice as expensive as most other shoes of the time. It's difficult to find today, and that rarity made it one of the more expensive shoes for Kayser to add to the collection.

As we go through boxes, we dive deeper into history, at one point coming across a simply designed Keds sneaker with a black canvas upper, white fabric stripes, and rubber outsole—and no cushioning whatsoever. Kayser guesses it dates back to 1963 or so, a time when athletic shoe brands were just starting to manufacture shoes out of materials other than leather. "This is what people ran road races in back then," Kayser says, shaking his head at the lack of midsole cushioning.

The Keds shoe is a stark contrast to the model beside it, a well-preserved pair of 1930s leather track spikes from British brand Fosters. Based in Bolton, England, J. W. Foster and Sons got its start when John William Foster, the teenaged son of a shoe cobbler, started building spiked competition shoes to provide more traction on the cinder tracks of the day. The business grew, and the company became the first to mass-produce athletic shoes in a factory. The shoes were worn by many top British track and field athletes, including 1924 Olympic 100-meter dash champion Harold Abrahams, who would later be memorialized in the Oscar-winning film *Chariots of Fire*. In the late 1950s, some 25 years after this set of spikes were built, the brand changed its name to Reebok and eventually became one of the biggest athletic footwear brands in the world.

In one of the last boxes, I spot a shoe I had been hoping to see: the legendary New Balance Trackster. Introduced in 1960, more than a decade before the recreational running boom started in earnest, the Trackster is credited with being one of the first American-made shoes designed exclusively for everyday running on the roads as opposed to more general-use sneakers or track-specific shoes. Made with a soft leather upper and a saddle to help cinch the shoe around the midfoot, it conformed to a runner's foot. It also had a flexible rubber outsole with a ripple pattern that enhanced traction and helped cushion a runner's impact against the ground. Furthermore, the Trackster was the first athletic shoe available in multiple widths. At the time, it was advertised as a shoe that would help prevent shin splints, although there was never any validity to the claim. Nonetheless, Kayser insists, the Trackster was a key model in the evolution of running shoes because of its advanced functionality.

We go shoe by shoe through Kayser's entire collection. His wife, Sheila, waits patiently for us to finish, and we enjoy a twilight dinner next to the well-manicured gardens in their backyard. Our conversation moves away from running and on to the flowers and vegetables they're growing, the Red Sox, and other items they collect: antique packaged goods; baseball cards; and anything related to Goofy, Disney's anthropomorphic cartoon dog who speaks with a Southern drawl. They have several hundred figurines, pictures, posters, and other Goofy items on display in their basement—a far bigger collection than the set of vintage running shoes, in fact.

"The Goofy stuff got a little bit out of hand," Sheila admits with a laugh. "But the running shoe collection is amazing. Maybe it's a little nuts, too, but there could be a lot worse habits. His passion for old shoes is a good one."

Spending several hours handling and discussing classic running shoes with Kayser is a huge personal thrill, of course, but more importantly, it provides an intriguing 10,000-foot perspective on the evolutionary path of running shoes from their formative years to the present. In Kayser's collection, it is easy to spy design elements and performance features that are still present in modern running shoes. It's also easy to see what is not present.

As I examine the older shoes in the collection, I'm reminded of how minimally designed running shoes once were. The most popular running shoes of the 1960s—such as the Trackster and the Onitsuka Tiger Marathon—had almost no cushioning at all, just a flat rubber outsole; a barely-there insole layer between the runner's foot and the ground; and a wafer-thin, lightweight upper made from leather, canvas, or nylon.

These minimalist designs are a bit of a head-scratcher, considering all of the great runners and road running performances that came before modern design. How could runners have trained so hard, run so many miles, and run such fast marathons wearing shoes that offered so little protection and virtually no cushioning underfoot?

Consider Australian Derek Clayton. He trained for years in flimsy canvas-and-rubber Dunlop tennis shoes, yet he became the first runner in history to run under 2:10 for the marathon in 1967, clocking a 2:09:36 in Fukuoka, Japan, in a pair of Onitsuka Marathon shoes. Two years later, he lowered the record by more than a minute in a similar pair of shoes.

Elite American runner Amby Burfoot wore a pair of the popular Onitsuka shoes when he won the 1968 Boston Marathon. Four years later, American Frank Shorter won the 1972 Olympic Marathon in a pair of custom-designed Adidas road racing flats that also had scant cushioning. That was the order of the day—and a stark contrast to the way shoes would evolve over the next 40 years—but runners found a way to run times that are still considered relatively fast in the 21st century. Shorter's Olympic-winning time of 2:12:19 in 1972 while wearing minimally designed shoes remained a competitive time in every Olympics through the 2016 Games in Rio de Janeiro.

"It was all we had," shrugs Burfoot, who would go on to serve as editor in chief at *Runner's World* from 1985 to 2004. "Nobody had ever heard of a midsole, and therefore we could never have even conceived of one. It's a chicken-and-egg situation. Did we survive because we were the efficient guys who didn't need built-up shoes? Or was there something good about those shoes back then—what we would now call minimalist shoes—that made us hearty and healthy and kept us going?"

Burfoot's question is an intriguing one but, like the chicken-and-egg puzzle, is perhaps not solvable, certainly not in hindsight. No one could have predicted where the evolution of running shoes would lead, Burfoot says, but with the changing demographics of the running boom, an increasing number of runners were interested in comfort and cushioning. Shoe brands glommed on to the trend, knowing it was one of the keys to increased sales, even if it would begin a divergent path toward marketing-fueled hype and away from the purity of performance-oriented running.

—————

In the late '60s, Onitsuka Tiger was the top brand for racing and training shoes. The Japanese company's bare-bones Marathon racing shoe—with its lightweight nylon upper and thin rubber outsole—earned praise for a snug fit and flexible, "barefoot" sensation. But the company's top training model, the Cortez, with its thin leather upper and firm rubber outsole, was lauded for a feature that was novel at the time: midsole cushioning aimed at creating a softer "ride" by reducing harsh foot-strike impacts.

At the time, Portland, Oregon, businessman Phil Knight with his fledgling Blue Ribbon Sports start-up was the U.S. distributor for Onitsuka Tiger shoes, and his former University of Oregon track coach, Bill Bowerman, was his business partner. Bowerman had been tinkering with shoes for his collegiate charges for years, always looking to shave off ounces, increase traction, and promote stride efficiency.

The first shoe designed by Bowerman for the Japanese brand that was intended for the American market, the Cortez, debuted at the 1968 Olympics in Mexico City. It had a thin, soft, rubber layer of midsole cushioning from heel to toe and a beveled wedge of even softer rubber foam at the rear of the shoe to absorb impact and reduce stress on the Achilles tendon. It was the first shoe designed with that purpose, and the midsole cushioning feature would be copied in nearly every new shoe model that followed until the minimalist revolution of 2007–2012 would lead to the rebirth of level or "zero-drop" shoes.

Kayser has a beat-up pair of Cortez in his collection, but he's more proud of the cloth Blue Ribbon Sports bag that he acquired. Blue Ribbon Sports broke away from Onitsuka in 1972 as Knight and Bowerman began manufacturing their own shoes under a new brand that they named Nike. After a court battle with Onitsuka, Nike retained the right to the Cortez name, while its former partner renamed its version the Corsair. The shoes were virtually identical save for the corporate logo—Onitsuka with its crisscrossing red and blue stripes and Nike debuting a red "swoosh" emblem when it showed off its Cortez to American retailers in March of 1972 at a sporting goods trade show in Chicago.

Burfoot recalls the sensation of running in shoes with midsole cushioning for the first time. "The first midsoles were minimalist and provided a little bit of cushioning that felt good but didn't alter your stride. When you felt that cushioning, you couldn't not appreciate it."

That midsole is one of the reasons the Cortez became a huge hit with runners in the United States—especially among its growing population of joggers—and one of the shoes that subsequently set off a cushioning revolution that would continue into the 21st century.

The shoes were immortalized in the 1994 Oscar-winning film *Forrest Gump* when the title character wore them while running across the country, inadvertently sparking the American running boom of the 1970s. It may not have happened quite that way outside Hollywood, but Nike's innovative footwear certainly made a strong contribution to the rise of recreational running. Meanwhile, TV star and pin-up girl Farrah Fawcett donned a pair of the women's Senorita Cortez while riding a skateboard on the Charlie's Angels TV set in 1976, helping spark an overnight frenzy that led to the shoe selling out nationwide.

With the success of Nike's Cortez, other top brands of the day scrambled to devise their own version of cushioning in order to remain competitive among this growing population of recreational joggers.

After consulting American mile champ Marty Liquori, Brooks president Jerry Turner met with the Monarch Rubber Company in Baltimore to discuss developing a new kind of midsole compound. "I wanted more rebound, better shock absorption, and lighter weight," Turner recalled in *Runner's World* years later. "The guy said, 'I think I've got just the thing for you,' and the next day he comes back and shows me EVA."

Ethylene-vinyl acetate (EVA) had the properties that Turner was seeking. He gave the green light to Brooks to put the soft, bouncy, air-infused foam in its Villanova training shoe in 1975.

EVA wasn't brand-new to the running shoe scene. It is a simple, two-part material that's easy to make (and therefore not proprietary), but it can be blended many different ways by varying the amounts of vinyl acetate and ethylene to create softer or firmer compounds. Nike had used a version of EVA a year earlier in several models designed by Bowerman but called it something else. New Balance would use a similar version of the foam in its 320 trainer the following year.

EVA foam became the midsole darling and sparked a full-on running shoe cushioning war that played out via advertisements, running store promotions, and elite athlete endorsements. It would become the most prevalent cushioning compound in running shoes for the next 40 years.

In the fever of explosive growth and innovation of the early 1970s, manufacturers began tinkering with other parts of the shoe, too. In a race to outdo one another, brands began searching for a way to garner runners' favor (and dollars) by providing better traction, more support, more resiliency, and lighter weight with the stated goal of improving performance and reducing injuries.

In one of the more creative attempts at innovation, Bowerman started melting rubber in a waffle iron to create outsoles that offered more energy return and traction. A huge hit for the upstart brand, "waffle" outsoles soon graced several Nike models, including the Waffle Trainer and Boston models of 1973. Nylon fabric replaced leather and suede as the primary upper material by 1975, and even more versatile and breathable synthetic meshes debuted shortly thereafter.

Other popular innovations included the use of Italian-made Vibram rubber outsoles, which were grippier than traditional outsoles; the development of women-specific lasts to fit the common sizes and shapes of women's feet; new midsole compounds; shoes with springs built into the midsole; and, most controversially, various forms of stability and motion-control devices aimed at slowing the rate of pronation (the inward rolling of the ankle after the foot impacts the ground). We'll focus on that particular decades-old conundrum in Chapter 5, when I tackle running injuries. But for the moment, suffice it to say that the quest to control how a runner's foot moved was one of the central focuses of the running shoe evolution and marketing hype of the 1970s.

But the biggest innovation of the decade was the advent of Nike Air-Sole cushioning.

The concept was devised by Marion "Frank" Rudy, a former NASA aeronautical engineer who patented a cushioning system that encapsulated inert gas inside a polyurethane sole using a technology called blown rubber molding that had been used to create helmets for NASA's Apollo missions.

In March 1977, Rudy and his business partner, Bob Bogert, another aeronautical engineer, pitched Nike on the idea of building running shoes with pressurized air packets in the heel for optimized cushioning, promising that this technology would create "the ride of a lifetime" and would become the next big thing in the running shoe world.

Knight was skeptical, but Rudy and Bogert were persistent and explained with enthusiastic detail that an air-injected insole would never go flat and would never lose resiliency, as foams did. They showed off prototype samples of air-encased insoles, which only made Knight more skeptical.

"Air shoes sounded to me like jet packs and moving sidewalks, comic-book stuff," Knight recalled in his 2016 memoir, *Shoe Dog*. Knight was ready to turn Rudy and Bogert away until he heard that they had already pitched the concept to Adidas—the number-one running shoe brand in the 1970s—and had met with similar skepticism. "That was all I needed to hear," Knight said.

Knight inserted the makeshift air insoles into his own running shoes and laced them up. After a 6-mile run, he was convinced that the idea was worth pursuing. Within a few weeks, Knight and his Nike cohort reached a deal that would allow Nike to license the technology and pay Rudy and Bogert about 15 cents for every shoe sold with the air-encapsulated midsoles.

Nike then fast-tracked a design project to incorporate this proprietary "Air" technology at its Exeter factory, and a little more than a year later, the first Air Tailwind shoes were built.

The Air Tailwind launched in limited quantities at the Honolulu Marathon in December 1978, creating a huge buzz in the running industry. Already well versed in the product promotion game, Nike told the running world that this was more than a next-generation shoe; it was a postmodern work of art.

Mike Fanelli, a competitive runner who worked for several running retail stores and shoe manufacturers between the '70s and '90s, recalls the excitement around the Tailwind, a dazzling silver-painted shoe with an electric-blue swoosh. Stores couldn't keep it in stock in the spring of 1979, he says, and it was on pace to surpass the previous sales records Nike had set with its Waffle Trainer five years earlier.

But despite the fanfare, the initial production run of the Tailwind was highly problematic. "It was a disaster when it launched," Kayser recalls as I gingerly examine the pair of crumbling Tailwinds that he bought on eBay. The midsole has broken apart like angel-food cake over the past four decades, revealing the edges of the Air-Sole. "I heard stories about all kinds of problems."

Following huge preliminary sales the first spring, running stores were inundated with disappointed customers and returns. In addition to complaints of popped and deflated Air-Sole units, the silver paint was reportedly flecking, and tiny shards of metal in the paint were rubbing against the nylon upper, creating microtears in the fabric. As a result, runners were experiencing shredded and blown-out uppers within their first few runs in the shoes.

Nike recalled the shoes and offered full refunds, admitting that the launch of the greatest innovation in running shoes was a failure.

"We'd learned a valuable lesson. Don't put 12 innovations in one shoe. It asks too much of the shoe, to say nothing of the design team," Knight remembers. "We reminded each other that there was honor in saying, 'Back to the drawing board.' We reminded each other of the many waffle irons Bowerman had ruined."

Despite the failure of the original Tailwind, Nike recovered from the challenges and grew the Air-Sole into one of its most successful running shoe technologies over the next 25 years. The design also fueled a wide range of innovation throughout the industry, a period that coincided with even greater reliance on marketing hype. By the time I got my first pair of Nike Air shoes in 1984—the second-edition Pegasus—Nike had turned "air" into the top buzzword in running shoes.

"Every shoe company went for some kind of technology that would be proprietary to them," Fanelli says. "Every brand was in search of something they could call their own."

―――――

With all these innovations, the price of running shoes rose dramatically as the cost of making and marketing them increased. While the Onitsuka Tiger Marathon retailed for $10.95 and the New Balance Trackster for $15.95 in the 1960s, shoes were selling for between $25 and $40 by the mid-1970s and for as much as $50 by 1978, when Nike debuted the Air Tailwind. The New Balance 990 took the price up to a cool $100 in 1983.

Along with a new price tag, running shoes got a new home as running specialty stores opened across the country in the mid-1970s. Prior to that, running shoes were sold in sporting goods shops and department stores or via mail order through ads in *Runner's World* and *Track & Field News*. These specialty shops were staffed by experienced runners who could instruct and advise customers on how a shoe should fit and feel. Even America's running heroes were getting in on the business side of the sport. Marathon champions Frank Shorter and Bill Rodgers were among that first wave of retail shop owners, opening their own branded stores in Boulder, Colorado, and Boston, respectively.

"The running shoe business quickly became a much bigger business by the end of the 1970s," recalls Carl Brandt, who cofounded Movin Shoes in 1977 in San Diego. "Every brand wanted a hook, something that said, 'This will help you run better.' Every company was trying to develop something to use for a marketing scheme."

As recreational running grew, shoe models became more sophisticated, and choices increased exponentially. *Runner's World*, the sport's dominant media voice of the day, saw a need to provide readers with a reliable evaluation to guide their footwear purchases.

Consulting an eclectic mix of runners, coaches, podiatrists, and shoe brands, the magazine developed principles for what composed a good running shoe and scored shoes accordingly. The criteria favored shoes with soft cushioning, durable outsoles, and a high heel lift that were also relatively lightweight and flexible. Sturdy heel counters, rigid arch support, and pliable uppers also earned praise for providing a more stable ride.

Beginning in 1975, *Runner's World* began releasing an annual ranking of the best-selling shoes on the market. In the first report, the Adidas SL-72, a modestly cushioned German-made shoe, earned the shoe-of-the-year award. It got high marks for its half-inch heel lift; rigid heel counter; soft, supple nylon upper; and flexible forefoot, though it was criticized for being cramped in the toe box and inadequately cushioned compared to other models.

The reviews quickly became a catalyst for conversation and controversy. Getting a good review in *Runner's World* naturally resulted in increased sales, especially for a top-ranking shoe. While the shoe reviews were said to be entirely independent of advertiser influence, they put the magazine on a treacherous path between publishing positive reviews and trying to collect increasing amounts of ad revenue from those brands every year.

Fanelli says many in the industry suspected that the ratings were fixed. "A Brooks shoe would win the top award, and, coincidentally, Brooks would spend a ton of advertising dollars [with *Runner's World*]," he says skeptically.

To combat this negative buzz and increase the rankings' reliability, *Runner's World* publisher Bob Anderson hired Penn State University biomechanist Peter Cavanagh to conduct objective measurements of cushioning, flexibility, and durability. Cavanagh's figures, which first appeared in the 1977 shoe review, were an improvement over the previous procedures, which had relied on more basic measurements of shoe thickness and weight as well as hand-tested flexibility and collective fit assessments that were combined to produce highly subjective values of good, fair, and poor. But the new system was neither entirely data-driven nor objective. A panel of experts ranked each model based on their own subjective interpretations of the shoes, creating a two-score system that was then totaled to determine the winner. "The shoe that had the highest score was the winner," Anderson recalls.

Given the importance of the rankings, brands were soon developing shoes to meet the specific criteria in the evaluation process, and more skepticism ensued. Soon *Runner's World* abandoned numerical rankings altogether and initiated a more general ranking system that would show deference to the good, better, and best shoes while downplaying the not-so-great shoes. Five stars meant "excellent and highly recommended" while the rare one star was a harsh vote of no confidence and "better left in the box."

The new system helped spread a positive gloss over more shoes, but it didn't end the hullabaloo. The four- and five-star ratings resulted in huge commercial success for those shoes, but brands that received fewer-than-expected stars for a particular model felt the sting of lower-than-expected sales. As soon as the reviews were published, *Runner's World* found itself trying to placate some of its top advertisers with make-good deals in future issues. Nike, growing ever more powerful while still struggling with quality control issues, legal battles, and a quest to become a publicly traded company, pulled its advertising for several years beginning in the late 1970s because of a belief that the results were unfairly rigged against it.

Despite its rankling of shoe brands, Anderson calls the ranking system a big win for *Runner's World*, consumers, and the industry. "There was a huge range in shoes that were available at the time as far as style, weight, construction techniques, and overall quality," he recalls. "I think, for the first time, [the reviews] helped shoe manufacturers and retailers figure out what runners needed and wanted."

The rankings, albeit imperfect and flawed, created a buzz that runners, too, were keen to follow. Amid all of this excitement, focus, ad dollars, and innovation around shoes, running participation grew exponentially in the 1970s. With the jogging craze tantalizing the United States, marathon participation exploded in a single decade, from an estimated 7,000 in 1970 to 143,000 in 1980. Running shoe sales skyrocketed from $3 million in 1970 to a whopping $100 million by 1980.

"All of these things brought more people into running," recalls Burfoot, who oversaw shoe rankings and reviews as the magazine's top editor at the time. "There had never been anyone to talk to about running; then suddenly everyone at the cocktail party wanted to talk about it!"

———

Initially, Kayser hung his retired shoes on a fence post in his backyard—he literally created a "shoe tree" by nailing shoes and insoles over thin strips of wood in an array to resemble branches—but when his passion for preserving history carried over into running, he became the serious shoe aficionado that he is today. He took down the shoe tree, salvaging what he could but tossing out key models that had been wrecked by exposure to the elements. (Interestingly, a pair of original Nike Waffle Trainers sold for $437,000 at an auction in 2019.)

"I could kick myself now," he says, looking at a weathered pair of late-1980s Pegasus with nail holes and a midsole that crumbles like chunks of blue cheese. "Some of the models survived, but I had to get rid of a lot of them because they were covered with moss and just trashed. Man, I wish I still had some of those shoes in my collection."

He says it with a laugh, but it's clear that he had a serious connection to those long-ago shoes. I find myself wondering what happened to a few

SIX PATENTS THAT CHANGED RUNNING SHOE DESIGN

Stan Hockerson has spent his career examining, innovating, and selling shoes. After running competitively and studying kinesiology in college, Hockerson worked in some of the first running shops in California in the mid-1970s and started looking at shoe designs with a critical eye. He began sketching ways to improve the functionality of shoes and received his first patent in 1979 at the age of 24. He has worked for several brands and continues to consult with shoe companies while also owning several running stores. Here, he describes what he believes are the six most influential patents that have changed running shoe design since the mid-1970s.

❶ Bill Bowerman's Waffle Outsole

When Bill Bowerman created the waffle outsole for Nike, everyone had to make their own version of it because it improved traction and cushioning and was so visually striking. Not long after Nike's waffle with the square lugs made a splash on the market, Puma came up with a version with round lugs, Saucony made triangle lugs—and so it went. The waffle outsole was what's called a "disruptive patent" because it disrupted the industry and forced other brands to follow a new way of doing something.

❷ Nike's Air-Sole Cushioning System

The Air bladder midsole concept that Frank Rudy designed and licensed to Nike was unlike anything before or after it. It immediately spawned new midsole ideas and innovations from other brands. Nike grew enormously after it perfected the ability to put Air packets in the midsoles of its shoes, and the evolution of the Air Max and the cross-training category that followed were a big part of that. Nike hit the market at the right time, with innovation that made everyone else react.

③ Stabilizing Midsole Design

"I filed this patent in 1979 for a supportive midsole design that came up around the side of the foot and eliminated the collapse around the void between the heel counter and the flare of the midsole. When I tried to sell the patent in 1980 to 1982, there wasn't much interest. I remember the letter that Jeff Johnson [Nike's first employee, who served many executive roles with the brand] sent me telling me it was 'cosmetically unsound,' which meant it looked ugly," Hockerson says. But as running changed and people started craving one shoe that could do more than just run, brands started to design with a midsole that wraps the foot for more lateral stability. The Air Max and cross-trainers were two initial ways it was used, but there's not a shoe made today that doesn't use this design.

④ Barry Bates Pronation Plugs

Barry Bates designed and patented shoes for ASICS in 1980 that had midsole inserts with varying levels of firmness to cater to the rate and severity level of pronation. A footwear guru from San Francisco named Jeff Sink was doing it before Bates, but he didn't put the patent out there the way Bates did. Ultimately, it changed the industry, and every brand wound up creating its own version of multidensity midsoles and, later, more dynamic midsole designs that could avoid inserts altogether.

⑤ Decoupled Outsoles

South African Johnny Halberstadt (who cofounded the Boulder Running Company stores in the United States) was the first to create and patent a decoupled outsole with a longitudinal groove under the heel. The design created a left and right side of the heel, allowing the shoe to compress into that void. This changed how shoe developers thought about how to disperse heel impact forces because it segmented the heel for the first time. "I took it a step further by putting sipes all the way across to create small independent squares that allowed a wide range of natural movement that a structure or posted shoe could not, and that wound up being a big part of how the Nike Free was designed," recalls Hockerson.

⑥ Articulated Toes by Vibram FiveFingers

FiveFingers, with its low-to-the-ground design and individual pockets for each toe, disrupted the industry big-time, whether good or bad. "I thought it was a good thing because it made shoe companies aware that shoes had gotten too high off the ground, disallowing feet to move naturally. At the time, designs were hiding air and gel packets, and shoes were really high off the ground. Now, running barefoot was a dangerous thing. We've been wearing elevated shoes our entire adult lives, so trying to go down to zero probably means you're going to get injured. Still, in my opinion, FiveFingers were good for our industry because they led to the minimalist movement and forced everyone to think differently," Hockerson says.

of the models I wore during my own formative years as a runner—those Adidas Oregons; my old Nike Zoom spikes; and my favorite shoes ever, Nike Air Edge distance racing flats.

If there is one thing that's clear from Kayser's colorful, wide-ranging collection, it is that the running shoe business is fickle, even among the top brands. While Nike, Adidas, New Balance, ASICS, and Brooks have remained industry stalwarts for 40 years, each of those brands has suffered deep valleys along with peaks, caused by poor designs, missed trends, bad reviews, manufacturing challenges, and shifts of company resources from running to other sports. Smaller brands—often the ones that have spurred innovation—can't always survive those downfalls, and many have disappeared into history.

Within Kayser's collection are plenty of brands that have long been extinct, at least on the American market: Etonic, Turntec, Osaga, EB Brütting/Lydiard, Pearl Izumi, and Pony, to name a few. Interestingly, I spy a few original models from Brooks, New Balance, and Nike that have returned in recent years as nonrunning "vintage" replicas amid the retro-styled sneaker craze. However, I don't see any shoes from Fila, Diadora, LA Gear, Kangaroo, Zoot, or Patagonia, all bygone brands that came and went.

As I drive away from Beverly that night, listening to the last of the Red Sox game on the radio, I feel grateful for the time spent with Kayser and his thoughtfully curated collection. But I'm a bit somber, too. In tracing the evolutionary timeline that his shoes represent, it's evident that brands have long been on a conflicting path: tripping over themselves and each other to make optimal running shoes that help customers run better even as they are hugely distracted by shiny objects and false flags that allow them to sell more running shoes. While those two criteria seem to mesh just fine in the corporate boardrooms of fast-growing running shoe brands, they may sometimes entirely undermine each other when the rubber hits the road on a run.

3 **RUNNING SHOE** COOL

Fashion is a mirror, reflecting the culture.
BILL ROBINSON, FASHION PHOTOGRAPHER

In March 1995, I was in my mid-20s, and, hoping to get out of a postwinter malaise, I had committed to getting back to serious running, regaining a fit runner physique, and training in earnest for a race. I had moved from Chicago to Boulder, Colorado, and felt inspired by being in one of the epicenters of American running, where some of the world's best runners lived and trained.

I headed to Runners Roost running specialty shop on Pearl Street, Boulder's popular pedestrian mall. I had been out of touch with the running scene for a while, having been buried for a few years while getting my career going. But as I approached the store, I felt those old familiar feelings of inspiration and excitement.

The shop was located in a small, subterranean space below street level, which added to its cool factor. It was like a hidden den, and the extra effort required to maneuver the short flight of steps kept tourists at bay, relegating it to a place only runners would visit. Every time I went in, I found lanky, lean athletes hanging out, talking about races, trying on shoes, and planning workouts. It had an authenticity that oozed running culture.

The store had history, too. Formerly known as Frank Shorter Sports, the shop had been started by the 1972 Olympic Marathon champion, who had moved to Boulder in 1970 and still lived in town. Like the old Competitive Foot store in the Chicago suburbs, the shop had autographed posters of famous runners on the wall, running magazines scattered about, a table with race entry forms, and a sizable shoe wall showing off bright and colorful new models.

I knew the shoe I wanted to buy before I even entered the store. The new Air Max from Nike had been highly touted in shoe reviews and ad campaigns that spring, gracing the pages of *Runner's World* and *Sports Illustrated* and showing up in flashy TV ads on ESPN. Even before I saw it in person, I knew it was innovative, cool, and special—a shoe that would not only turn heads but turn me into a better version of myself. Or so I hoped. I was certain this latest model would get me into shape to run a marathon faster than my mediocre attempt a few years earlier.

Conceived by Sergio Lozano, a talented young designer who had been working in Nike's other sport categories in the early 1990s, the shoe was originally intended for a larger, more powerful runner who demanded maximum cushioning when pounding the pavement. But by the time the shoe hit stores, it was a work of art that far transcended running.

The Air Max was an eye-catching, thickly cushioned shoe with a tricolor fade design, but what really set it apart was the small feature at the rear of the foot, a cutaway "window" that revealed the Air-Sole unit in the heel. The unique peekaboo feature had become known as "visible technology" in the footwear industry after Nike had debuted it in the original Air Max in 1987.

At $140, the Air Max cost $50 more than most of the top-priced running shoes in the store, and it felt heavy compared to the shoes I had typically worn. But a former college teammate had raved about his pair, and, yearning to rekindle my running vibe, I bought into the hype.

At the time, $140 was a lot of money for me—and, let's face it, it still is—but I justified the purchase as an investment in my well-being. I knew that building a solid aerobic base of fitness would lead to better health and, ultimately, new opportunities. Buying a pair of Air Max would be worth every penny, I reasoned, even if it meant I'd be eating dry cereal and ramen noodles as my primary sources of sustenance just to be able to run in them.

I was an impressionable consumer at the time, unaware of the tidal wave of change that had been sweeping over the world of running shoes and had brought me and the Air Max to this moment.

From the late 1980s through the mid-1990s, running shoes had gone through a period of radical innovation, with new technologies, new materials, new construction techniques, and new ways of thinking resulting in groundbreaking new shoes every season. The 1995 edition of the Air Max that I held in my hands epitomized this creative period.

The evolution was happening for one simple reason: money. Participation in running was growing year after year, and increasingly outside its original customer base of core runners. That meant there was more money to be made—and a lot of it—by shoe brands. As running increasingly became a mainstream activity, and new, leisure runners joined the herd, running shoes became more trendy in pop culture. As a result, much of the design and innovation—and the marketing budgets—were trending away from performance running.

For me, though, running was still about speed. Sure, I needed to lose 5 pounds, but my focus was not to run for the sake of losing weight. What I wanted was to run a faster Bolder Boulder 10K than I had the previous year and to break 2:50 in the marathon. For me, that meant starting with a new pair of the right running shoes.

Because of my track background, I had always favored a "less is more" approach in shoes, which meant wearing lightweight, low-to-the-ground racing flats for most of my workouts. The Air Max model for which I was about to lay out a significant chunk of change was bold, brash, and innovative, to be sure, but it was anything but low to the ground. Or lightweight. Or nimble. Or an ideal high-mileage running shoe for marathon training. To me, it felt hefty and too clunky to produce a smooth running gait.

That said, it looked soundly built and fit my foot well, and it was undeniably eye-catching. And that ad campaign was just so inspiring. So I bought it—both the hype and the shoe.

The good news was, I got a lot of compliments on the shoe. "Those are the coolest running shoes I've ever seen," a former college teammate told me one night as we headed out for a beer. Then he laughed. "They look a little big and bulky for running, but they sure look good with jeans."

The bad news was that he was right, and running 10 miles in them felt laborious and tiresome. I gave up on them as running shoes after about two weeks and relegated them to casual wear, which was the growing trend.

With no more cash to spare on shoes, I started training in two older pairs of Nikes from my closet—the light and fast Air Skylon and Air Huarache, both from the early '90s. I had already logged more than 300 miles on each, yet every time I slipped them on, they felt the way I thought a running shoe should feel. I was not nearly as fit in the spring of 1995 as I'd been when I'd worn those shoes originally, but they still provided me with that reassuring proprioceptive connection to the ground that I knew and appreciated.

As I embarked on my training program, stuck with an expensive pair of shoes I wished I hadn't bought and instead running in old kicks, I wondered whether the evolution of running shoes was headed to a place that I didn't understand or wasn't going to like.

The late 1980s and early 1990s were a time of sweeping change in pop culture, from music to design to athletic gear. Pop music was transitioning away from aging British crooners and American rock legends to frizzy-haired heavy metal rockers; the somber, self-indulgent sound of Seattle grunge; gregarious boy bands; and the rise of urban hip-hop. The fall of the Berlin Wall signaled the end of the Cold War, ringing in a new sense of freedom and self-expression throughout the Western world. Feathered hair gave way to mullets and shoulder pads, a rainbow of Day-Glo colors became a thing in fashion, and low-definition computer-generated graphics and Beavis and Butthead rose to prominence.

Running was in transition, too, as the original running boom hit a plateau amid the rise of aerobics and other gym-based fitness trends.

A second phase of that boom was surging, however, and this one would make running inviting and accessible to anyone willing to lace up and hit the roads. While the first phase had been largely about top-tier athletes and early adopters running a marathon or 10K race as fast as possible, this phase was about just getting out there and participating. Instead of a pure performance mantra about training harder to run faster, running was increasingly about just finishing. America's elite runners were no longer the face of the sport. If you were a new runner in those days, *you* were the face of the sport.

The pro scene was changing, too. Despite a few significant high points and all-world athletes such as Bob Kennedy, Lynn Jennings, Steve Spence, and Mark Plaatjes, U.S. competitive distance running began a steady decline that would continue through the 1990s. As East African and other international runners began to dominate the Olympics, the track and field world championships, and the world's biggest marathons, America was transitioning into a nation of hobby joggers.

None of this was bad news for brands because these runners came en masse, and they brought their wallets. As running participation grew, the sales of running shoes, clothes, and accessories skyrocketed.

With this new approach to running came new needs, new vibes, new aesthetics. These modern runners weren't interested in looking like competitive runners—because they weren't, nor did most have the typical wiry physique of an elite—and so apparel went through dramatic changes. Tiny split shorts, skimpy singlets, and revealing tights were replaced by more comfortable, less revealing clothes that limited exposure and boosted confidence. More supportive sports bras; longer, roomier shorts; cushier socks; and baggier running pants hit the scene, and sales soared.

The subdued color palette that had been the tradition for gear also went out the window, exploding into a rainbow of bright colors, hues, and design elements never before seen on running shoes—purple, pink, Day-Glo fluorescents, pastels, speckles, fades, splatters, and more. I rocked a pair of pastel-blue-and-bright-pink Nike Air Flows in 1989 and remember feeling really good about them.

But the biggest changes came in the expansion (and promotion) of running shoes.

Sneakers were becoming in vogue, both as something to wear casually and something to covet. The trend started with the release of the Air Jordan basketball shoes in 1985 and became increasingly widespread among brands until by the late 1980s, athletic shoes—specifically running shoes, aerobics shoes, and basketball shoes—were *the* casual shoes of choice for Americans.

Wearing athletic shoes as everyday wear—to run errands, at work, to pick up the kids, to a cocktail party—became popular both because those shoes were far more comfortable than the traditional dress shoes or casual shoes that most people had worn before then but also because of what it said about you. Wearing running shoes on a regular basis gave the impression that the wearer was an active and fit person.

The trend took off in the 1980s as the percentage of the population identifying as a recreational athlete grew to a critical mass, says Matt Powell, a respected athletic footwear industry analyst. As consumers started thinking of athletic footwear in ways other than its intended use (i.e., in sports), brands jumped headlong into the new design and marketing opportunities presented by that shift.

Nike, the dominant leader in the early '80s, found itself facing strong competition from Reebok, a British brand making a splash with its running and aerobics shoes. Nike upped the stakes with a unique limited-supply tactic aimed at stoking demand for its coveted Air Jordans, creating hunger and hype in key American markets, and then shortly thereafter feeding the masses by flooding the market with the $65 shoes. Nike also began to invest huge amounts of money in ad campaigns—campaigns that went a long way toward helping this casual trend create a bona fide cultural shift, Powell says.

Nowhere was this trend more prominent than with Nike's new running shoe, the Air Max, in 1987.

The original Air Max wasn't just cool; it was a genuine revolution in running shoes—a soft, supercushioned trainer that sported a chunky avant-garde design with a rockered profile from heel to toe but was still light and capable enough for long runs. In essence, it was the world's first maximally cushioned running shoe, although 20-plus years later, a new French brand called Hoka One One would get credit for revolutionizing running shoes by creating the "maximalist" category of running shoes.

The shoe was the creation of a design team led by Tinker Hatfield, an imaginative young designer who had put creative pizazz into some of the early Air Jordan basketball shoes.

What really made the Air Max explode in popularity, though, not only among runners but also among the greater athletic shoe-buying universe, was the energetic advertising campaign that helped launch it. Conceived and produced by Widen+Kennedy, a small Portland, Oregon, ad agency that had made a name for itself when it began working on the Nike account in the 1980s, the campaign featured a series of eye-catching, two- to six-page glossy magazine ads and heart-thumping TV spots unlike any that had ever been seen before in the running world.

In one, a massive image of the Air Max is featured prominently across a two-page spread. A bright light shines through the Air-Sole unit under the heel. A callout in smallish print reads, "NIKE-AIR IS NOT A SHOE." On the next page, bold type screams, "IT'S A REVOLUTION."

The ad went on to describe the Air cushioning system and its many benefits to runners, such as reducing shock-related injuries to bones, muscles, and tendons. Over the next several pages, the ad explained how the technology worked and how Nike had tested it against the best-selling running, aerobics, and basketball shoes of the day from top brands. It said that Nike's best athletes across all sports, from marathon to basketball, had been using Nike shoes with Air-Sole cushioning to achieve greatness all along, although that Air cushioning system had been hidden in the midsole of their shoes.

When you saw that bold ad, it was impossible not to feel inspired. But that was nothing compared to the impact of the TV ad. In flashy quick cadence and grainy black-and-white, with the Beatles' "Revolution" blasting in the background, the ad showed a flurry of recreational athletes and top Nike pros engaging in more than a dozen sports amid repeated close-ups of an Air Max impacting the ground in slow motion. The 60-second spot was electrifying. Powerful, provocative, and moving, it offered something for everyone, from the doers to the doubters, across all walks of life.

That campaign helped Nike make "visible air" bigger than just a running conversation and thrust the Air Max into the popular consciousness in a way no running shoe had been before. In every way that the original Tailwind had failed, the Air Max hit it out of the park.

Nike caught a lot of flak for using the Beatles song, partially because it had done so against the wishes of Apple Records, which had been the Beatles' recording company. Nike had paid Capitol Records, which held the North American licensing rights to Beatles songs, a cool $250,000 to use a rendition of the song. A court battle ensued, and Nike stopped running the ads after settling out of court, but the impact had been felt, and that controversy wasn't going to unring the bell. Nike sold more than five million pairs of the original Air Max, breaking every record in the book for athletic shoe sales.

Running shoes were hot, and Nike was on a fast track to reclaiming its throne as king of the sneaker world, which Reebok had briefly stolen. But even with its cool factor at an all-time high, Nike couldn't rest easy. It needed a way to catapult the success of the original Air Max through sustainable messaging. And in 1988, Dan Wieden of Wieden+Kennedy helped it do so with a phrase that would become one of the stickiest in ad campaign history: "Just Do It."

Although Phil Knight was skeptical of the phrase at first, he acknowledged that it touched on one of the original tenets on which he had founded Nike: that everyone was an athlete, regardless of age, gender, or athletic ability. "Just Do It" encouraged more people not only to become more active but to flaunt that active lifestyle as a fashion statement. It didn't matter how fast or strong or athletic you were, what your racial makeup was, or how old you were. It didn't even matter what you were doing to get your athletic fix. All that mattered was that you were out there just doing it—or were willing to start.

The first Nike "Just Do It" TV commercial from 1988 portrayed iconic San Francisco runner Walt Stack running shirtless across the Golden Gate Bridge. "I run 17 miles every morning," he pants as a text bar announces that he's 80 years old. "People ask me how I keep my teeth from chattering in the wintertime," he says as he waves to cars passing him on the bridge.

And then the punchline: "I leave them in my locker." The witty, authentic ad paid homage to Stack as just another ordinary guy out there just doing it like millions of other Americans.

The slogan, a simple but powerful call to action, helped Nike transcend its success in running to become a global sportswear giant, putting itself on the path to grow into the $30 billion company that it is today. Decades later, "Just Do It" is recognized as one of the most successful marketing taglines in the history of American business. While the catchphrase certainly encouraged more people to run, the many iterations of the "Just Do It" campaign encouraged consumers not just to run but to do a bit of everything. It suggested a different mentality about how they spent their time exercising—one that demanded a different type of footwear.

Capitalizing on these changes in running, fitness trends, popular culture, and self-expression, Nike catapulted its "visible air" success into an entirely new category of shoes called "cross-trainers." As interest in hardcore running waned, Nike created cross-trainers to be the consummate athletic shoes for the recreational athlete. The category was all about versatility, with smartly designed training shoes that carried a do-everything vibe—you could go to the gym, go for a run, lift weights, play tennis, play basketball, or do aerobics in cross-trainers.

Perhaps just as importantly, the shoes were designed with crossover lifestyle aesthetics and appeal that made them conducive to casual wear and passed the "looks good with jeans" test that had become increasingly important in athletic shoe design.

The launch of the cross-training category took America by storm, thanks in part to a series of captivating TV commercials that featured versatile two-sport star Bo Jackson and included Michael Jordan, John McEnroe, Joan Benoit Samuelson, Wayne Gretzky, and the music of Bo Diddley. Nike's cross-trainers crushed Reebok's aerobics shoe business, turned the athletic footwear industry upside down, and returned Nike to its dominant perch once again.

===

The story of "visible air" didn't begin with Hatfield's design of the Air Max. Rather, it started when David Forland, Nike's director of cushioning innovation, began constructing new encapsulated Air-Sole prototypes by hand, molding the air-injected polyurethane packets so that they fit inside a shoe yet could be seen by the outside world. He stumbled upon a critical moment when he rotated the bag, placing the seams on the top and bottom instead of on the perimeter. "A light bulb turned on," he recalls. "I built a new prototype right there on the spot."

Prior to that eureka moment, the design trend had been to make Air-Sole units thinner and thinner in order to make burying them in the midsole easier and to keep running shoes as light and lean as possible for optimal performance. But Forland knew that runners—especially new runners—desired more cushioning, not less. With this change, along with the innovative shoe designs from Hatfield and Lozano, Nike shifted the way running shoes were made throughout the 1990s.

With "visible technology," the thinking at Nike was that if consumers could actually see the Air cushioning unit, they would understand it, crave it, flaunt it. They were right. The feature was a huge hit and an early precursor of the look-at-me (and my cool shoes) approach to fitness pursuits and gear that social media would tap into many years later.

As Nike went, so went the industry. The advent of the first Air Max shoe and the cross-trainers that followed sparked a visible technology revolution, forcing brands to develop not only their own innovative cushioning system but also a way to show it off. By the late 1980s, how a running shoe looked was as important as how it performed. Maybe more important.

With those undertones as a backdrop, running participation continued to soar in the 1990s, with the number of marathon finishers rising from 224,000 in 1990 to 353,000 by the turn of the new century. A growing trend of charity running helped spur that growth as people who had never run before suddenly found a way to become a marathoner. Led by groups such as the Leukemia & Lymphoma Society's Team in Training, which trained runners who were raising money for the organization's cancer research efforts, suddenly everyone could finish a marathon.

An explosion in women's participation provided another notable growth spurt. While running had once been a male-dominated sport and recreational activity, the '90s significantly altered the ratio. In 1980, 90 percent of marathon finishers in the United States were men and 10 percent were women. By 1995, the percentages had shifted to 74/26, and by 2000, they were 62/38, a trend that would continue through 2019, when the percentages are currently 54/46. Women's participation in shorter-distance races has actually been greater than men's since the start of the 2000s.

When Oprah Winfrey finished the 1994 Marine Corps Marathon in 4:29, it was a national come-hither to women, even more so than Joan Benoit Samuelson's victory in the 1984 Olympic Marathon had been. That Oprah had trained for a year and lost 83 pounds in the process was secondary to the fact that she ran 26.2 miles and did something that many women thought impossible. While Samuelson's Olympic win helped inspire women's competitive distance running in the United States, Oprah's marathon finish—more than 2 hours slower than Joanie's—was far more relevant when it came to inspiring women to run. If Oprah could do it, so could you.

======

As running's popularity grew and changed, median marathon times began to slow. In 1980, when 143,000 people ran a marathon in the United States, average times were 3:32 for men and 4:03 for women. By 1995, when the total finisher number approached 300,000, the times had slowed to 3:54 for men and 4:15 for women. By the early 2000s and nearly 400,000 finishers, men had slowed to 4:20 and women to 4:56. As the marathon hit its high-water mark of 550,000 finishers in 2014, the median time for men was 4:22 and a slightly faster 4:47 for women.

As for shoe design, the performance aspect moved further and further off the radar for the average runner. Shoes had to look good or unique to be considered credible or cool. The shoes that sold the best were those with the most plastic, metallic, and technology additives.

"In the 1990s, sheer bulk translated into a perception of cushion or stability or some kind of premium product," says Sam Winebaum, publisher of the running shoe review site RoadTrailRun.com. "It was kind of a dead period in design as far as performance running was concerned."

It wasn't that brands were going out of their way to make shoes that weren't fast or efficient; it was more that running was changing, with a premium placed on comfort, stability, and looks. New runners didn't necessarily want to run as fast or as often, so lightweight, minimally designed shoes were lost on them. What they wanted was to feel comfortable and avoid soreness and injuries. And they wanted to wear their running shoes while doing things other than just running. So how a running shoe looked became paramount and a reason for brands to push the envelope of design in new directions.

This new thinking coincided with the advent of affordable personal computers and new software tools—specifically Photoshop in 1990—which together helped unleash a whirlwind of design breakthroughs across pop culture in everything from electronics and album covers to apparel and footwear. When it came to running shoes, aesthetics were crucial to sales.

Through the end of the 1990s and into the early 2000s, performance-oriented shoe design slowed tremendously. The true shoe innovations that led to improved performance weren't able to gain much fanfare outside an increasingly shrinking base of core runners. So naturally, brands sank their money elsewhere, trying to gain more appeal with the masses.

But it wouldn't be accurate to say aesthetics was the sole focus. While it's easy to paint the late 1980s and 1990s with a broad brush based on the wild, eye-grabbing, colorful trends that were produced during that time, there was at least some focus on helping to solve a problem, increase comfort, or add to the performance value of shoes.

Some particularly innovative shoes of the era included the Nike Air Stab, a motion-control shoe with reinforced see-through heel slashes that not only revealed the shoe's Air-Sole cushioning system but also restricted the heel from rolling inward after impact with the ground. Nike's Air Huarache, which utilized design cues from traditional Mexican footwear, had a neoprene interior bootie and a futuristic heel tab that was more than just cool to behold: It also created a precision fit and a lightweight, smooth ride, again proving that innovation had its place in the performance-oriented category, too.

While Nike was the innovation leader from which other brands took cues, those brands were busy in this time period, too, striking out on their own path of creativity and modernization. The Reebok HXL used an air-pump system designed to fill in gaps between the foot and the interior of the shoe and thus create a semicustom fit. Reebok borrowed the design from Ellesse International, which was known for its innovative tennis gear. It was a huge success. Nike followed Reebok's lead on this element but, unable to match the success of Reebok's iconic red-black-and-neon-yellow InstaPump Fury, eventually dropped its air-infused fit technology.

Puma joined the innovation fray with its Disc system that used a dial and internal wiring system to tighten a shoe around a wearer's foot. Although Puma never gained the level of mass appeal that Reebok and Nike had, it did gain notice with the Disc Blaze. Other quirky innovations of the time included shoes with interchangeable outsoles, multicolored wear-indicator lugs, and metal springs in the midsoles.

Meanwhile, ASICS countered Nike's Air cushioning technology with its own GEL cushioning technology. Like Air, GEL doesn't break down or lose its cushion over time, but ASICS had kept this technology buried within its shoes. After Nike's success with visual tech, ASICS followed suit with visual GEL packets in its Kayano in 1995. But, sticking to its conservative Japanese roots, it continued building performance-oriented running shoes. Unlike many other brands, ASICS remained loyal to committed runners, mostly avoiding mixing its running silhouettes with lifestyle cues. Its GEL-Lyte III was as popular for that cool GEL-infused midsole as for the innovative, split-tongue closure system and trend-bunking lightweight design. (Well, at least it was lightweight for the time.)

These models proved that the performance category wasn't dead, but the mainstream popularity of running shoes had definitely created a split within shoe companies. While brands still developed a few lightweight, performance-oriented shoes every year, the '90s were known primarily for heavier, overbuilt shoes meant to have visual and crossover appeal.

"Some of the shoes were good, some were crap," recalls Mike Rouse, a running industry veteran who worked in retail as well as various sales, marketing, and development stints with Brooks, Mizuno, K-Swiss, Zoot, and On Running. "Every brand was trying to keep pace with Nike and looking for the next big thing. Everyone was chasing the shiny prize that would make their shoe and their brand cool, because cool was what was selling in the 1990s. You had to be doing something different or you were dead in the water."

KARA GOUCHER || Adidas Adistar LD spikes

Two-time U.S. Olympian

Back in high school, my friends and I always loved the track guy in the blue Adidas that we'd see in running magazines and on TV. It was Haile Gebrselassie, the great Ethiopian runner. Of course, I've known for a long time now that he was a multi-time world record holder and Olympic champion before moving on to the marathon with huge success and setting the world record. Back in high school, we didn't understand the significance of who he was or how great he was, yet we knew he was awesome, and we loved the little guy in the blue shoes.

I told my mom I really, really wanted blue Adidas spikes, and she went on a mission to find them. Between the limited selection available in Duluth, Minnesota, and whatever was available from the Eastbay catalog, she did her best and got me some black Adidas spikes. I freakin' loved those things! I thought I was so cool, like some kind of great Ethiopian athlete! My teammates were like "What?! You've got Adidas spikes!" Prior to that, we all had Nike spikes, and those were fine, but we wanted Adidas spikes because of him. I ran every cross-country and track race through the last two years of my high school career in those shoes. I have no idea what model they were, but I'll never forget them and all that they meant to me.

Nothing exemplified this split between souped-up performance and design-enhanced lifestyle shoes better than Nike's 1994 Air Max Triax. Designed to be a comfortable, high-mileage training model for performance-oriented runners, the Triax was cushioned, supportive, and not as bulky or heavy as many of its contemporaries. It was flexible and had plenty of energetic pop as well. But it also had an overtly fresh and stylish look, with a mesh-and-leather upper, a large, visible Air-Sole unit in the heel, a padded tongue and collar, and a variety of bright colors.

Committed runners gobbled it up, making the Air Max Triax the number-one-selling shoe at running specialty retail stores across the United States. This was a huge distinction for a shoe at that time, given that running retail shops were selling a much larger percentage of high-level kicks than they are today, so the competition to be first was fierce and meaningful.

The shoe's aesthetic highlights helped make it the number-one shoe at mall-based Foot Locker stores, too, which meant that casual mainstream enthusiasts were buying it in droves as well. This dual-pronged success of a single model had never happened before and has not happened since.

"The Triax helped on both sides of the business," recalls Fritz Taylor, who has overseen shoe design at Brooks, Mizuno, Under Armour, and Descente and got his start at Nike. "It was comfortable, good to run in, and looked good. But after 1995, you didn't see that happening in one shoe anymore."

Nike started chasing the fashion side of the business, Taylor says, a choice that had a positive effect on Nike's bottom line in the lifestyle category but came at a cost. Its lean toward fashion in the mid-'90s helped rival ASICS emerge as the new leading brand among committed runners. It ascended to the top of the ladder among brands sold at specialty stores and wouldn't relinquish that position for more than a decade.

======

As the "visible air" packets embedded in the heel of Nike shoes got bigger, so too did a shoe's silhouette. The original Air Max—which was a decent high-mileage training shoe—was followed by the Air Max 90 (1990), Air Max 180 (1991) and Air Max 93 (1993), shoes that continued the design motif built around the rearfoot Air cushioning system but all of which were successively more built-up, higher off the ground, and heavier than the previous version.

"If you look at the history of Air Max, one of the main differences among models was that each version held a greater volume of air than the last one and the least amount of foam," Forland says. "Foam breaks down; air doesn't."

That simple fact, along with a design-first mentality, put Nike on a quest to develop a foamless running shoe. But to do so, it needed to figure out how to get its air capsules into the forefoot. That aim led to a new Air-Sole construction method called "blow molding." The technique, which allowed the creation of Air-Soles in three-dimensional shapes that didn't depend on air pressure, paved the way for Air-Soles to be crafted to fit the curvature of a shoe's forefoot.

The Air Max 95, which featured two separate blow-molded Air-Sole units, was the first to include visible Nike Air cushioning in both heel and forefoot. It also sported a colorful gradient pattern on the upper that coincided with a lacing system inspired by a set of ribs, a spine-inspired outsole, and a mesh-and-suede upper representing muscle fibers. "It was meant to have a provocative look and draw attention to the innovation of forefoot air," says Taylor, who was involved in the initial design brief process.

It may not have been a very good running shoe—too heavy, too clunky—but it oozed cool to the consumer. More than any other running shoe before it, that edition of the Air Max was coveted by urbanites, suburban teens, pro athletes in other sports, Hollywood actors, music personalities, and just about everyone in between.

Fashion tastes, along with interest in running not to race but to finish as well as pursue a range of other athletic pursuits, continued to pummel performance-oriented design. Lifestyle-inspired shoes were making a whole lot of money, so that's where the bulk of brand attention was directed. Performance-oriented running wasn't dead, but fewer people cared, and many runners were taking their own approach to reaching finish lines and spending their money accordingly.

At the same time, trail running was gaining mainstream popularity. Although a small community of off-road running fanatics had been around since the 1970s, most runners wore road running shoes or lightweight hiking shoes when running trails. But as the sport started to grow, brands recognized the need to create trail-specific shoes with features providing agility, protection, and traction on natural surfaces. Initial models that appeared in the mid-1990s came from both running brands and hiking boot brands. The Adidas Response Trail was the most popular trail shoe of that era, although the New Balance 801 trail runner would soon become one of the best-selling running shoes on the market as it gained surprising mainstream appeal with mall walkers, soccer moms, and other lifestyle users. Meanwhile, a new brand called Montrail developed a supercushy shoe called the Vitesse that became the top brand among dedicated trail ultrarunners. Nike, Salomon, Brooks, La Sportiva, The North Face, and Merrell would all eventually get into the fray, as would flip-flop maker Teva, when it debuted a trail running sandal with a grippy outsole. Over the next few years, the trail running category—once thought of as a marginal niche—would grow to 15 percent of the overall running shoe market. Their design and construction would be influenced heavily by marketing, sales, and pop culture, too, at times resulting in zany-looking and ill-performing models out on remote trails.

As the dawn of a new century approached, running was more fashionable and more popular than ever before. But were there consequences? People were running more slowly, and more were getting hurt—including me. Between inconsistent running, buying inappropriate running shoes, and a lack of running-specific strength, I increasingly found that I simply wasn't running well, regardless of what cool shoe I bought. Worse, my body was starting to revolt.

I never did run the marathon I had hoped to train for and run that fall. After years of running injury-free, I had started suffering what felt like an endless string of aches and pains, and my body was starting to feel broken down. Something had to change for the better. I was in need of some serious running reinvigoration, but maybe, I thought, it had nothing to do with my shoes.

4 DOING WHAT COMES NATURALLY

Don't follow trends, start them.

FRANK CAPRA

"Hi, I'm the mover your landlord hired to help one of your neighbors," said a tall man with long, scraggly blond hair when I opened my apartment door. "Do you know which apartment I'm working on?"

Life sometimes works in peculiar ways. People appear in our lives unexpectedly and without explanation or context, and while those meetings may seem to be random or insignificant at the time, often they are anything but.

Such was the case when Michael Randall Hickman knocked on my door in the summer of 1995. I spotted a small, beat-up pickup truck through the window of my apartment and opened the door to a tall, robust hippie on my doorstep. He appeared to be a throwback to the 1970s, complete with mangy hair, frayed blue jeans, a threadbare T-shirt, and a pair of funky-looking sandals.

At the time, I was wearing torn jeans and a worn-out T-shirt myself. Working out of my apartment as a freelance writer, I was busy pitching my first articles about running to *Runner's World*, *Running Times*, and a variety of other magazines and newspapers. It was a lean living, and to make ends meet, I had taken a gig as an on-site apartment manager of a 16-unit complex about a mile from Chautauqua Park at the foot of Boulder's iconic Flatirons. It was a sweet, rent-free scenario. I got paid a few bucks to do maintenance, operate the sprinkler system, and generally keep things in order for a few hours every week while having a solid home base from which to sleep, work, and run.

Happily, my running had revived after what had been a long, tough spring dealing with injuries. I was inspired anew by the contagious running vibe that emanated from the fitness-crazed utopia that was Boulder. But the biggest reason for my newfound energy was the affinity I had developed for running the trails that snaked around and above the city. I was taken in by the sensation of trail running, so distinct from the road and track running I had done for nearly 15 years.

Several times a week, I found myself heading up the road to Chautauqua Park to run a rocky, rooty singletrack trail that would eventually bring change to both my life and my career path. But, just as when Michael Hickman knocked at my door, I had no idea at the time how all of the pieces would fit together.

The Mesa Trail is a rolling, 6.8-mile dirt trail that starts at Chautauqua and passes beneath the mountains that make up Boulder's western horizon line: Green Mountain, Bear Peak, South Boulder Peak, Flagstaff Mountain, and the rugged, distinctive rock formations called the Flatirons. As I had begun to discover that summer, Boulder has an abundance of off-road running options and 300 miles of singletrack trails, dirt roads, and craggy mountain ridgelines to explore in running shoes. As a trail newbie, I had glommed on to the popular, approachable Mesa Trail. It was my only point of reference, in the way someone going to the gym for the first time does some lightweight lat pulldowns and leg curls before heading to a treadmill or StairMaster.

"Looks like you do some running," the mover said, glancing at a neatly organized row of running shoes just inside my door.

I nodded. "I run almost every day, a lot on trails lately. Do you run?" I asked, making polite small talk but pretty sure there was no way that this guy, as gangly and unkempt as he looked, was a runner.

"Yeah, I've been running trails around here for a while," he said. "If you ever want to go on a long trail run, let me know. I usually go out for three to four hours a couple of times a week."

Three or four hours? I was dumbfounded. *Who was this guy?*

I'd soon learn quite a lot about this guy, including that he went by another name—Micah True—and that he was a vagabond citizen of the modern West. He had taken to trail running in his late 20s after moving to Boulder. Trail running barely existed as an organized sport in the early 1980s, but that made it a good match for the counterculture roots True had developed while studying Eastern religions and Native American history at Northern California's Humboldt State University in the early 1970s. It also made True a distinctive figure as a trail runner in the early days, especially because his appearance and running preferences offered such a stark contrast to the elite marathoners who had been training in Boulder for years.

But I didn't know any of that when he showed up at my apartment that day. Google didn't exist yet, and Yahoo! was woefully ineffective as a search engine, so there was no easy way to dig up background on this guy. But I got a good feeling, so I took him up on his offer to go running. A few weeks later, he showed up at my apartment early on a Saturday morning—shirtless and wearing a ragged pair of navy-blue nylon running shorts, a red bandanna around his forehead, and a pair of funky-looking, huarache-style sandals that appeared to be made from old tires.

"What are you wearing on your feet?" I asked skeptically, wondering what I had gotten myself into with this character.

"Best trail running shoes I've ever had," he replied. "I bought these in the Copper Canyon of Mexico for about two bucks. But I've learned how to make them myself. Everybody wears them down there."

I was wearing a pair of brand-new Adidas Trail Response shoes. Although trail running had been a niche activity in the United States for years—it dates back to the 1970s in a few sparse pockets—trail running footwear didn't exist until the late 1980s, when a few brands began making what were essentially road shoes with more traction-oriented outsoles. The latest edition of the Adidas I had on had been touted by *Runner's World* as one of best trail running shoes ever made. I liked the traction they offered on Colorado's steep mountain trails and the cushioning and protection that kept rocks, roots, and pebbles from becoming annoying protuberances into the bottom of my foot. Clearly, True's sandals offered none of that. I shrugged and kept my comments to myself.

The forecast was for hot weather, so I had filled a mountain biking hydration pack with water. Noticing that he had nothing, I offered to get him a plastic bottle from my recycling bin to carry water. He declined. "I'll just drink from streams when I get thirsty," he said.

We started jogging at a meandering pace through the alley behind the apartment complex, but we didn't take my usual route along the sidewalks adjacent to the road. Instead, we cut through a cemetery and popped out on a trail I hadn't known existed behind a government building and eventually headed up to my familiar (and relatively flat) Mesa Trail for a short stretch, only to then veer up a steep route through Bear Canyon and head up the even steeper trails toward the 8,459-foot summit of Bear Peak, a mountain I had hiked up only once and never considered running.

Although I was gassed going up the trail, True seemed to be barely breathing as he told me about all the races he had run—and won— around Colorado, the places he had lived, and his recent winter trips to Guatemala and Mexico. He was a strong, robust athlete, yet clearly also very agile. It made perfect sense when he told me he had been a semipro boxer in the 1980s before he discovered trail running. He also told me about his experience running alongside the Tarahumara Indian runners at the Leadville 100 trail race in 1993 and volunteering to help pace some of the runners the previous summer.

True talked in detail about the Tarahumara, who he informed me were known among themselves as the Rarámuri—which meant "running people"—because of their long heritage of long-distance running. They had subsisted by running great distances for centuries, he said, as we ran along the rugged trail between Bear Peak and South Boulder Peak, the highest of the mountains on Boulder's western horizon at 8,549 feet. We were a little more than 90 minutes into the run and my legs were trashed, and yet I was becoming more and more energized and intrigued by my running partner.

From his weathered looks, I figured True to be in his mid-40s, but I couldn't really tell given how fit and strong he was. What was clear, though, was that living simply and minimally amid the complexities of the modern world came easy for him. Although it didn't become his calling card until years later, "Run Free" was clearly his mantra for life.

I asked him to tell me more about his unusual footwear, and he said he'd begun running in huarache-style sandals made from pieces of old tires and leather straps because that was what the Rarámuri ran in. He said the primitive sandals allowed him to run more nimbly and feel a greater connection to the earth and the trail. Besides, he added, they didn't cost much, certainly not $100 like most running shoes.

I couldn't help thinking of the pair of Air Max shoes I had foolhardily shelled out $140 for earlier that spring but no longer ran in because they felt too heavy and too clumsy. All the same, this sandal talk sounded a lot like hippie-speak and didn't make much sense to me, especially because I was enthralled with the comfort, protection, durability, and traction that my well-cushioned Adidas were providing.

After reaching the summit of South Boulder Peak, we retraced our steps past Bear Peak and down to Bear Canyon and then made our way up to the summit of Green Mountain. By then, I was cooked. My hydration pack was empty, and my feet were killing me. As we descended the north side of Green Mountain along Gregory Canyon, True stopped to drink from a clear-flowing stream, and as thirsty as I was, I gladly joined him. *Giardia be damned*, I thought, as I slurped cold water that I'd gathered in my cupped hands.

From there, we passed through Chautauqua Park and, finally, down familiar sidewalks back to my apartment. As True drove away in his beat-up truck, I relished the magnitude of what we had just undertaken. The circuitous run had taken more than four hours—by far the longest and most invigorating run of my life. I was grateful to have taken those few sips from the stream, but I was even happier to take my shoes off and crash on my futon while sipping a cold beer.

I ran with True a couple more times that summer and would occasionally see him driving around town with a truck full of furniture or chatting with friends at the Trident Café on Pearl Street. He started spending six months of the year living among the Rarámuri in the Copper Canyon, returning to Boulder to see friends, earn a few bucks, and perhaps give himself more inspiration to head south of the border the next October when the days grew darker and shorter, his body grew tired, and his spirit started to fade.

Years later, I found an old article from the *Rocky Mountain News* about True that quoted him as saying, "I have a theory that to breathe is to live— and the more you breathe, like on a long mountain run, the more you live. That sounds cosmic, but it's really a simple statement: when you run up in beautiful country, breathing all that clean air, there's no better way to live."

Although I might not have entirely understood True's free-spirited ways at the time, I was intrigued by his passionate immersion in trail running at the most primal level and, of course, his mystifying choice of running shoes. At the time, however, I didn't connect those dots to recognize that True was a visionary, running long distances in minimally constructed footwear. I was aware that long-distance running was a key aspect of many ancient cultures in Africa and Asia and even among some Native American tribes that lived in what is now the western United States, but I still didn't understand how running in minimally constructed footwear was at all practical for modern runners as the dawn of the next century beckoned.

I was to learn much more on that count, but that enlightenment was still years away. What True did do that summer was open my eyes to what trail running was all about and could be, an inspiring catalyst that eventually led me to start running up and down Colorado's 14,000-foot peaks, entering ultradistance races, and running across the Grand Canyon and back. I was all in, and in December of 1999 helped launch *Trail Runner* magazine, beginning in earnest my total immersion in the burgeoning sport, the trail racing scene, and a brand-new facet of the booming running shoe business.

—————

More than a dozen years later, I walked into the Boulder footwear lab of Danny Abshire, a running form guru widely acclaimed for making custom orthotics for some of the world's best runners, triathletes, cyclists, and mountaineers. He had been known to tinker with shoe designs, and that day I was there to learn about an innovative new model he was crafting.

An accomplished runner and ultramarathoner, the self-taught entrepreneur had learned what he knew about running gait efficiency and foot stability by observing and doing. When he was transplanted to Aspen from Tennessee in the late 1970s, he fell into a gig at a ski shop and became a sought-after ski-boot fitter because of his ability to custom-mold insoles that gave customers a more balanced platform for skiing. He eventually figured out how to adapt those same concepts to running and helped athletes by improving the fit, feel, and ride of their shoes.

In the late 1980s, he took those learnings to Boulder and opened Active Imprints, a company that aimed to help athletes of all types and ability levels to perform better and move more efficiently with improved posture, stability, and biomechanics. The business took off. By the time I met Abshire, Ironman® champions Paula Newby-Fraser, Mark Allen, Peter Reid, Lori Bowden, Natascha Badmann, and Scott Molina were among his high-profile clients, as was former Denver Broncos quarterback John Elway.

Abshire had been toying with running shoe designs for a decade, with ideas that bucked the popular design trends of the day. At the time, most mainstream running shoes were still based on design edicts that dictated fashion over function. Generally speaking, this meant that how a shoe looked—both its aesthetics and how added technology affected a runner's *perception* of how a shoe would perform—was arguably more important than how it actually performed.

Like Abshire, a few brands had been dabbling with an alternate approach. Nike was the first to commercialize natural running footwear, or barefoot-style shoes, with its Free line in 2004. The line was developed, in part, by observing the barefoot running drills and workouts of the elites on the Nike-backed Farm Team postcollegiate running program in Palo Alto, California, along with eight years of research conducted in Nike's innovation lab in Beaverton, Oregon.

The Free shoes were lighter, less structured, and less controlling than most shoes on the market; had a low heel-to-toe offset; and were flexible in all directions. Those properties were intended to allow a runner's feet to move naturally and uninhibitedly, as if barefoot, while offering just enough cushioning and protection against impact with the ground. Although Nike didn't specifically promote the line with cues for improved running, the minimally designed shoes were the first to break the overbuilding trend (multiple overlays, highly raised heels, excessive weight, parts to control or limit a foot's natural movement) that had persisted over the previous two decades.

The Free line became hugely successful, but the design created a new worry for Nike. It soon got feedback that many runners were getting injured after running long distances in the shoes, which prompted the brand to include a warning inside shoe boxes advising that developing additional strength and fitness would be helpful before running in the Free shoes.

Another striking design gaining traction in this new area were the Vibram FiveFingers—quirky, glovelike shoes with an individual compartment for each toe, extremely thin rubber outsoles, and no cushioning whatsoever. Unveiled in 2006, FiveFingers were little more than an oddity at the time. They weren't even touted as running shoes but rather as casual shoes that were even greater outliers than the various "shape-up," or buttocks-toning, shoes developed by Reebok, Skechers, and MBT (Masai Barefoot Technology) during the same era. Ecco, a seasoned Danish shoe brand, also joined the fray, developing low-to-the-ground shoes made for running with a barefoot gait.

Most of Abshire's tinkering focused on unique propulsion activators aimed at increasing energy return. When I met him at his downtown Boulder digs in the summer of 2006, he handed me a well-refined prototype of a shoe he had been working on. The shoe was certainly eye-catching: extremely lightweight, with modern stretch-mesh uppers and a dazzlingly bright fluorescent color palette. But when I flipped the shoe over, I discovered something odd: four rubber lugs about the size of my pinkie protruding from the outsole.

Was this guy nuts? Interested in wasting my time? The peculiarity was unlike anything I'd ever seen in a running shoe, and I was immediately skeptical of the design and of Abshire's claims. It all seemed pretty gimmicky.

Dubious, I asked him to break it down for me. Abshire described how, upon impact with the ground, the protruding lugs pushed into a taut membrane hidden under the lugs, momentarily storing energy before discharging it into the forward momentum of the foot as it entered the toe-off phase of a stride.

But wouldn't the lugs create a weird and highly abnormal sensation of the forefoot being higher off the ground than the heel? I wondered. Not at all, Abshire assured me. Rather, the design would allow a runner's foot to move naturally and meet the ground as if it were barefoot. The extension of the lugs gave the shoes a near-level profile, he explained, similar to how a foot meets the ground when unshod. The key, he said, was running with the tenets of good form: an upright, slightly forward-leaning posture; consistent upward drive of the knees; a tight, consistent arm swing; and one more thing that would become the hallmark of everything Abshire was about—a proper landing.

Numerous studies had shown that heel striking created a dramatic peak impact force that reverberated up a runner's kinematic chain from feet to ankles to knees to hips, eventually even reaching the head. While the human body is designed to attenuate some of that impact with its pliable and resilient soft tissue (ligaments, tendons, and muscles), many researchers have agreed that a heavy heel-striking gait is exacerbated by running shoes with thickly cushioned heels. Running with a midfoot gait has been shown to exert much less impact force on the body. Thus Abshire's focus.

"The key is running with a midfoot- or forefoot-style gait in which a foot hits the ground softly in a position that is almost parallel to the ground," he said, mimicking the action in slow motion with a shoe he held in his hands. "I call it the Land, Lever, Lift technique. Your foot lands softly instead of braking with a hard heel strike, momentarily stores the energy from impact, and then returns that energy as you lever your body mass forward and lift off to start a new stride."

This technique, Abshire told me, would improve the proprioceptive communication between the foot and the brain, allowing a runner to run with a more upright, slightly forward-leaning posture and more efficient running mechanics. And while most running shoes had a heel that was 12 to 14 mm higher than the forefoot, Abshire's models offered a far more balanced platform with a 1 to 2mm heel-toe offset, thus helping reduce or eliminate the negative aspects of a heel-striking gait and, as a result, allowing a runner to run more naturally and efficiently.

This idea of natural running wasn't new to me. Running guru Danny Dreyer had recently popularized it with a concept he called ChiRunning. But Abshire was one of the first to develop footwear that espoused and promoted a specific style of running gait. At the time, I had never heard anyone speak about heel-toe offset, or "heel drop"—or even talk about forefoot technology at all, given that most innovations at the time were happening around the heel—but it was something that would increasingly come into play among shoe manufacturers.

I could tell that Abshire was a disrupter, eager to go against the grain of conventional thinking, maybe even for the sake of being a contrarian. Nevertheless, I was inclined to think he was on to something, largely because of my own disenchantment with many new running shoes.

I ran in the sample pair that he gave me to test, and although it took a while for my body to sync up with the technological features of the shoes, I couldn't deny the unmistakable energetic pop when I made a point of running with more optimal running form. I also loved how light they were and how my feet interacted with the ground. Those qualities harkened back to my track days and my love of running on the roads in racing flats.

Abshire's new brand would be called Newton Running. The shoe I'd tested, the Gravity, was named after 18th-century British scientist Sir Isaac Newton and his third law of motion. That law is based on the notion that for every action, there is an equal and opposite reaction. Thus, in every interaction, there is a pair of forces acting on the two interacting objects. The size of the force on the first object equals the size of the force on the second object.

Newton Running translated that nugget of science into its proprietary Action/Reaction Technology, the trampolinelike cushioning from its propulsion-enhancing lug system that it claimed provided greater responsiveness than the EVA foam found in the midsoles of most running shoes on the market.

In addition to the design of the shoes, Abshire was promoting a midfoot-style running gait and better running posture and mechanics. This approach was a considerable departure from the mainstream thinking of most brands, which were still focusing millions of dollars of research, technology, and materials on thickly cushioned heel crash pads.

"Almost all of the so-called technological advancements in running shoes have been focused on the heel," Abshire said. "Almost every shoe boasts some kind of oversized heel cushioning unit aimed at lessening the damaging impact that comes from the foot hitting the ground."

Abshire saw this as fruitless and even dangerous. "All it does is promote heel striking and braking in the middle of every stride, and that just creates bad, inefficient running form. What we're doing is focusing on the forefoot. I really believe in the next 10 years, the focus will shift to the forefoot and how better running form will contribute to healthier, more efficient running."

Led by Abshire and his business partner, Jerry Lee, Newton Running launched in the spring of 2007, unveiling its first shoes at a triathlon in Oceanside, California, to much acclaim. It quickly sold out of the first

1,000 pairs and gained traction with an online-only sales model as word spread through the triathlon community, Internet message boards, and then-new social media sites such as MySpace and Facebook.

Newton, one of the first brands to trend toward a zero-drop, or level, platform, helped spur the development of lightweight shoes with bright color palettes and premium pricing of $155 to $175 per pair. It offered running form clinics and coaching certification to promote its message about efficient running form. But the biggest thing Newton did was help set the stage for the minimalist revolution that was about to go mainstream.

=====

Once in a great while, something comes along to disrupt the status quo—something that makes people change the way they view things that once didn't seem to need rethinking. When the book *Born to Run: A Hidden Tribe, Superathletes, and the Greatest Race the World Has Never Seen* was published in 2009, author Christopher McDougall hit the nail right on the head. It might well have hit me on the head, too, given that the Boulder moving man Micah True was unexpectedly one of the book's star characters.

In Mexico to report on another story, McDougall had met True—known locally as Caballo Blanco ("the White Horse"), a reference to True's large size and blond locks—and witnessed the race that True organized with North American ultrarunning standouts and local Tarahumara greats. He marveled at how Rarámuri people of all ages ran long distances in huarache sandals and were rarely injured. McDougall, himself a broken-down and oft-injured runner, became a convert to minimalist footwear, and the Mexico experience sent him on a journey that became a deep and critical look at the running shoe industry.

In the book, he asserted that running shoes are the cause of most common running injuries that coincided with the original running boom of the 1970s. It was a bold claim, and it had a massive impact on the running industry, runners, and shoe design. Whether he was right or wrong, McDougall hit on a hot-button topic and poked the bear just as it was waking up.

The book sold more than one million copies in the first six months and ignited a firestorm of discussion and controversy about how people should be running and what they should be wearing on their feet. Although it contained considerable hyperbole, the semiautographical book earned its due (and rave reviews) because McDougall's vivid storytelling, compelling character development, and in-depth reporting appealed to everyone from new runners and veteran ultrarunners to nonrunners and couch potatoes.

McDougall had originally set out to write an adventure book in the same genre as *Into Thin Air* or *The Perfect Storm*. He wanted to tell a story about what had been going on in the Copper Canyon of Mexico, which he did, but he also ignited a social movement that turned the running shoe business on its head.

The book became a primary catalyst for the minimalist running shoe revolution that spurred brands to develop lighter, lower-to-the-ground shoes using less material. When Harvard scientist Dr. Daniel Lieberman published a study about how humans run in *Nature* in 2010, it supported McDougall's claims and further ignited the minimalist running fervor.

Lieberman's study suggested that runners who land on their forefoot do so with far less force and far greater efficiency than heel strikers. It found that modern running shoes, as comfortable and cushioned as they may have felt, encouraged a heel-striking gait and did little to mitigate the impact of running or the common injuries associated with running.

Part of Lieberman's study drew evidence from a test of rarely shod East African runners that showed that they landed with a lighter mid-foot gait when unshod but immediately switched to a harder heel-striking gait when running in modern running shoes. The study concluded that running with a barefoot-style gait promoted greater proprioception, even in lightweight, minimally designed footwear, and might reduce impact, stress, and injuries.

As *Born to Run* was hitting its peak of popularity in 2010, minimalism hit the mainstream. After 30 years of shoe design focused primarily on controlling how the feet moved while running or offering more cushioning and technological add-ons, there was suddenly a categorical shift in thinking about how running shoes should be designed.

Almost every brand fast-tracked products intended to accommodate the natural movement of a runner's feet and to provide a tool for optimally efficient running form. At the crux was the notion that the foot can do a better job of self-stabilizing and balancing the weight of the body when it can move freely and is allowed relatively unencumbered contact with the ground than when it's in a shoe that is thickly cushioned or overly corrective by design.

Shoes lost a lot of weight, too. Whereas 11- to 13-ounce training shoes had been the norm in the 2000s, brands quickly found ways to make similar shoes in the 7- to 10-ounce range—and some considerably lighter than that. Runners responded eagerly and with open wallets. Newton, New Balance, Saucony, Nike, Merrell, Brooks, and other brands found their new lightweight, low-to-the-ground models soaring in popularity.

Running stores started selling the Vibram FiveFingers popularized by McDougall and couldn't keep them in stock. The Italian brand claimed that the shoes could strengthen runners' feet and improve their running form. They became all the rage, especially after newspapers, TV stations, and blogs, taking Lieberman's study out of context, started suggesting that it was literally better to run barefoot (or in FiveFingers) on city streets than in traditionally cushioned running shoes.

I tried on a pair and was astonished—and a little alarmed—at the barefoot-style running experience they served up, with no protection other than a slim piece of rubber; reinforced toe caps; and a thin, durable mesh upper. I could feel every piece of gravel on the road. I didn't dare take them on any trails that weren't of the smooth dirt variety. Plus, they were very hard to put on. Aligning my toes in FiveFingers reminded me of trying to put my fingers into gloves too small for my hands. Yet runners were buying them—and running in them—in droves. I wasn't sure what to make of this. Did they know something I didn't know, or were people blindly following a hot trend, perhaps at their own peril?

At NRC in Naperville, the demand was outrageous. Hartner recalls getting new shipments of FiveFingers with the majority of the shoes already sold in advance. "It was crazy," he recalls. "We couldn't keep them in stock. Some buyers were longtime runners, but there were a lot of people who bought into the fad and started running because of it."

Along with Vibram's FiveFingers, Newton's Gravity and Distance models, and Nike's Free shoes, New Balance found success with its 101 model and Minimus line. Saucony's Kinvara (2010) was one of the first training shoes with a 4-mm offset and a good amount of cushioning, and the brand's Virrata (2013) took it a step further with a zero-drop design. The movement spawned the advent of new companies, too, as upstart brands, such as Vivo Barefoot, Altra Running, and Topo, entered the fray with minimalist designs.

Brands that were slow to react suddenly took a dive. ASICS, which had been the number-one brand at specialty running stores for more than 15 years, saw sales evaporate because it didn't have new products that fit the mold. If a brand didn't have a minimalist story to tell with a new model, it was soon off the back and answering to corporate bean counters or angry shareholders.

Of course, some of these hot new shoe design concepts weren't really so new at all, given that most of the original running shoes of the late 1960s and early 1970s were light, low to the ground, and minimally designed. And similarly built modern racing flats had always been an alternative to the heavier, overbuilt everyday trainers that had dominated the market since the mid-1980s. The natural running philosophy wasn't new, either; there had been a tiny percentage of runners wearing minimalist shoes since the 1970s, be they Earth Shoes, racing flats, self-modified shoes, or sandal creations.

What differentiated this new genre of shoe design was that, more than ever before, it was based on biomechanical science and running performance rather than comfort, aesthetic appeal, or streamlined race-day simplicity. Shoe companies started taking cues from academic studies and using high-speed video stride analysis and advanced impact measuring devices to better understand how a foot moves naturally, both while running barefoot and inside a shoe. Combined with new materials and construction techniques that created lighter, stronger, and more flexible shoes, it was the dawn of a new age.

"It was about going back to basics with more minimal, performance-oriented designs," J. F. Fullum, a shoe design manager at New Balance, tells me. "We reached a plateau in the early 2000s with putting so much junk on shoes and [started] going back to what made sense a long time ago. We went back to the idea of form follows function, even though we're using modern materials and techniques."

A shoe's platform, specifically the differential between heel and toe, became a key area of focus for designers. For decades, starting with the Nike Cortez and Onitsuka Tiger Corsair that Bill Bowerman had developed in the early 1970s, most everyday training shoes had been built with a 12- to 14-mm heel-toe offset, meaning the heel sat 12 to 14 mm above the height of the forefoot. The intent was to add cushioning, ease the tension of the Achilles tendon and lower calf muscles, and put the foot in a forward-leaning position.

But academic studies and shoe company research showed that this geometry can perpetuate inefficient, heel-striking form, both because it continually forces the body to rebalance in an unnatural position and because the built-up heel is the first part of the shoe to strike the ground even if the foot approaches the ground in a horizontal position. In contrast, many of the modern minimalist shoes had heel-toe drops between 4 and 8 mm, though a few more radically designed models with 0- to 2-mm offsets were on the way.

A lot of experts got behind this minimalist trend. "It's different for everyone," says Jay Dicharry, MPT, director of the REP Lab in Bend, Oregon, and a leading biomechanist, running gait expert, and shoe company consultant. "But most experts agree that it's easier to avoid hard heel striking and the risk of straining deconditioned muscles and soft tissue in the more forgiving moderate minimal shoes without built-up heel crash pads."

A lot depends on the individual. Whether a runner lands at the forefoot, at the midfoot, or even with a slight heel strike in these new shoes is based on the pace of the run and also on the runner's physical makeup, which includes relative foot, ankle, and lower leg strength as well as the ability to engage the core, glutes, and hip flexors while starting a new stride, Dicharry says. Repeating that natural form in a treadmill test is one thing, but doing it continually for 10 to 12 miles is quite another, he says. And running 26.2 miles with that kind of form is typically possible only for the world's fittest athletes, though numerous studies (and high-speed photography) have shown that even most elite runners revert to a heel-striking gait in the latter stages of a marathon.

Form mattered, making the minimalist running revolution about more than just shoes. Alongside the new shoe designs was a growing movement from shoe brands, retailers, coaches, bloggers, and technique gurus to preach the tenets of more efficient, natural running form in the same way that Abshire had in 2006. Developing core strength, relentlessly doing form drills, and the notion that there's more to running than high mileage and a little stretching finally hit the mainstream.

=====

While some argue that "barely there" shoes led many runners to run with insufficient cushioning and protection underfoot, there's no question that the paradigm shift helped runners rethink how much (and how little) they really needed in a shoe. It also spurred manufacturers to seek out new materials and construction techniques to build lighter models across all categories.

But the rocketing movement wasn't without growing pains. Shoe brands and running shops were eager to meet the demand of the mini-malist movement, and runners flung themselves into the new trend with abandon. But the shift happened too quickly, Dicharry says. "I wasn't sur-prised to see a spike in injuries. People were buying FiveFingers and New Balance 101s and other minimalist models and going out and running 10 miles in them. Two days later, they could hardly walk, let alone run. And those were the lucky ones who didn't get hurt."

Many runners found out the hard way that running in minimalist shoes required stronger foot, ankle, lower-leg, and core muscle groups than did traditionally cushioned trainers. A proper changeover took more time and effort than many people allowed, Dicharry recalls, result-ing in sore calf muscles, strained Achilles tendons, aching feet, and other pains and injuries.

The transition is key, he says, and can take up to a few months. Numerous other factors, including a runner's weight, body composition, past injury patterns, level of fitness, and running goals also need to be considered before making a drastic change in running footwear.

Newton, Vibram, Nike, and other brands that had seen sales of minimalist models skyrocket soon got word of injured runners returning those shoes, swearing they'd never fall prey to such a fad again. And it wasn't just injuries that consumers were complaining about; many felt they couldn't—or didn't care to—adapt to the stark feeling served up by most minimalist shoes.

As a result, the trend evaporated nearly as quickly as it had appeared. Minimalist shoe sales peaked in 2012 with about 11 percent of the market but fell off the table almost overnight as sales plummeted to less than 4 percent of the market by 2013.

=====

Born to Run remains one of the most popular and inspirational running books of all time. It stayed on the *New York Times* best-seller list for more than 178 weeks, eventually selling more than three million copies worldwide. Its impact on the running shoe industry continues to be felt. More than a decade after it hit bookstores, it still sells at a steady rate, and shoe manufacturers continue to push design innovations that have roots in the minimalist era. The long-awaited *Born to Run* movie, starring Woody Harrelson as Micah True, is expected to be released in 2020 or 2021.

McDougall was humbled, if not surprised, by the book's success. "My thought was, 'There are so many runners out there in the same position I'm in that if I can just deliver the story, then why wouldn't a lot of runners want to read it?' To me, the story was so real, so compelling, that I just didn't want to mess it up."

He says he stumbled into a vibrant undercurrent of thinking from people who had figured out that there was a more efficient way to run. He didn't intend to spark a minimalist revolution but rather just to relay what he—and thousands of other runners—were experiencing.

"I truly feel like just the messenger," he says. "I was the mailman. Someone wrote the letter, and I happened to be the one to drop it off. Why should running be the only physical activity on planet Earth that is immune from the laws of physics? In every physical activity, there is a more or less efficient way to do it. It was the same with running."

After meeting Micah True by chance at my apartment complex so many years before, I'd often seen him around Boulder, usually during the summer months, working his one-man moving operation, running up and down the local trails, or hanging out at the Trident. I caught up with him in fall 2010, a year after the book was published, on the day that he was going to drive back to Mexico for the winter. I was gratified to see that he had somehow maintained his simple, nomadic lifestyle, even though Boulder had become much more of a yuppie enclave than the hippie outpost it had once been.

When the book came out, he became an instant celebrity, albeit begrudgingly. Despite his fame, True seemed unchanged, insisting that he was nothing more than a common man who cared about those around him. What he was for sure was a stubborn, streetwise survivor, often witty and seemingly carefree, though he took life as seriously as it needed to be taken. He used his celebrity to bring awareness to the struggles of the Rarámuri people and to get more corn, blankets, and supplies donated for prizes in the increasingly popular ultramarathon that he organized every spring.

He still ran in minimalist footwear, although by then he had been given dozens of pairs of FiveFingers; modern barefoot-style running sandals; and lightweight, minimally designed models of Saucony shoes. But like everything else in life, he gave most of those shoes away, keeping just a few pairs for himself.

True said someone had given him a copy of the book when he'd returned to Boulder in the spring of 2009 and that he had read it cover to cover in one night. If there were two things True thought McDougall got right, they were the passages about minimalist running shoes and the notion of living more simply.

"When I read the first 40 pages, I thought, *What the hell?* But it was a really good read," True told me that day in October. "He drew you in with a character that was supposed to be me. He made me out to be some sort of badass, but it's far from the truth. But as the book went on, it captured all of us well. It did take some liberties with all of our personal lives, and some of it was very controversial. But I think it's a book that inspired people to come run with us, and that's great."

True died with his minimalist running shoes on at age 58, doing what he loved to do most. He was on his way back from Mexico in the spring of 2012 when he passed away from negative effects of an enlarged heart during a run in New Mexico's Gila Wilderness. He traveled light and moved freely through life, as he did on the trails, but his simple and sometimes primal messages made lasting impressions and connected people—in life and in death.

Minimalism didn't go extinct, but the category shrank back to a tiny segment of the running market as runners and shoe manufacturers reverted to cushioned shoes. Still, the legacy of *Born to Run*, Micah True, and the minimalist revolution lives on in the many changes in running shoes and the innovative ideas that continue to spring up today.

Running shoes are no longer overbuilt to the degree that they were in the early 2000s. Gone or dwindling are plastic support shanks, firm medial posts, and rigid vamps in place of more flexible, naturally moving shoes. Thick sewn-on suede, leather, and plastic upper overlays have been replaced with airy, seamless mesh or stretchy knit uppers with lightweight heat-welded thermoplastic polyurethane. Most shoes are lower to the ground and have less of a slope from heel to toe. And while there are still some heavy, overbuilt shoes with flashy features offering little or no performance value, most modern running shoes are built with performance and natural foot motion as two of the primary design criteria.

Longtime retailer, running form guru, and shoe tinkerer Hawk Harper, who has owned and operated the running specialty store Runner's Corner in Orem, Utah, for more than 30 years, has seen positive impacts on shoe design, new studies that indicate runners have their own specific gait pattern, and a raised awareness about the connection between a runner's brain and feet and how shoes connect to the ground.

"I think McDougall was spot-on with a lot of what he wrote in the book," says Harper, once a 2:22 marathoner who formerly worked for Nike and Saucony. "We see evidence of it day in and day out, year in and year out. He wasn't wrong; he just made it sound a little more glorified than it was. We were all born to run, but running in barefoot-style shoes just isn't the answer for everyone."

5 IT'S ALL FUN AND GAMES UNTIL SOMEBODY GETS HURT

There is no ghost so difficult to lay as the ghost of an injury.

ALEXANDER SMITH, SCOTTISH POET

Running along the Foothills Trail on the north end of Boulder, I don't immediately recognize the runner coming toward me, but I do notice his wonky gait. It's hard not to. A little hunched and leaning slightly to the left, he runs with slightly wobbly, compromised mechanics—so much so that I grimace as he approaches and passes me.

Frank Shorter might not run with the tall, proud posture he once had, but he's still an inspiring legend, and seeing him puts a spring in my stride. The elite marathoner, credited with being a pioneer of the 1970s American running boom, has lost the fluid gait, smooth cadence, and silent footstrike that helped him win the 1972 Olympic Marathon in Munich and earn a silver medal four years later in Montréal. But give the guy a break—he's had a hip resurfaced, surgery to repair a meniscus tear, two vertebrae fused to fix a back problem, and a knee replacement since his retirement from pro running in the early 1980s.

Still, Shorter continues to run 20 to 30 miles per week—as well as swim and lift weights—and at 71, he is a picture of health and fitness. While many people believe that years of running long distances eventually takes a toll on our bodies and our running form, Shorter blames his off-kilter form not on running but rather on age, long-term wear and tear, and surgeries. In fact, he credits running for his excellent health. "I think the running has actually forestalled and held off a lot of the orthopedic problems that people get as they get older."

Shorter is right. Studies show that people who remain active later in life tend to remain stronger, healthier, and more limber than those who don't. While it's a fact of life that bodies become weaker and wear out over time, just as cars, clothing, and appliances do, if you compare Shorter to the average American in his age bracket, he's arguably superfit.

Along with living in Boulder for many years, I have a few other things in common with Shorter. We've both run a lot of miles over the years, both worn thousands of different running shoes, and both dealt with a handful of minor overuse ailments and major injuries resulting from long-term damage.

At age 50, I have recently begun to wonder how my body will hold up for running (and life) over the long haul given that in the last decade, I have dealt with several lingering bouts of Achilles tendinitis, a painful stint of iliotibial (IT) band syndrome, a functional leg-length imbalance that led to an angry case of sciatica, a debilitating case of runner's knee, one frustrating case of shin splints, and an excruciating ruptured Achilles. Not all of those injuries were caused by running, but each one presented itself when I ran.

This has led me to think a lot more about the shoes I choose to wear and the marketing promises that accompany them. Can they really help me run longer, healthier, and injury-free? Conversely, might they be causing my problems?

Shorter started running in the 1960s, when running shoes had little cushioning underfoot save for a thin layer of rubber on the outsole. In contrast, I started running in the 1980s, about the time he was retiring from racing, when shoes were not just well cushioned but going through a cushioning revolution.

We've both spent the past 30 years running in shoes with various cushioning mechanisms—EVA foam midsoles, Air-Soles, GEL capsules, and a variety of new materials—yet we've both wound up with a variety of gait-altering aches, pains, and injuries.

Frank and I are not oft-injured outliers, unfortunately; rather, we're part of the norm. Despite the continued evolution of running shoes since the 1970s, the rate of injury among runners has remained high and, depending on which report you read, might even be climbing. Reports of annual injury rates vary widely, from 20 percent to 92 percent, but the average rate is somewhere around 50 to 60 percent. That means more than half of the running population gets dinged up in some fashion every year. Imagine that as every other runner in your local running group, or fully half of the 50,000 participants who line up to start the New York City Marathon every November.

It's a startling injury rate. Might shoes be the culprit? Absolutely not, says Jay Dicharry, who authored *Running Rewired: Reinvent Your Run for Stability, Strength & Speed*.

Dicharry has published numerous research studies about running mechanics, and he insists that running shoes don't cause injuries. "There are better and worse shoes for an individual runner based on their gait characteristics, but running shoes are not the cause of injuries," he says.

There has never been a correlative link between injuries and running shoes, he points out, which sounds like a convincing exoneration of shoes from where I sit, though it's important to note that there also haven't been many studies. In fact, in the only study that has remotely produced some interaction between running shoes and injury rates, 81 female runners were categorized by foot type (neutral, pronated, highly pronated) and randomly assigned neutral, stability, or motion-control shoes. After basic information about their gaits was recorded, the runners were put through a 13-week half-marathon training program. Of the 194 training days missed by the test subjects due to pain or ailments, 79 were missed by runners wearing motion-control shoes, followed by 64 by neutral-shod runners, and 51 by stability-shoe wearers.

The neutral runners reported greater pain values while running in neutral shoes than in stability shoes; runners with pronated gaits reported greater pain values while running in stability shoes than in neutral shoes. No significant effects were reported for runners with highly pronated gaits. Ultimately, the study concluded that the "current approach of pre-scribing in-shoe pronation control systems on the basis of foot type is overly simplistic and potentially injurious." But the researchers admitted that the study was too small and didn't take into account enough factors to be conclusive.

=====

When I stood in front of the massive running shoe wall at the NRC, it was hard to fathom—yet easy to see—how far running shoe design and development had come in 60 years. Today's running shoes are leaps and bounds ahead of models produced even just 20 years ago and light years ahead of the first "modern" running shoes made in the late 1960s.

New materials, new manufacturing techniques, and new understand-ings of movement have resulted in shoes that are lighter, more durable, and more responsive. We can surmise that, based on the improvements in manufacturing, materials, and data collection, shoes today are nothing like they will be in 10 or 20 years.

Yet, even with the advancements in kinesiology; the study of biomechanics, the human body, and materials science; and massive investment and vested interest from shoe companies, relatively little is known about how shoes actually impact our ability to run, no matter whether it is 100 meters, 100 miles, or somewhere in between.

There is no universal understanding of or agreement on how shoes should be designed and built to improve efficiency, maximize energy return, and reduce the risk of overuse injuries that, some research shows, may be caused by the repetitive motions of a running gait.

In the 1970s, there was tremendous focus on stability and motion control. Despite the fact that at the time, there was little science related to human running mechanics, brands became obsessed with the notion that pronation could be harmful to a runner's heath.

Although high-speed video cameras and force-plate treadmills weren't yet available to analyze running gait, biomechanists, podiatrists, coaches, and shoe developers pointed to this inward rolling as one of the causes of common running injuries. As a result, the shoe war encountered a brand-new battlefield, one concerned with how to control the movement of a runner's feet—an idea that, although never grounded in science, has lingered into today. Science or no science, it has been a powerful marketing and sales tool.

In 1977, Brooks introduced several shoe models that supported the interior side of the heel with its Varus Wedge. The firm foam piece was engineered to provide greater stability, increase heel and foot protection, and improve running efficiency while decreasing muscle and tendon fatigue.

The Brooks Vantage was the first shoe designed to control the inward rotation of the foot, a motion that would soon be known by the industry-wide catchphrase "overpronation." Under the guidance of renowned podiatrist Steven Subotnick, who would later author *Cures for Common Running Injuries*, Brooks attempted to counter the rolling of the foot toward the medial side with a wedge that not-so-subtly canted the foot outward to the lateral side.

Brooks's innovation sparked dozens of imitators and eventually led to a whole new category of shoes based around stability and motion control. But it also led the industry down a misdirected path of self-help without compelling scientific evidence or quantifiable results. Soon every brand had its own feature designed to restrict overpronation—the most common being the medial post, a firmer-density midsole foam located under the arch of the foot. Worse yet, it also prompted the unsavory practice of brands hiring scientists and paying for the lab results they needed for their marketing programs that supported their new shoe models.

While innovation can be good—and even imperative at times—the problem was that a lot of the innovation was being fueled not by science but rather by marketing hype and copycat imitation, neither of which necessarily led to better performance or more efficient running, even if they decidedly did lead to selling more shoes and developing a vernacular to support three types of shoes (neutral, stability, and motion control). Worse, the new trend didn't reduce a growing epidemic among recreational runners: overuse injuries such as shin splints, Achilles tendinitis, plantar fasciitis, patellar tendinitis, and runner's knee.

"Shoe companies started adding as much cushioning as they could because that felt good to many new runners," says Burfoot. "And then they started throwing in all sorts of biomechanical and antipronation devices because the new runners were getting injured, and brands wanted to be able to say they were doing something to prevent it."

Dicharry doesn't think shoe brands are really listening to what science—specifically kinesiology and anatomy—is telling them.

"For a long time, the running shoe industry has had a bias that suggests a running shoe has to stop parts of your body from moving and force something to move in a different way," he says. "That's based on unfounded ideas that evolved 40 or 50 years ago. Science shows that doesn't exist and never did. People are variable and move differently, and that's OK."

Dicharry says that until brands stop trying to control or limit movement, shoes will never fully move forward. "The foot is an adaptively controlled lever; it's not just one rigid thing that moves one way. It's all about adapting and conforming." His insights beg the question: If every runner has his or her own preferred path of movement based on specific anatomical variances and irregularities, is it even possible to mass-produce a commercial product that will actually improve performance and reduce injury risk for a wide range of runners?

Dicharry insists that it is possible, but "you would mostly have to scrap the model of how shoes are built and marketed." There is sufficient technology and understanding of how to do it, he says; however, mass production and an entire recategorization of running shoes are still significant inhibitors.

In Chapter 9, we'll explore how some brands are working on "personalized" shoes that incorporate a runner's specific foot size and shape and leg movements based on digital data captured from high-tech scanning devices. A few brands have even produced wearable prototypes with 3-D printing machines and heat-moldable components, but to date, it doesn't appear that any brand will have a semicustom shoe available on a widespread basis for a few more years.

Until that happens—if indeed it ever does, at least for a wide audience— the biggest challenge facing running shoes may be that they're not keeping runners from being injured. Despite numerous advancements in outsole rubber, midsole foam, training philosophies, and understanding of how the body moves, there has yet to be a shoe that has shown the ability to reduce injuries. The incidence rate of common running injuries has remained constant since they began being monitored, with most surveys and studies showing an average of 50 to 60 percent of runners being injured every year.

An essential piece of the puzzle cannot be ignored: Running shoes are a commodity, and every running shoe company is in the business of designing and manufacturing shoes for the sake of selling as many as possible. The A-goal is not improving performance or reducing injuries—and perhaps with good, or at least justified, reasoning. Because while running shoes have both functional and aesthetic cues—along with loads of marketing hype—consumer purchasing surveys have shown that the color or aesthetics of a shoe often influences a runner's purchasing decision more than its perceived ability to help that individual run better. Ultimately, it's not in the best interest of a shoe brand to really hone a message about training better, becoming stronger, and fixing one's mechanics because that proves that it's *not* about the shoes, or at least makes shoes a secondary factor in healthy running. Plus, it's too risky for a running shoe brand to make a claim even remotely suggesting that its running shoes can reduce the chance for injuries. Instead, it is in every brand's financial interest to make shoes that look good and feel good and come with a good marketing story.

"In a perfect world, shoe brands would design and make shoes based on how a foot naturally moves when it runs, and tune the models to match different runners based on their size, weight, and pace," Dicharry says. "But that's not how it happens. It starts with a bean counter at the brand telling the footwear team they need to develop a shoe for this niche addressing X, Y, and Z. Until that changes, most shoes are going to be all about marketing, and runners are going to keep getting hurt."

═══

When it comes to running's extraordinarily high annual injury rate, many people want to blame their shoes, but that's like blaming the tires on your car when the engine won't start, insists Reed Ferber, PhD, the founder and director of the Running Injury Clinic at the University of Calgary. "Running shoes are definitely not the cause of injuries," he says, echoing Dicharry. "Shoes are a small piece of the puzzle that people have focused on as being the cause or salvation of running injuries, but that's just not the case."

Ferber says that the one thing the running research community agrees on is that the most common running injuries, especially those suffered by recreational runners, are caused by doing too much, too fast, too soon. In other words, overuse injuries such as shin splints, Achilles tendinitis, runner's knee, IT band syndrome, plantar fasciitis, and many types of stress fractures are caused by user error: running too many miles or running too hard during workouts without adequate aerobic fitness, leg and foot strength, or flexibility.

When it comes down to it, most recreational runners aren't nearly as aerobically fit or as functionally strong as they could be. "Not even close," says Mark Plaatjes, a Boulder, Colorado–based physical therapist, coach, and owner of In Motion Running, a running specialty store. The former world-class runner—and 1993 world champion in the marathon—points to the stark difference between how elite runners train and how the average runner trains.

Not only are elites leaner and stronger, he says, but they're also running higher-mileage weeks—thus becoming much more aerobically fit and efficient—and dedicating equal hours every week to strength training, form drills, therapeutic work, and recovery. The majority of recreational runners don't have the time or interest to do those things, he says, and they often pay the price through the resulting overuse injuries.

Generally speaking, recreational runners are less interested in running fast than they were 20 or 30 years ago. That's obvious by looking at growing marathon participation numbers alongside the continual slowing of average marathon times during that span.

Although running has grown in popularity over the past 30 years, it has also transformed along with lifestyle trends and societal changes. Today, a greater percentage of the running population approaches training in a less structured or performance-oriented way, meaning they run fewer miles, run fewer times per week, and do fewer challenging workouts while also choosing to engage in other fitness activities on a weekly basis.

"You have a lot of people participating but fewer competing," Plaatjes says. "They are not as interested in running fast, and so they're not doing all of the training required to be faster marathon or half-marathon runners. That's one of the biggest factors in the high incidence of running injuries."

He says most recreational runners don't make the time, don't have the time, or just aren't interested in doing the regular core strength work, drills, and plyometric exercises that can help prevent common overuse injuries. He notes that most of the runners in the group he coaches are busy professionals who make just enough time before or after work to squeeze in a run.

"Most people just want to meet and go for a run," Plaatjes says. "It's time-intensive to do more than that. And it's a different era. People don't have as much time or as much interest."

I certainly recognize myself in Plaatjes's assessment. As a high school and college track athlete, I spent as much time on the extra stuff as I did on my running workouts. But through the years, I have become busier and less interested in the grind that goes with being the best runner I can be. It's not that I've become content with mediocrity; it's more that I'm just not as interested in running as fast as possible as I used to be. That's especially true as I've focused more time and passion on the experiential joys of trail running and ultrarunning, participation in both of which has grown exponentially over the last decade.

Even when I have tried to focus on a 12- to 15-week training block of a marathon, I haven't gone all-out. I've toed several starting lines undertrained and without the optimal core strength, speed, or agility that I had when I set my PR in my late 20s. As a result, I haven't run as fast as I had hoped to do in those races, and, more tellingly, I've been injured almost every time. That's on me.

Plaatjes points out that this lack of comprehensive training is also the reason that the minimalist shoe revolution was a disaster for many people. The shoes weren't the problem, he insists. In fact, there were merits to the idea that minimally constructed shoes would help build foot strength and cue better running form. The trouble was that few people were willing to take the time to ease into wearing those kinds of shoes and do the considerable amount of work it would take to prepare their bodies to adapt.

He also acknowledges that minimalist shoes aren't for everyone. "Most recreational runners need cushioning and protection," he says. "What the minimalist trend did was put runners who weren't strong or fit enough into shoes more minimally constructed than even the racing flats an elite runner might wear. It didn't make sense as a mass-market trend."

In March 2012, just weeks after minimalist shoe evangelist Micah True's death, Massachusetts runner Valerie Bezdek brought a class-action suit against Vibram, alleging that the brand deceived consumers by advertising that the FiveFingers could reduce foot injuries and strengthen foot muscles without any scientific basis for those assertions. (Similar lawsuits had been brought against Skechers, Reebok, and MBT for the claims behind their "shape-up" shoes.) Additional class-action suits were subsequently filed against Vibram and were eventually absorbed into Bezdek's case. The company settled the suit in 2014, agreeing to pay $3.75 million in refunds to more than 155,000 claimants who joined the class-action suit.

The lawsuit never suggested that minimalist shoes such as FiveFingers were not good for runners, only that Vibram had overreached in its advertising claims. However, numerous subsequent studies published between 2011 and 2018 have shown that minimalist footwear might lead to injuries because of the drastic gait changes it prompts, especially if worn without proper strength training. That's still not to say that minimalist shoes aren't the right tool of choice for some runners, some of the time. But these studies indicate that most runners need some degree of the cushioning and protection that the minimalist shoe movement so dramatically eschewed.

===

While minimalist shoes weren't to blame for injuries, the movement simultaneously proved that running shoes couldn't *prevent* injuries, either. Yes, running shoes can be a tool to improve your running, but the most vivid takeaway from the minimalist revolution was the reminder that most runners need an ample amount of cushioning and protection between foot and ground, and that good running form (and the proper strength, posture, and flexibility that go with it), not newfangled running shoes, is the key to healthy, efficient running.

"Running shoes can't prevent injuries," Dicharry says. "There is no shoe on the market that will solve a raging case of IT band syndrome. It doesn't exist, and it never will."

What does work and always did, long before bells and whistles were piled on shoes, is having a detailed understanding of your own running gait and anatomical idiosyncrasies. Dicharry says the human body is indeed born to run based on the elastic system of muscles, ligaments, tendons, muscles, and bones in the feet, ankles, hips, lower legs, upper legs, and hips. That elasticity and the ability to produce forward propulsion faster than a walking gait haven't deteriorated as we've evolved from chasing down our meals as sustenance hunters millions of years ago. But every single runner uses that system slightly differently based on the unique ways his or her body moves.

Doing core strength work, drills, and plyometric exercises can give you a general boost toward running better, more efficiently, and maybe even faster. But the only way to create a specific program for improving as a runner is to gain a detailed understanding of how the individual body operates as it runs—how it moves, where it is strong, where it is weak, where it is asymmetrical. These mechanics can be revealed through a high-tech gait analysis.

At his lab in Bend, Oregon, Dicharry uses state-of-the-art force-plate instrumented treadmills and high-speed cameras to analyze a runner's gait data in real time. The lab is one of only a handful of places in the United States where advanced running science can be applied to any runner—professional or recreational—in a clinical setting.

Dicharry and his team interpret a wide range of precise digital measurements—everything from stride cadence and degree of inward roll of a runner's foot to ground contact time and ground impact forces—to create an individualized biomechanical analysis, strength assessment, and functional mobility evaluation. He has examined both elites and recreational athletes. Some find their way to the clinic because they're trying to recover from an injury; others seek to become more efficient and faster.

By studying a runner's gait, Dicharry can determine what kind of anatomical weaknesses or dysfunctional patterns that runner might be falling prey to and ultimately what is causing him or her to run with unbalanced form and less efficiently. For example, a runner might not be able to properly stabilize a foot when it hits the ground and rolls from footstrike to toe-off, to rotate the hips effectively, to use the core stabilizing muscles effectively, or to fully extend the hips. All of those deficiencies can lead to minor ailments or major injuries.

Postanalysis, Dicharry and his team of physical therapists and coaches provide exercises and drills to help cue improvement in those areas.

"Some issues have nothing to do with running," Dicharry says. "They might be lifestyle problems developed from everyday life, but they show up in running or other things you might do, whether it's walking or riding a bike or swimming."

Many runners have specific running form problems, too, he says. He routinely tests fit and functionally strong runners who move efficiently and stabilize their body effectively but have a specific gait aspect that needs improvement. It might be subpar cadence, poor running posture, or a propensity to overstride. Again, he prescribes a series of drills and exercises to cue more efficient form.

Many athletes have both lifestyle and running form challenges. Ultimately, Dicharry says, the goal of the lab is to examine runners at a specific point in time and correct the factors that are working against them. Sometimes the changes are easy to fix with drills and form cues, but sometimes it takes months of drills, weight training, and physical manipulation. Very rarely, however, is footwear part of the equation.

"It's like baking a cake, and the icing on the cake is footwear," Dicharry says. "I don't get into talking about shoes until we're talking about the rest of the details about how they run."

Generally speaking, Dicharry believes most runners can benefit from running in "less" shoe, especially models that don't inhibit the natural motion of a foot. But he cautions against making big changes—to a more minimally designed shoe or a shoe with a lower heel-toe offset—too quickly.

He offers runners insights into which shoes might be better suited for their gait style by determining which models allow them to run most efficiently. However, he points out, running in a variety of different kinds of shoes on a weekly basis is the best scenario for a runner, and there is science to back up that statement. A 2013 study conducted in Luxembourg showed that recreational runners who rotated among multiple models of shoes during a 22-week study had a 39 percent lower risk of running injury than those who almost always ran in the same shoes.

"Having a quiver of shoes exposes your body to different ways of interacting with running surfaces, different muscular responses, and different neurological reaction timings," Dicharry says. "Variability is a good thing, so switching up your running shoes several times a week is a very good thing."

Ferber says about 85 percent of the running population should be capable of running in neutral shoes, based on studying thousands of runners' gaits in his clinic, but it is only recently that his numbers have synced up with running store shoe sales. While stability and motion-control shoes made up the vast majority of sales from the mid-1980s to the early 2000s, the industry averages today have shifted to a point where the majority of sales are of neutral shoes. Like Plaatjes, Ferber believes most runners can make headway by improving their overall fitness and functional strength to become less injury prone, but he doesn't necessarily believe in overhauling a runner's gait. Plaatjes, in contrast, is concerned about the industry-wide shift and strongly disagrees that most runners should be running in soft, flexible neutral shoes, insisting that many runners still need some support and stability, especially as they become fatigued during longer runs. The best way to provide that support, he says, is via stability shoes or after-market insoles.

"I was out of the retail business for five years, and the industry shifted from selling 75 to 80 percent stability shoes to selling 75 to 80 percent neutral shoes," he marvels. "How did that happen? They're the same runners that were running five years ago, and during that time, my injury-treating practice has increased by 30 percent."

The answer is likely a combination of marketing hype and the new shoe designs that emerged after the minimalist revolution subsided.

Dr. Irene Davis, PhD, founding director of the Spaulding National Running Center at Harvard Medical School, believes that gait retraining can go a long way toward removing the influences that lead to chronic running injuries. She says running is a natural, instinctive act, not a learned activity such as playing golf or hockey, changing a tire, or playing piano. But, she says, every individual moves differently, based on the anatomical structure we are born with, the mechanics we run with (or how we put that structure into motion), and the training we do on a regular basis. The cause of running injuries is multifactorial, often the result of one or more of those aspects, and because of those variables, there isn't a one-to-one relationship between any single factor and an injury.

The key to avoiding or reducing the chance for injuries is to reduce loading rates—excessive impact stress and rotational forces—with "well-aligned soft landings" on every stride, she says. That's best done by retraining a runner's gait—specifically building proper strength in the feet and lower legs and cueing form changes—and not by forcing a midfoot footstrike pattern or changing a runner's cadence. Indeed, a 2018 joint study at the Hong Kong Polytechnic University and Boston University showed that gait retraining led to a 62 percent lower risk of injury.

Forefoot striking greatly reduces impact forces, Davis says, but she admits it's not easy for most runners to adapt to a forefoot gait style. No matter what type of shoes you run in, she cautions, you have to do it right. You should not rearfoot strike in minimal shoes or try to forefoot strike in conventional shoes.

"Changes in mechanics require a commitment," she says. "It's not a quick fix."

Over the decades, running shoes have continually evolved, ostensibly with the aim of improving the experience of runners—to run better, to run more comfortably, to run faster. But for brands engaged in this multi-billion-dollar industry, it's really about selling as many shoes as possible. That has typically meant trying to find the best solution for the widest range of runners. Do these aims complement one another or collide?

Although the minimalist trend is viewed as a flash in the pan or a failure, it did more than sell a lot of shoes; it spawned a new way of thinking. It also shone a light on the importance of running form, the natural movements of a runner's feet, and the "aha" realization that every runner's gait pattern—how that person moves from feet to hips—is unique to his or her own physical makeup. The trend not only forced brands to think differently in order to create lighter, more flexible, and more functional shoes; it also opened the way to innovation. Small brands burst on the scene with new ideas, forcing bigger brands to entirely rethink how they approached shoe design.

In 2011, Brooks embarked on a new "Run Signature" paradigm for shoe design, one that recognized that every individual runs differently. Like a signature or fingerprint, each runner leaves his or her own personal mark on the ground with every single footstep. But the deeper the Brooks research team delved into the project, the more they realized they were dealing with more than merely how a runner's foot interacts with the ground.

During the minimalist era, discussion focused on the need for runners to land lightly near the midfoot at a point slightly in front of the center of the mass of their body. Heel striking was decried as destructive and wrong, and midfoot running was considered the goal for most runners to aspire to. Although rare and hard to replicate, forefoot running was considered the ultimate in efficient form, even if only to mimic what everyone believed the world's fastest and most efficient runners were doing.

But the Brooks research led to something entirely new. The footwear team studied thousands of runners' gait patterns and found . . . no pattern whatsoever. Not only were every runner's footstrikes different, but so were the movements of their ankles, knees, and hips. This revelation meant that no longer was there a need for every runner to chase some elusive notion of ideal running form. Instead, runners should embrace the natural movements and mechanics that they had evolved throughout their lives. Brooks concluded that irregularities in that unique movement pattern will misalign the joints and cause friction and resistive forces to joints and bones. That can lead to a risk of injury, so maintaining the path of least resistance is desirable to prevent such wear and tear.

Around the same time, biomechanics specialists changed their assessment of pronation, which had long been blamed for many running injuries. In his book *Biomechanics of Sport Shoes*, Canadian biomechanics researcher Benno Nigg explained that pronation is an entirely normal phenomenon. In fact, it's the way humans are designed to walk and run. Excessive, harmful overpronation is rare, Nigg said. A 2014 study in the *British Journal of Sports Medicine* confirmed his position by following 927 novice runners for a year and finding that the overpronators had fewer injuries than the nonpronators.

Nigg's research found little or no scientific evidence to connect pronation and running injuries or any evidence linking cushioning to injury prevention. Instead of focusing on correcting every runner's stride, the study recommended that running shoes should support each runner's preferred movement path. More importantly, it asserted that the best way to assess how a shoe fits your running style is through the highly subjective filter of "comfort." Turns out what feels good on our feet might just be the most important criterion to finding a path to running better—and may offer a greater chance to avoid injuries. Your brain apparently knows best.

These revelations led to a radical shift in the running shoe paradigm, debunking a lot of the previous thinking about stability, cushioning, and support that for years had led to shoes that controlled, guided, and steered runners to a "right" way to run. Brooks' work on shoes that would allow runners to embrace their individual running mechanics was based on a theory it called "natural habitual joint motion." It was a new starting point from which a runner could begin to pursue his or her own ideal form, posture, and alignment while also adhering to personal preferences about how a shoe feels and performs.

"The answer to reducing injuries, enhancing comfort, and improving performance is not to change or fix a runner's 'flaws' but to work with the natural and highly individual motion paths of the joints," says Carson Caprara, senior director of global footwear product management at Brooks. "The focus then becomes keeping a runner in this path of least resistance for as long as possible during a run. For some runners, the variables of shoe geometries, midsole hardness, or excessive stabilizing technologies can push them outside of their preferred motion path. The task of modern running shoes should be to help these runners stay within their unique motion corridor at all times."

Brooks outlined a holistic approach to designing and fitting running shoes that would optimize efficiency, reduce injury, and enhance comfort. Instead of breaking down its shoes into neutral, stability, and motion-control categories that took into consideration one factor—the level of pronation at the ankle—it came up with new categories based on four biomechanical silos related to cushioning, energizing, connecting, and propelling a runner's experience. And it acknowledged that the individual's preference had a lot to do with what shoe would be best for that person. The brand concluded that shoes allowing runners to run in their natural preferred state on the path of least resistance, rather than attempting to correct perceived problems or deficiencies, would provide the best experience and be the most comfortable. Brooks became the first brand to ditch medial posts to control overpronation in favor of a new system of guiderails that offer just enough support for that particular runner's feet and gait style.

In the same spirit, Salomon debuted a shoe in 2019—the Predict RA—that aimed to reimagine how a runner's foot interacts with a shoe and the ground and to create stability through geometry rather than added materials. The design was based on the notion that the foot (and its ability to proprioceptively "sense" the ground with the help of the brain) is able to inherently stabilize while barefoot or shod in minimally designed shoes, but it's more difficult for it to do so in shoes with various layers of foam and rubber because of the increased torquing forces that can inhibit a runner's natural movements.

The Predict RA claims to reduce those forces by "decoupling" the sole with deep grooves on both the exterior and interior of the shoe that reflect how the major joints of the foot move. The result is a firm sole with 10 "platforms" that can adapt independently, cushioning and supporting when needed as forces change throughout the stride—just as the foot does. During the shoe's first months on the market, reviews have been favorable, although sales have been modest.

While all of these new shoe designs are aimed at changing the game, it has also become increasingly clear that there is no magic bullet, and that ultimately, it is less about shoes and more about how a runner is training and taking care of his or her body on a daily basis.

———

Advancements in running shoes continue amid new science, new materials and construction techniques, and a deeper understanding of how a runner's gait is as individual as a fingerprint. But the industry hasn't let go of marketing hype and outlandish claims, so how then is a runner to know what shoe is truly best? It's not an easy process, to be sure. Without the aid of a high-tech gait analysis or the ability to test shoes with digital analytics as a reference, it can feel like a guessing game.

"I like to say I don't sell shoes, I sell solutions," Plaatjes says. The physical therapist has a sophisticated understanding of how the human body moves, how to fix common and complex running injuries, and how to fit runners with shoes that meet their specific needs. He views every runner as a study of one, which is why he's earned a reputation as a sort of shoe whisperer and one of the most renowned shoe fitters in the country.

Plaatjes's Boulder shop is at the front of a growing trend in running retail stores, one that includes a full-service in-house physical therapy and sports massage clinic.

After retiring from professional running in the mid-1990s, Plaatjes became one of the first running retail store owners to examine runners' gaits using a treadmill; video cameras; and expert, anatomically based insights. "Early in my career, when I started doing gait analysis as a physical therapist, I realized there were few running stores doing anything specifically to help runners find the right running shoes for them," Plaatjes says. "That's why I wanted to get into the running retail business in the first place."

Plaatjes puts runners on a treadmill as part of a basic gait analysis, which he then analyzes with the help of a digital app that records the runner's movement pattern and offers insights into where and how that runner's alignment is out of balance. He then has customers try on several different shoes before recommending the one best suited for their style of running and comfort preferences. The goal is to help every runner run with efficient form, a neutral position that allows his or her feet to track straight, and as little knee and hip rotation as possible.

That goal is accomplished by understanding runners' unique movement patterns, helping them strengthen their body and improve their mechanics for running, fixing any ailments, and properly fitting them with the right shoes for the type of running they do.

"You can't just put a runner in a shoe and ask if it feels comfortable," Plaatjes tells me. "Comfort has to be part of the equation, but you really have to understand an individual runner's mechanics, how they move, how they run, where they run, their foot shape, how the surface of their foot interacts with the interior of a shoe, and then synthesize all of that and come up with some proper options for that particular runner."

Plaatjes says he stays current on the latest running shoe and biomechanical research and tries to apply as much of it as possible with his customers and patients, but he admits he's at the mercy of the shoes that are available to sell. Plaatjes and his footwear buyer meticulously determine which shoes they'll bring in to the store from each brand, with an aim of offering a wide range of possible solutions for customers. Ultimately, he says, it's not just the shoes but also the research, gait analysis, after-market insoles, custom orthotics, and experience gleaned from years of shoe fitting that are the tools he employs to keep runners on a path of healthy, efficient running.

He knows that runners can and do buy shoes on the Internet, often for a cheaper price and free next-day shipping. But he's confident that online sales can never provide the specialized service and individualized shoe-fitting process that his store can. "Every person is an experiment of one," he says. "So when we help a person, we do it on an individual basis, using as many tools as we have at our disposal to figure him or her out. It's a matter of working through the maze to solve the puzzle, finding which tool is going to work for that particular customer that you're working with."

Everyone close to the running shoe industry predicts that greater individualization is on the horizon. As biomechanical science and running shoe design continue to evolve, new shoes—including the first truly custom shoes that match an individual runner's gait attributes—are already on the way. Shoe brands know how to make a personalized shoe one at a time via 3-D printing, but to date manufacturing viability and pricing remain big obstacles. We'll look more closely at this issue in Chapter 9.

Meanwhile, more retail stores are developing relationships with physical therapists, podiatrists, doctors, and biomechanists to add individualized gait analysis as a service for their customers. Plaatjes hopes to bring an advanced force-plate treadmill into his store to offer an even higher level of running form analysis, akin to what's offered at a research lab.

Running—whether training for a fast marathon or just running some miles a few times a week—remains a fairly rugged physical pursuit. Runners, including me, will continue to set ambitious new goals and train as best they can in the time they have. Sometimes that will mean bouts of undertraining or moments of overtraining and the consequent injuries.

Advances in footwear, training, and technology might have an effect on how a runner moves, but how and whether those changes will impact the rate of injuries remains a big question mark. In the end, running is both a very simple and an extremely complex activity, a polarizing set of parameters that leave it open and vulnerable to the interpretation, style, and experience of each individual runner. The key to healthy, efficient running has less to do with shoes than with the time, effort, care, and passion that each of us puts into it.

"Don't spend time opening your wallet; spend time opening your mind to making yourself a better athlete," Dicharry says. "There are multiple ways of improving as a runner and getting faster, and none of them require spending money on a piece of footwear. Make your body better and you'll run better."

DAVE MCGILLIVRAY || Hoka Clifton 5
Boston Marathon race director

Over the years, my favorite shoes have changed based on what I'm racing and how fast I am. But right now, it's the Hoka Clifton 5. That's the shoe I live in, train in, and race in—even though it's not really a racing flat. My pace these days doesn't require a racing flat anymore!

When I first got the Cliftons, I was skeptical. When I saw them in the box, I thought they weighed 900 pounds because they were so thick. But when I held them, I thought, *Wow, that's an optical illusion.* They look a lot heavier than they are. When I put them on, they felt more than just pretty good. They're very light, and the cushioning and flex and the way they move is amazing. I'm older, slower, and not as flexible as I once was, and my Achilles is tight. The Cliftons seem to take the stress off and help me feel better after long runs. It's like having a sixth man on a basketball team.

I took four pairs with me on the World Marathon Challenge in 2018, where we ran a marathon on every continent in seven consecutive days. I was thinking I'd have to rotate them around, but I wound up wearing the same pair for all seven marathons. It just felt good, and I thought, *Why mess with a good thing that is working for me?* When we got to Perth for the third marathon, I decided to try on a different pair to see if it would feel even better. I did one out-and-back with a new pair of Cliftons on, and it didn't feel right. Not that they were bad; I just didn't feel as comfortable as I did in the ones I had been wearing. Lucky for me, I had brought the original ones in my bag, so I put those back on and wore them for the rest of the week. They just worked. I never really felt fatigued or had any challenges, and I felt those shoes had a lot to do with it.

6

MINIMALISM TO MAXIMALISM: A TALE OF TWO INNOVATORS

Imagination is more important than knowledge.

ALBERT EINSTEIN

Twenty-five years before *Born to Run* and the minimalist shoe revolution took the running world by storm, Kenneth "Hawk" Harper already knew quite a bit about the importance of lightweight, low-to-the-ground running shoes. But his interest in natural running mechanics and trial-and-error shoe tinkering were way ahead of their time—and, for that matter, his time. The Utah native and devout Mormon didn't find his true calling in running until his mid-30s, and to say his journey to becoming a national-class runner, influential retailer, and shoe guru took some obscure and unexpected twists and turns is an epic understatement.

Hawk had been a talented baseball and football player in high school and college, earning his nickname as a ball-hawking center fielder willing to dive through the air to catch any line drive he could get close to. He was good enough to be recruited by the California Angels organization out of high school, only to have a badly blown-out knee prohibit a pro career from getting off the ground. Moving on from traditional team sports, the determined and crafty Hawk tried his hand at other athletic challenges and stunts—from weightlifting (he set a Utah state record in the bench press) to cliff jumping to busting through wooden doors for charity. He was nothing if not tenacious. Although he once leaped more than 100 feet into 6 feet of water, he also once broke several bones jumping 80 feet into 3 feet of water. Perhaps his most physically demanding gig ever, though, was spending 10 years as a river-rafting guide on the Colorado River through the Grand Canyon.

Still, believe it or not, it was distance running that almost did him in.

Built like a football player, Hawk had never been a runner and considered running more of a punishment than something to be enjoyed. But it was the late 1970s, after all, and he fell prey to the jogging craze. He tried his first marathon on a dare, pledging to run 26.2 miles after receiving a postcard touting the Las Vegas Marathon with a handwritten note from a friend that said, "Hawk, if you're a real man, you'll run a marathon."

As with any physical challenge in those days, Hawk was gung-ho and ready to go—despite having the muscle-bound physique of a 240-pound weightlifter and no endurance training to his credit whatsoever. "How tough could it be to run 26.2 miles?" he remembers thinking. That the race was only a few weeks away didn't make a difference, nor did the fact that he was hobbled with a bad knee that didn't align, and had no meniscus, resulting in painful bone-on-bone friction with every stride. At the time, he says, he couldn't even run around the block without stopping.

Grossly undertrained, he finished near the back in Las Vegas that day, finally crossing the finish line after toiling for nearly five long hours on the course. "Old ladies with shopping carts were passing me," Hawk jokes as he recalls the race. It was a frustrating scenario, but, true to his dogged spirit, he refused to let running get the best of him. Instead it only encouraged him.

He entered a second marathon, and saw a small improvement. And then another, which went slightly better, and so on, each race helping him become more inspired—and more fit—along the way.

It wasn't long before Hawk found himself fully immersed in running, not only as his passion but as his career. He worked as a tech rep for Nike in the late 1970s, wear-testing the original Nike shoes with Air cushioning packets built into the midsoles. In the '80s, he was the western sales manager for Saucony, overseeing a massive territory that included dozens of running shops and sporting goods stores between Colorado and California.

Along the way, Hawk became a student of running. He read books and watched VHS tapes about running, talked to runners, learned from coaches and elite athletes, and kept training harder—and better—while running numerous marathons. He knew his form was plodding and painful, and marveled at how elite Kenyan runners ran so smoothly that they were almost floating. "If I ran like those guys, my knee wouldn't hurt so much," he recalls thinking. "And I'd be more efficient and a heck of a lot faster."

It took him several tries to break the 4-hour mark (which in the late-'70s running boom was considered a rather pedestrian effort and well below the average for male marathoners in the United States), but he kept at it and kept improving, dropping below the 3-hour plateau and eventually under 2:30.

About that time, he had a serendipitous run-in with a runner named Cheryl Howlett while training on the track one fall evening at Brigham Young University. "The joke at BYU was that Cheryl Howlett would never marry because she was so fast, no one could catch her," Hawk says. "It's possible I would not have caught her, either, but. . . I was running the track in the opposite direction, and I literally bumped into her. I took one look and was smitten."

Hawk and Cheryl married 11 months later and within a few years had a growing family. That was impetus for Hawk to leave the travel-heavy sales gig behind and invest in Runner's Corner, a neighborhood running shop originally located in Provo.

Working in the running shoe industry taught Hawk a lot about shoes, but it also taught him a lot about the marketing and the hype that went along with each pair he sold. He discovered quickly that not all advancements were made in the name of performance and efficiency. Some were hype, some were misleading, and some were downright phony.

Despite the massive propagandalike excitement, he says he wasn't a fan of the original Nike Air midsoles because the soft, pillowlike cushioning made his stride feel more plodding. Moreover, the shoes tended to fall apart. He discovered after a few years of running that he wasn't in search of a shoe with more cushioning but instead a shoe with less—and, more importantly, one that helped him run better, more efficiently, and with less pain.

Not finding what he wanted on the shelves, he became a hobbyist shoe cobbler, modifying his own shoes to make them fit better, feel better, and run better. He did everything from lacing them differently in order to allow his toes to flex and splay more naturally to coating parts of his shoes with glow-in-the-dark paint for greater visibility at night.

A favorite tweak was drilling holes laterally through the thick heel portion of the midsole to make the back half of the shoe lighter and to create a more evenly balanced ride. He found that taking weight and bulk out of the back half helped keep his feet level when they struck the ground, which in turn helped eliminate the practice of landing with an acute bend at the ankle. That bend (called extreme dorsiflexion) typically produces a harsh heel-striking gait and a tendency to strike too far out in front of the body with excessive force. Studies wouldn't confirm that to be true for 25 years, but Hawk was big into trial and error and had great instincts. He didn't know precisely *why* it was working, but he did know that ultimately it made his knee feel better, and that was what mattered.

His cobbler's instincts must have been sound, because after eight years of running and numerous attempts at the 26.2-mile grind, he won the St. George Marathon in an impressive time of 2:22:03 at the age of 38 in 1984.

I ask him how someone could run a marathon within 14 minutes of the world record at the time just seven years removed from a soul-scorching, back-of-the-pack sufferfest in Vegas. The key, he says, was training smarter, running with better form, and modifying running shoes to mimic his natural gait patterns.

Before St. George, Hawk had worn a variety of shoes from myriad brands, made from a wide range of materials. But what almost all of the shoes shared in common was a raised heavy heel with copious amounts of cushioning.

Brands had increasingly focused on heel cushioning with the idea that the additional cushioning would alleviate the shock caused by heel striking and also ease the stress on a runner's Achilles tendon. While those aspects might have been true, Hawk believed that the raised heel design was leading to his bad form.

He was up to his usual tinkering one day when he looked at his Saucony Dixon Racers—a lightweight, low-to-the-ground shoe—and a light bulb went on in his head.

"I took part of the outsole off and removed some of the midsole in the rear foot and then put a patch of rubber from a car inner tube under the heel and glued it all together," he says. "When I started running in that shoe, I found I could suddenly run smoothly and not with a hobbling, broken-down gait."

Those were the shoes he wore when he won St. George, and they were the inspiration to take his successful "experiment of one" to a broader clientele.

At Runner's Corner, he started working with customers on a one-on-one basis to help improve their form and reduce ailments and injuries. More than a decade before discussions about good running form became commonplace following the advent of Nike's Free shoes, Newton Running, and the release of *Born to Run*, Hawk and Cheryl Harper, and eventually their young son, Golden, were having those discussions with runners on a regular basis in their family shop.

"When people came into the store, they would get a lesson on how to run better and protect their bones and joints when they run," Hawk says. "That was pretty rare for the early- to mid-1990s. Back then it was all glitzy, unneeded overlays and built-up heel cushioning that contributed to shoes being heavier and more unbalanced than they should be."

=====

As the son of one of the country's most innovative running retailers, Golden Harper was born with running—and a fascination with running shoes—in his genes. He started logging long miles with his parents at an early age, running his first marathon at age 10 in an astounding 3:08. A true running prodigy, he went on to set a world-best marathon time for a 12-year-old of 2:45:34 in 1994 (a record that still stood as of early 2019), won two Utah high school cross-country titles, and was an Academic All-American runner for Brigham Young University and BYU-Hawaii.

While he loves to run, shoes and how people run in various models have always intrigued him the most. The precocious Golden started working at Runner's Corner at 8 years old, sometimes manning the store by himself and selling shoes without adult supervision when he was as young as 10.

"People would come into the store and ask, 'Can someone help me find some shoes?' and I'd say, 'Sure, I'd be happy to help you,' albeit in a voice two octaves higher," Golden remembers, laughing.

He says that if they saw there was no one else to help them, typically they'd turn to walk out the door. "I'd watch their gait and say, 'I can see you have some right foot eversion in those Sauconys that's probably causing you some knee discomfort. I might be able to help you out with that.'"

At that point, they'd usually turn back around, he says. "I'd get them some shoes to try on and eventually sell them a model that worked much better for their gait."

Golden met Brian Beckstead in 1997 on the first day of cross-country practice at the start of their sophomore year of high school. They immediately hit it off. Not only were both already superior runners, but Beckstead was equally nuts about running shoes.

They could name every running shoe they spotted—whether worn on a teammate's feet, on a passing jogger's, or on an elderly walker's at the mall.

"We were running shoe geeks way back then," says Beckstead, who started working part-time at Runner's Corner in 1998 while he was in high school. "It was just one of those things that gets in your blood."

A lot of young runners have a favorite pair of kicks, and these guys are no exception. Years later, they still unanimously agree that the "glory" shoe of their high school years was the Reebok 3D Fusion DMX Lite, a tricked-out circa-1999 shoe with six futuristic outsole pods and a seamless blue-and-gold upper. It came out when they were juniors and among the best runners in the state. "It looked so cool," Beckstead recalls. "We thought that was the greatest shoe ever."

Like most running shoes, the model lasted just a year in that incarnation before it was morphed in favor of the next season's latest and greatest colors and design style. But Golden did honor the shoes by wearing them with a tuxedo to his prom at the end of the school year.

As the years went by, their fascination with running shoes continued. Both worked countless hours at Runner's Corner in high school, fitting thousands of runners with new shoes. They continued working at the store during and after college—Beckstead earned degrees in exercise science and recreation management, while Golden studied exercise science with a focus on biomechanics and kinematics—eventually becoming general managers and shoe buyers for the store in their early 20s. The latter role allowed them to attend the semiannual Outdoor Retailer (OR) trade show 40 minutes to the north in Salt Lake City, which was akin to releasing two kids into a candy store.

They attended the show to check out the next season's shoes from the top brands, all in the name of researching the new models that would be sold at the store. But as their interest in shoes—and, more importantly, in helping runners find shoes that could help them run better, more efficiently, and healthier—grew, so too did the realization that a lot of running shoes were poorly designed and doing a disservice to runners and their attempt to run with good form.

In August 2005, at about the time Christopher McDougall was immersing himself in the culture of the Rarámuri people and their centuries-old running traditions in the Copper Canyon of Mexico, Golden and Beckstead, just 24 years old at the time, were visiting the OR show and came across the bustling Vibram booth.

The brand known primarily for its Italian-made rubber outsoles was debuting its FiveFingers shoe. What launched as a novelty lifestyle shoe quickly developed a small group of niche fans. Yacht racers found it ideal for maintaining grip on slippery boat decks without compromising the agility of a barefoot experience. And athletes who competed in skyscraper races such as the Empire State Building Run-Up took to wearing it for precise cornering when charging up stairwells. Soon, the barefoot running community would get hold of it—including Barefoot Ted, a character highlighted in *Born to Run*—and FiveFingers would explode on the running scene, but in 2005, the shoes existed quietly on the periphery.

Golden and Beckstead received samples of the brand's newest models, although FiveFingers weren't being marketed as running shoes. After trying them out that same night, they returned to the Vibram booth the next day, and Runner's Corner became the first running store in the country to place an order for FiveFingers.

What intrigued them about the shoes was not the unusual glovelike design and toe pockets but the fact that the design allowed a wearer's foot to sit level inside the shoe and maintain its natural barefoot position. The "stack height" of the material in the heel was virtually the same as that of the forefoot under the metatarsal heads. Yes, there was an intriguing low-to-the-ground barefoot sensation about them; however, it was that lack of a built-up heel that was most interesting, Golden recalls.

The young buyers didn't know at the time that the running world would be swept away by a minimalist revolution in a few years, but they did understand early on that FiveFingers allowed runners to run with optimal form and a very natural gait pattern. It was never the intent to have customers run long miles in them, they said, but rather to have the shoes serve as a training tool.

"Our goal was to have runners use them to learn how to run with better form and strengthen their feet and lower legs," Golden says. "We would have runners wear them for short laps on the grass, very short runs, and drills to improve the strength of their feet. We never intended to sell them as full-time running shoes, even though that's what they became known for and why most running stores started selling them."

———

In the 1990s, when low-tech video gait analysis became more widely available at running stores, Runner's Corner was among the first to utilize it for the purpose of understanding the individual running gait patterns of its customers. A runner's feet and lower legs were video-taped from behind while running on a treadmill, and then a shoe-fit expert would watch the tape in slow motion to determine whether and how much that runner was pronating (rolling inward) or supinating (rolling outward).

For much of the previous 25 years, the running industry had been obsessed with how runners pronated. Studies had long shown that most runners pronate when they run, but how much and how potentially inju-riously has always been a wide-ranging debate based on hearsay among form gurus and running shoe marketing directors.

The general idea was that overpronating, especially severe overpro-nating, led to many of the most common running injuries because it caused additional twisting of the ankles, lower legs, knees, thighs, and hips. While the twisting is a fact, overpronating versus severe overpronat-ing has never been clearly differentiated, nor has a causal relationship to specific injuries been established.

But that didn't stop shoe companies from taking this so-called calam-ity and running with it as a sales mechanism.

To solve this supposed gait malady, the thinking went, runners who overpronated needed to be fitted with supportive shoes—a mildly sup-portive stability model or a highly supportive motion-control model—that would limit the degree of rolling and thus greatly reduce the chance of overuse injuries. The rare runner who didn't show signs of excessive pronation would be fitted with neutral shoes.

The process was well intentioned but flawed for a few reasons. One, true video gait analysis is effective only with high-speed cameras that can record super-slow-motion images, which was not the tech being used in running stores at the time. Two, and more importantly, the idea was based on the false notion that what was happening at the foot and ankle was the most important aspect of a runner's gait. The reality is that pronation is

The Naperville Running Company in suburban Chicago has earned a reputation as one of the best running specialty stores in the United States.

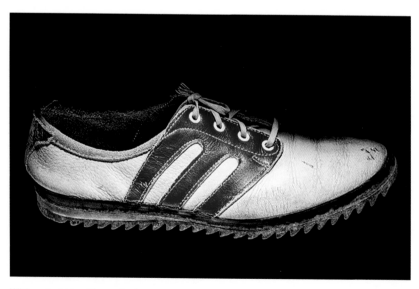

With a rippled rubber outsole, the New Balance Trackster was one of the first running shoes made for running high mileage on the roads.

The EB Lydiard Marathon shoes were codeveloped by renowned New Zealand coach Arthur Lydiard and Germany's EB Brütting company. The shoe featured an upper made from kangaroo leather.

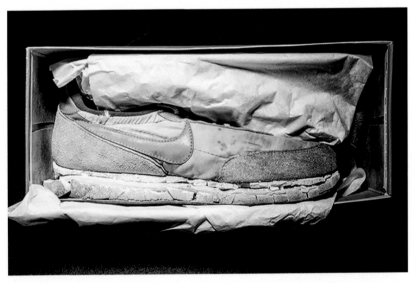

The Air Tailwind was the first shoe to feature Nike's proprietary Air-Sole cushioning technology.

The late 1980s and early 1990s saw numerous innovations in running shoes. Reebok's Pump had an airbag system to create a semicustom fit by filling up interior volume with air.

Customatix, a start-up founded in 2000, allowed consumers to customize shoes via the Internet.

The New Balance 420 was a lightweight, cushioned shoe built for marathon running in the early 1980s.

Dave Kayser's running shoe collection has more than 120 vintage models. Each acid-free box contains 10 to 12 pairs of shoes from the 1930s to the 1990s.

New Balance employs about 1,500 factory workers in New England who produce four million pairs of shoes annually in its five U.S. manufacturing facilities.

Shoes are built around hard plastic placeholders known as "lasts." Each last represents the size and shape of a corresponding men's or women's foot size in the production run.

At the height of the minimalist shoe revolution in 2011, Hoka One One turned the running shoe world upside down by unveiling maximally cushioned trail running shoes to provide increased comfort, protection, and natural running features. The Speedgoat 3 was created with input from ultrarunner Karl "Speedgoat" Meltzer.

Altra Running was founded on principles to ensure a runner could run with natural biomechanics. The shoes feature a level platform known as "zero-drop" and a wide, foot-shaped toe box that allows the toes to splay.

Swiss company On Running offers an innovative approach to cushioning with its unique CloudTec system of specifically "tuned" cushioning "clouds."

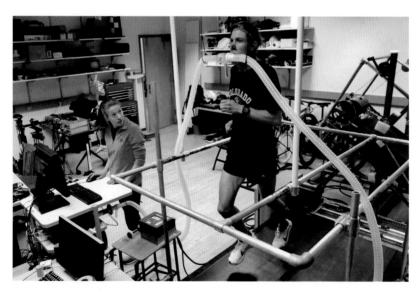

Nike spent years working on a shoe to help runners break the 2-hour marathon barrier. Lab tests at the University of Colorado showed the metabolic cost of running at specific paces was 4 percent less than in comparable racing shoes.

Nike's Zoom Vaporfly 4% shoes dominated marathons and half-marathons in 2016–2018—including Kenyan Eliud Kipchoge's 2:01:39 world record at the 2018 Berlin Marathon.

Specially designed versions of a brand's top models (known as SMUs, or special makeups) are increasingly popular at marathon expos. Saucony and Dunkin' Donuts collaborated to create this shoe to commemorate the 2019 Boston Marathon.

a natural movement pattern for many runners, and trying to control it or slow it with a restrictive shoe that was heavy and limiting only caused more problems up a runner's kinematic chain.

Not surprisingly, Hawk said, the return rate of shoes at Runner's Corner doubled when the treadmill gait analysis was at its peak and stability and motion-control shoes were being regularly prescribed, as did the number of runners who returned to the store complaining of injuries.

Once those trends became apparent, they removed the treadmill from the store and reverted to teaching runners how to run with good form and be proactive about protecting their bodies from overuse injuries—mainly through form drills, core strength work, greater agility through dynamic stretching, and some barefoot running.

"As soon as we pulled the treadmill out of the equation and started watching people run outside again, the way they normally would, and giving them lessons to run with better form, returns and injuries went way down," Hawk recalls.

Furthermore, sales of stability shoes—which running shoe brands had pushed for decades as a way to lessen common running injuries— dropped like a stone, he said, and the store went back to selling neutral shoes to 85 percent of its customers. Instead of relying on medial posts and other controlling devices in structured shoes, they started allowing a runner's natural stride habits to dictate how the foot moved through the gait cycle. "That's when we knew that not everything taught to us by shoe companies was a good thing and that there was, indeed, a better way," Golden confirms.

Runner's Corner invested in a high-speed digital video camera in 2006, and Golden and Beckstead filmed runners running in FiveFingers and then in traditional running shoes. Watching them in FiveFingers (or other minimalist shoes built on a level platform) was like watching a child running through the grass with perfectly efficient form, they recalled.

When running in a Brooks Adrenaline, ASICS GEL-Kayano, Nike Pegasus, or other top-selling shoes with traditionally built-up heels, most runners reverted to a dramatic overstriding gait with a hard-hitting heel strike that caused more impact force on their bodies.

The experiment was another kernel of knowledge leading to a new way of thinking about running shoes. "With all of this modern technology and expensive running shoes that are supposed to reduce injury, still as many as 83 percent of people are not running well. In some studies, injury rates are actually higher than ever before," Golden realized.

He also realized that he had been, to some extent, lying to people. "Not intentionally, but I had been taking what brands told us and passing it along to customers even though we were trying to preach good running form. Every time I sold someone shoes, I knew they had to undo everything I'd just taught them every time they went running. Something had to change."

The seeds for a new way to build running shoes were now firmly planted.

Golden and Beckstead began tinkering with shoes and footbeds for customers with the aim of engaging the preferred movement path of their natural running mechanics based on their individual anatomical needs. They wanted to create shoes that essentially stayed out of the way and allowed the foot to behave naturally, as if running unshod over a smooth, grassy lawn.

Although Beckstead eventually moved on from Runner's Corner and took a job managing an outdoor gear and apparel shop in Ogden, the friends remained close and continued to talk about newfangled shoe ideas. Golden, with Beckstead's constant input, decided to build a shoe of his own, one in which the foot could stay relatively level to the ground and land lightly under the knee.

Relying on the most current and best-understood research he could get his hands on, he began his shoe experimentation in 2008 by holding to a handful of science-backed truths about running shoes, including the following ideas:

- Cushioning protects (but weakens) your feet, and also magnifies the forces on the joints.

- Overpronation doesn't cause common overuse injuries; a weak kinematic chain is the primary catalyst of those ailments.

- Stability and motion-control shoes don't fix pronation; instead they weaken and limit the natural motion of the feet, lower legs, knees, and hips, causing an unnatural and sometimes catawampus gait pattern.

- Good running form is facilitated by strong feet, ankles, and lower legs as well as lower limb agility, allowing knees and hips to track consistently in the sagittal plane.

- An efficient running gait results in a foot hitting the ground lightly just below the body and not far out in front of it in a heavy heel-striking fashion.

Using a toaster oven and a butter knife, Golden deconstructed a pair of Inov-8 Roclite 325 shoes a size and a half larger than his own size 9. Once the heat of the toaster had melted the glue holding the shoe together and allowed him to delaminate the layers, he removed the foam midsole section, which was thicker in the heel than in the forefoot, and replaced it with a uniform piece of moderately soft Spenco foam that he cut to fit. He glued it back together to create a shoe with a level platform.

When it had set the next day, he slipped it on and skipped the laces on the bottom half of the shoe so that the toe box would open up, thus giving room for the toes and metatarsal arch to optimally splay, absorb impact, stabilize, and powerfully push off the ground.

As he ran in the newly constructed shoes, he noticed his feet landing softly, nearly level to the ground and right under his knee. High-speed video proved that this was precisely what he was doing. As a runner and as a shoe geek, Golden Harper had proven himself to be truly a chip off the old block.

"I felt like I was running in racing flats or FiveFingers while running in a fully cushioned shoe on the roads," Golden recalls. "It felt amazing to be running in a soft, supportive shoe that mimicked the feeling and good mechanics that occur when running barefoot in the grass."

The experiment was a huge aha moment. Golden immediately made five more pairs and asked staffers at the store to try them out. Their responses were similar. Within days, he had requests for 25 more pairs. He enlisted the help of a local cobbler, Robert Glazier, a certified pedorthist and third-generation shoemaker, and settled on the original Saucony Jazz as the shoe to deconstruct because it had two midsole foam layers, making it easy to remove the top layer.

After cutting the shoes apart and rebuilding them, Glazier would check the difference between the heel height and the forefoot height—essentially the difference between where the heel and forefoot sit inside the shoe—and make sure any "drop" from heel to forefoot was as close to zero as possible. Hawk gave the process a name: "zeroing."

"Up to that point, we were calling them 'hacked-up, modified shoes,' a horrible name," Golden says, laughing. "Then there's this moment of 'Robert, you're a genius! We'll call them zero-drop shoes.'"

By the spring of 2009, word had gotten out locally that Runner's Corner was making secret shoes that reduced pain and improved running form. They produced about 1,000 custom pairs of zero-drop shoes and still could barely keep up with demand.

Along with those early prototype shoes, Golden secured hundreds of surveys filled out by their wear-testers. Motivated by both a fear of being sued and the goal of trying to help their customers run better, they allowed runners to test their hacked-up shoes in the name of research, offering a $10 Runner's Corner gift card to runners willing to run in them for six weeks and then fill out the one-page survey.

The survey asked a variety of questions geared to providing insights into how the shoes performed and how runners ran differently while wearing them. *Do you run with a different gait? Do your feet land on the ground differently? Do you land more at the heel, midfoot, or forefoot? What muscles on your body do you use more? What parts of your body hurt more? What parts of your body hurt less?* The results were overwhelmingly positive, with 90 percent of runners suggesting that they were running better, more efficiently, and healthier than ever.

"We were getting feedback that showed that the common running overuse injuries—plantar fascia issues, shin splints, runner's knee, IT band problems, and lower-back discomfort—were being reduced dramatically," Golden says. "It wasn't independent research, but it was a really good way to validate what we were doing."

While Golden was doing most of the research, Beckstead was heavily involved in wear-testing and formulating a business model, with Golden's cousin Jeremy Howlett, around their new concepts. By the fall of 2009, Golden, Beckstead, and Howlett felt it was time to move forward and start a new shoe company in earnest. But how to go from building hacked-up shoes one pair at a time in a toaster oven to becoming a paradigm-changing, internationally distributed brand?

For two years, they continued tearing up and remaking shoes and knocking on doors with their shoes, their surveys, and their convictions. Finally, things started to come together. They eventually got help from some seasoned designers and developers—former Nike and Adidas employees—who were willing to take a chance on them. They also got assistance from an angel investor who invested $200,000 to cover the cost of their first round of shoes.

What started with a toaster oven and superglue was about to become a legitimate running shoe brand.

$$=====$$

It was a chilly, overcast afternoon in January 2010 when Nicolas Mermoud called my cell phone out of the blue. "Brian, I am over at the Boulder Running Company [BRC], and I have some new shoes for you to check out," he said in his thick French accent. "Can you stop by and go for a run with me? I promise you they're like nothing you've ever seen before."

Twist my arm, I thought. At the time, I was a senior editor for *Running Times* magazine and overseeing the publication's quarterly wear-test reviews of all of the new shoes. I was always interested in learning what was next in shoe development and particularly eager for peeks behind the curtain at future models before they came to market.

Mermoud had e-mailed the week before to tell me about Hoka One One, the new company he and former Salomon colleague Jean-Luc Diard had quietly been working on for more than a year. At the time, the minimalist shoe revolution was still a year away from hitting its zenith, and most brands were working fast and furiously to get new "barely there" models to market. But a full year before the April 2011 issue of *Running Times* hit newsstands with the headline "Minimalism Goes Mainstream," Mermoud was about to show me the thickest, cushiest shoe I had ever seen.

I had met Mermoud a decade earlier, when he worked for Salomon, the French sports equipment and apparel company known at the time for its leading-edge skiing, snowboarding, and hiking gear. In his role there, he worked with world-class athletes, but Mermoud was a legit athlete in his own right. Aside from being a great big-mountain skier, he was also an elite-level multisport adventure racer and mountain runner who could hang with some of the best ultrarunners on the European circuit. He once placed fifth in the highly contested Ultra-Trail du Mont-Blanc, a rigorous 104-mile trail running race that circles the highest mountain range in Western Europe.

When it came to playing in the mountains, Mermoud was skilled and fearless and always sported the latest and greatest gear. Still, knowing the zealousness that Mermoud exuded (or maybe it was just that his French accent made everything sound so full of zeal), I figured there was some hyperbole in his proclamation. Either way, I knew whatever he had to show me was something I should see.

I dressed to run and drove over to BRC, which was then considered one of the best running shops in the United States. Cofounders Johnny Halberstadt and Mark Plaatjes were known for being shrewd about stocking their store, eschewing fad technologies and marketing hype—they refused to sell FiveFingers or Newton shoes—while also taking risks on innovative new models that they believed in. At the core of their mission was the goal of helping customers run more efficiently and injury-free.

Halberstadt had been developing shoes for more than 25 years, initially in his native South Africa, and had earned several U.S. patents for shoe design since emigrating to the United States in the early 1990s. Plaatjes, the 1993 marathon world champion, was a renowned physical therapist with an intimate knowledge of how the human body moved while running.

Halberstadt and Plaatjes opened their Boulder store in 1996 with the intent of providing authentic products and shoe-fitting services for every level of runner in a city that very well might have had the highest number of runners per capita in the United States. Before long, every shoe brand in the world wanted to get its shoes into BRC.

When I arrived, Mermoud and Halberstadt were chatting near the store's massive shoe wall while handling a robustly cushioned model that looked like shoes on steroids, a cross between running shoes, moon boots, and something a Marvel Studios character might wear.

The story was that Mermoud had attended The Running Event trade show two months earlier in Austin, Texas, and had been wearing a pair of these oversized, trend-bucking shoes when Plaatjes spotted him.

"I asked if I could try them out," Plaatjes recalls. "I put them on and ran around the convention center lobby for about 30 seconds, and then I asked him if he had manufactured any yet."

Mermoud told him that the company had 600 pairs being produced in a Chinese factory, and Plaatjes said BRC would buy them all—the entirety of Hoka's initial production run—based entirely on that brief trial. "Clearly it was something new and very different, but it made sense," Plaatjes recalls.

After talking to Diard, who had formerly headed Salomon's design center in Boulder, Mermoud arranged the order and was in Boulder eight weeks later when the first shipment arrived.

The two innovators' original intent was to make trail shoes for the rugged mountain running races held in the European Alps, Pyrenees, and Dolomites. Early on, Mermoud and Diard had tinkered with a downhill-only, slip-on overshoe that could be carried in a backpack on uphill sections and attached to a traditional trail shoe on long, rugged downhills. But when it turned out to be a rather gangly working prototype, they decided not to waste time on a technical accessory and instead build a true running shoe.

The thick cushioning and wide-body design of the shoe were based on the oversized concept that had been successfully implemented in other sports gear: fat skis for powder skiing, 29-inch mountain bike wheels, and extra-large tennis rackets. A bigger sweet spot or considerably more cushioning would apply similarly to running, Mermoud posited, especially when running down steep mountain trails.

Given my own belief that less material led to greater agility, a more natural ride, and better feel of the ground, I was skeptical. Mermoud pushed back, arguing that a bigger platform would mean considerably less impact; less leg fatigue; more energy return; and, with the right mix of materials, more stability.

I respected his smarts, instincts, and experience, but this argument was hard to swallow, especially in a moment when the industry, the scientific community, and runners around the world were caught up in the front end of the storm swirling around the minimalist footwear revolution. It had been less than a year since *Born to Run* had hit bookstores and begun popularizing barefoot running, minimalist footwear, and a natural running gait. What was being discussed everywhere was the notion that *less* shoe—not more shoe—allowed runners to run with better mechanics and ultimately more efficiently.

When Hoka launched in 2010, uberminimalist running shoes were starting to trend in the mainstream. Yet here was Hoka, seemingly going in the opposite direction.

But while the shoes looked unwieldy, almost humorously so, Mermoud insisted that this did not mean they represented the polar opposite of minimalism. In fact, the shoe retained some of the key qualities of minimalist shoes, he assured me, namely, a design allowing for a smoother running gait that avoided heavy heel striking. Furthermore, the shoe was light. Given trends at the time, they knew that if they couldn't make the shoe light enough, it wasn't going to fly. So they eschewed traditional cushioning foam and sourced new superlightweight materials being produced in Asia that had not been used before in running shoes.

At the same time, he asserted, the shoe was an alternative to everything that people disliked about minimalism, not least the starkness of the ride.

Hoka's first models were the Mafate for trail running and the Bondi for roads, both strikingly unconventional in appearance, color, and shape.

It was the Mafate that Mermoud handed to me at BRC that day, asking proudly, "Well what do you think?"

I was genuinely flabbergasted, not only by the gargantuan thickness of the shoe's foam midsole but also by its surprising weight, given the size. It seemed almost impossibly light—lighter than many traditionally designed shoes on BRC's shoe wall at the time. Nothing with that much material could be that light, I thought.

He explained that the shoes had been built with 30 percent more cushioning than traditional models and that they featured a wide, stable platform and a rockered (convex) profile that he insisted would lead to less impact stress, better running form, and the smoothest ride I would ever experience. He whipped open his laptop and showed me slow-motion video of a Hoka-shod runner in a laboratory setting running with the smooth, effortless form of a nimble Kenyan marathoner.

"It's like flying, Brian," Mermoud told me. "Let's go for a run. I want you to try them out."

Having run in more than a thousand pairs of trail running shoes since the mid-1990s, I was a mix of excited, eager, and overwhelmingly dubious. It had been my experience that most of the initial models from the many running shoe and hiking boot brands that had ventured into the trail running category were flops—too heavy, too unstable, or just too wonky.

Halberstadt and Plaatjes, however, shared none of the doubts I was harboring. They suspected that all that cushioning would be a welcome benefit for many runners, especially those being beaten up by negligibly cushioned shoes and suffering from common overuse injuries. But it was the rockered profile that supercharged the BRC owners. It made great sense, Halberstadt said, because it smoothed out the gait cycle without the hard impacts of profound heel striking.

"It creates a very smooth, circular motion in a runner's gait," Halberstadt told me. "You can't land with a heavy heel strike in these shoes, so there's none of the hard slapping sensation when the foot transitions to the middle of the stride, and that's going to reduce impact throughout the kinetic chain and lower the chance of overuse injuries."

Mermoud and I laced up and went for a run up and down the popular Mt. Sanitas trail in Boulder. These shoes offered by far the strangest sensation I had ever experienced while running. They were much lighter, softer, and smoother than I expected, but at times they also felt unstable—for example, when one of my feet caught the edge of a rock. The marshmallow-soft cushioning offered little support if a foot started to roll left or right.

The real benefit of the Mafates became crystal-clear to me on our way down to the trailhead, however. We absolutely bounded down the final half-mile or so of technical trail with ease, running 2 minutes faster than I normally ran that stretch.

I still wasn't entirely sold on the shoe, but I could see that Mermoud and Diard were on to something. Behind it was a clever, innovative concept that made some good sense. But could it sell in the minimalist climate of the day? With the retail and shoe smarts of Plaatjes and Halberstadt, I thought it just might.

Hoka brought with it a divergent way of thinking that countered the prevailing barefoot and minimalist trend, but getting a foothold was initially an uphill battle. Although Mermoud and Diard signed top American ultrarunners Karl Meltzer and Dave Mackey the year they launched, it took Hoka a few years to gain mainstream acceptance and understanding, partly because it took time for the brand to hone the optimal size and shape of its shoes and improve the stability, durability, and aesthetics of its subsequent models. But a bigger factor was that the American running public was not an easy target: Some were still caught up in the minimalist craze, while others were smarting from jumping into that particular frenzy and hesitant to follow another fad.

Originally there was the perception that the shoes were built only for the slower paces and long hours of ultrarunning. But as the shoes were refined, additional models were built with more responsive and stable foam materials, and runners started logging fast times from the 5K to the marathon in Hokas.

By early 2013, the brand was red-hot, and sales skyrocketed, growing from fewer than 20 retail outlets in the first year to more than 850 three years later. Given that many runners couldn't tolerate or didn't like the impact of minimalist shoes and appreciated comfort in every step, the maximal cushioning concept seemed to come as a welcome change.

But there was—and still is—a divide on "maximalist" running shoes. For some, Hoka's thick cushioning, rockered design, and rolling sensation from heel to toe seem to provide relief from common aches and overuse injuries such as Achilles tendinitis. There are endless testimonials from broken-down runners who suggest that Hokas allow them to run consistently and feel better than they ever have.

But others, including many in the medical community, say the thick midsole prevents the foot from functioning as it is designed to—as a spring rather than a shock absorber—thus amplifying rather than attenuating impact loading.

Indeed, a 2018 study at Oregon State University concluded that runners experienced a higher impact peak and increased loading rate wearing maximally cushioned shoes. Increases in both factors are associated with a greater likelihood of injury such as plantar fasciitis and tibial stress fractures.

No question, though, that Hoka made a huge impact that continues to be felt. While it didn't single-handedly end the minimalist movement, it was a major catalyst that would lead to a cushioning revolution on the near horizon.

"Hoka swung the pendulum back and made it OK to like a soft, cushioned ride again," says NRC owner Hartner, whose stores felt the increase in demand for Hokas.

The brand doubled its sales every year in its first several years, growing so fast that at one point, it couldn't produce shoes fast enough to meet demand. It badly needed to continue growing, but it needed additional capital to do so; otherwise it would go out of business despite generating $4 million in revenue. That was when Angel Martinez, CEO and chairman of Deckers Outdoor Corporation, stepped in. The former elite runner and longtime shoe industry executive suspected that maximalism could be the next big thing in the running world. He led Deckers's acquisition of Hoka, with the Goleta, California–based company eventually taking control of the upstart brand in April 2013 for a reported $4 million and quickly building it into a $20 million brand.

KARL "SPEEDGOAT" MELTZER ||
Hoka One One Speedgoat 3

American ultrarunner, world's winningest 100-mile runner

One year, I was driving home from the Pikes Peak Marathon with my running buddies, and we saw this jackrabbit cross the road, and one of them said, "Hey, look, it's a speed goat," just to be funny. At the time, we were running in a shoe called the Fila Escapegoat, which is a shoe I liked quite a bit. That's where the "goat" name first started, and my buddies started calling me "Speedgoat." A bit later, I ran the Zane Gray 50 trail race, and the race director called me "the Wasatch Speedgoat" on the runner's list instead of my real name, and it kind of took off from there.

When I first started trail running, the Montrail Vitesse was my favorite shoe. I like a lot of cushioning on the trails because you need it for 100 miles. Once Hoka got into business, I was one of their first sponsored runners, so I ran a lot of miles and a lot of races in the Mafate. I liked it, but it was never my favorite shoe. Then I ran in the Bondi and a few other shoes and started giving Hoka input for a really well-cushioned shoe with sticky rubber for 100-mile races in the mountains. As it turned out, they kind of rushed the first Speedgoat to the market in 2015 before I really gave them much feedback. It was a good start, but it wound up being too narrow. They fixed that and made the shoe even better with the Speedgoat 2 and Speedgoat 3, and those became my favorite shoes because they have the right amount of heel-toe drop and the right amount of cushion. And yes, I had something to do with that, which was cool.

Back in the mid-1990s, me and my running buddies would always say, "Wouldn't it be cool to have your own shoe? One that was made just for you?" Well, here I am 20 years later, and they've made shoes for me, and it's pretty rad. Every race I go to now, there's a lot of people wearing Speedgoats. How good is that feeling? I'm no Air Jordan, but it's priceless.

At the OR trade show in August 2010, as Mermoud and Diard were getting considerable buzz about their oversized Hoka shoes from curious and bewildered running retailers visiting their small booth space, Golden, Beckstead, and Howlett were wandering the same show floor with a backpack full of obtuse-looking, foot-shaped prototypes to show running brands and retailers.

At previous trade shows, they had been split on their next best move. Should they try to sell or license their shoe designs to another brand or grow their own company in earnest? They knew working with an established brand would be an easier avenue into the market, creating instant credibility, but it also meant losing some control and the ability to innovate. But by summer 2012, they were ready to move forward with their own brand.

With the minimalist movement in full swing among mainstream runners, New Balance, Brooks, Saucony, Pearl Izumi, and ASICS were all exhibiting low-to-the-ground trail running and road running models for the coming year. Anton Krupicka, one of the first elite athlete proponents of minimalism and already a two-time Leadville 100 champion, was one of the biggest stars of the 2010 show, touting New Balance's forthcoming Minimus line. Meanwhile, the Vibram booth was packed with commotion as well, with new models of the FiveFingers toe shoes on display. Hoka One One was there, too, an outlier and newcomer to the scene, ready to buck the trends with its highly cushioned shoes.

Their aim was to have neither a minimalist brand nor a maximalist brand—indeed, it would soon have models in both categories. However, their idea was built upon deconstructing and discrediting one of the primary design precepts that virtually all running shoe brands had followed since the mid-1970s—namely, that runners should wear shoes with an elevated, cushioned heel.

Unlike Mermoud and Diard, who were longtime industry veterans with credibility, experience, and a few serious investors, Golden and Beckstead had never worked for a shoe brand, weren't very connected, and had little funding to get a new brand off the ground. Still, they were confident in what they had to sell, knowing that they'd already helped improve the running form and reduce the common overuse injuries and ailments of hundreds of runners at Runner's Corner.

As the trio walked past booth after booth on their way to their first meeting, they were hopeful, nervous, excited, and bewildered. Although they'd been to this spectacle of gear, clothing, and accessories in the past as buyers for Runner's Corner, on this day they felt a little like wide-eyed kids with paper airplanes setting out to explain aerodynamics to a bunch of rocket scientists at NASA. Would brands see that they were on to something with their zero-drop? Or was this little more than a fool's errand?

While a few running shoe brand managers understood the logic behind what Altra was trying to accomplish, many scoffed at the idea of building a brand around helping runners improve their form and become less injury-prone. After all, running shoes had always been built and sold on marketing hype, sharp designs, and the hottest colors of the season. The millennial entrepreneurs were repeatedly told that their shoes would never fit into a traditional brand's marketing campaigns with their newfangled heel cushioning foam and focus on mitigating impact.

The general skepticism and reluctance were perhaps understandable given the business model every brand had been built around for the past 30 years.

"We went from shoe company to shoe company, asking, 'Would you make a shoe like this?'" Beckstead recalls. "Most said, 'Look, guys, all of the cool cushioning is in the heel. We'd have to alienate our entire customer base and everything we stand for to do something like this, and we're definitely not willing to do that.'"

Beckstead also recalls questions along the lines of "You're getting people to land differently, and so none of the technologically advanced cushioning in our shoes really matters?" When the young entrepreneurs replied yes, that was what their data reported, and the runners who tested the shoes loved how their bodies felt, Beckstead says that, unsurprisingly, this response didn't go over very well.

They were laughed at, ridiculed, and scoffed at by several major running brands. But a belief in what they were doing, along with a plentiful dose of youthful resolve, didn't allow the decided lack of acceptance and understanding to become discouragement. In fact, it only encouraged them that they were on the right track.

That think-outside-the-box determination in the face of challenges was built into the genesis of Altra Running, the brand Golden and Beckstead soon founded to sell their shoes with the foot-shaped toe box and a "zero-drop" (or balanced) platform.

Their persistence and willingness to go it alone paid off. At the trade shows in the winter of 2010–2011, Altra launched in earnest and immediately had 40 retailers interested in carrying its shoes the moment the first shipment arrived from its Chinese factory. The brand quickly gained buzz in the media and at retail shops across the country.

"We believed in what we were doing, even when the industry was telling us not to," Beckstead says. Golden concurs: "A year later, a guy we had met with at the trade show came up to us and said, 'You guys have figured it out. What you're doing now, we'll be doing in 20 years, but we'll have to slowly take our time to get there.'"

It took Altra less than half that time to make a significant impact on the industry. It gained a much-needed boost in capital a few months later when Icon Health & Fitness gobbled up the brand, helping it continue to innovate, improve its design and production, and grow.

By late 2017, Altra was the eighth-largest running shoe brand in the United States, with more than 1,600 vendors worldwide and $50 million in gross revenue. It was such a hot company that VF Corporation, the owner of megabrands such as The North Face, Vans, Smartwool, Timberland, Wrangler, and Lee, bought Altra for a reported $130 million in 2018.

"We didn't set out to change the world or to make the biggest shoe company," Golden says. "Our mission was to get people to focus on technique instead of things that don't have scientific backing, like the negative connotations about pronation and cushioning being bad. We wanted to change the experience runners were having in shoes that we believed weren't built the right way. We believed we had discovered a better way, and it came from years of helping people run better and feel better."

A belief in the ability to make something better fuels innovation. And in a capitalistic society, new ideas and creativity spur competitive energy and, ultimately, fuel change. Why? Because money talks. Innovation and change are inevitable in consumer-facing industries because improvements—whether to advance the aesthetics or the functionality of a particular product, service, or organization—are what consumers are conditioned to want, to crave, and to buy. Whether phones, computers, automobiles, or running shoes, we all want what is new and improved.

In the case of running shoes, it took small start-up brands and fearless, tenacious entrepreneurs to bring about change—oftentimes disruptively so. Ultimately, the storm of unruly innovation set off by Newton,

Altra, and Hoka helped create a ripple effect among the bigger brands that had ruled the industry for 20 years. The success of these upstarts spurred Brooks, Nike, New Balance, and Saucony, among others, to dig deep, get creative, and reinvent their own product lines with innovative concepts and models.

The shift also severely damaged existing brands that were slow to react, including ASICS and Mizuno, and led to the demise of small brands such as Pearl Izumi, K-Swiss, and Fila that weren't doing enough to be different. And that made room for even more new brands, such as Skechers, On Running, Topo, Merrell, and Under Armour, to enter the running industry.

"You can come out of nowhere if you have innovation," said Dan Sullivan, national sales manager–performance for Skechers. "You can't be a me-too brand. You have to have a unique point of view. If you're trying to compare your shoes to another brand's great shoe and you come up with a good shoe, well, good doesn't beat great. That's the nature of competition, and that's why innovation has always played such a strong role in this industry."

7

A SHOE IS BORN

The competitor to be feared is one who never bothers about you at all,
but goes on making his own business better all the time.
HENRY FORD

Inside a plain, two-story industrial building on the outskirts of
Chengguan, China, I watch as a petite young woman wearing a colorful
printed blouse and a white cloth mask over her nose and mouth picks
up a curvy, die-cut sliver of white foam. Holding the slice of foam in her
left hand, she dips a small, well-worn brush into a plastic bowl of white
glue, spreads two small dabs on one side of the foam, and then sticks it
to a light-green plastic object that looks like a foot that's been cut off at
the ankle.

She finishes this task quickly and then sends the foot-shaped object
and its newly stuck-on foam companion on its way along a slow-moving
conveyor belt passing in front of her. She grabs another sliver of the precisely cut foam from a yellow plastic bin beside her and repeats the process, sticking it to another foot-shaped plastic object from a white plastic
bin. She repeats this again and again with the same methodical cadence.

Seated a few feet downstream on the other side of the conveyor belt, another young woman, this one wearing a pink acrylic sweater, designer jeans, and a face mask, picks up what appears to be two sewn-together pieces of black mesh and light-blue-and-black fabric from a yellow plastic bin beside her and coats the interior rim with a different-colored glue. Her finished product goes on the conveyor belt opposite the foot-and-foam modules.

Both items pass through a tunnel of heat to activate the glue and then are picked off the belt by an older man in a white T-shirt, ragged jeans, and a face mask. He turns the fabric inside out, revealing it to be the prelaced upper of a running shoe, and fits the two pieces together, ensuring that the glued fabric rim wraps around the bottom of the white foam stuck to the fake foot.

The heavy, hard-plastic foot piece is known in the footwear industry as a "last," a temporary placeholder object around which a shoe is built. Each last represents the size and shape of a corresponding foot size in the production run. A typical running shoe production run typically includes about 24 sizes (14 for men, 10 for women), depending on the product and whether it's offered in multiple widths.

Separately, the pieces on the conveyor belt look meaningless alongside each other, just random chunks of cut-to-fit synthetic materials. But when the man completes the task of gluing the fabric upper and foam strobel board around the last to create a foam-and-fabric bootie, I can start to see the shape and dimensions of the technical trail running shoes that are being built in this factory today.

A woman wearing a gingham-check blouse, jeans, and a face mask picks up the bootie and slides it onto the small platform of a mechanical device. The ancient-looking machine, with its dirty springs, hydraulic cables, and various levers extending from all directions, rattles and clanks as it closes around the bootie when the woman activates it with a foot pedal. In one swift move, the machine stretches, tightens, and smooths the fabric upper and applies pressure to ensure that the glued areas gain proper purchase before the shoe is put back on the conveyor belt to continue on its way through another heat tunnel.

The shoe that's being made today has a relatively uncomplicated design, but it still takes more than 60 individual steps to build it and 90 minutes for the assembly line to spit out the first pair.

The shoe has a single-layer EVA foam midsole, but it has a flexible plastic plate that's embedded in a comolding process. That piece was built offsite at a specialized foam plant, so it's an easy plug-and-play connection to the outsole at this factory. The upper is then reinforced with heat-welded overlays of TPU, a lightweight additive that adds support.

As it moves down the line, the shoe takes on more structure. The last is eventually removed, placed in a corresponding bin of lasts of the same size, and wheeled back to the start of the assembly line. I continue down the line to see the first of the finished shoes being examined by a quality-control inspector.

He looks over each pair, determining whether it's worthy of a grade A, and therefore good enough to proceed to the boxing and shipping area, or if it's a B (salvageable but in need of some refinements) or a C (failed beyond repair and bound for the scrap heap or sold in an off-market or factory outlet store for a lower price).

Grade A shoes are stuffed with cardboard inserts to maintain their shape, wrapped in tissue, and put in boxes. The boxes are stickered with labels that feature the shoe's model name, designated gender, and size, along with a serial number and UPC. Each box is scanned and put into a larger shipping box—usually 12 pairs per box—which is then put on a truck with dozens of other boxes for delivery to a cargo center at a seaport.

There, the boxes are loaded into shipping containers for a 10-day trip across the Pacific Ocean to a U.S. port of call—perhaps Los Angeles,

Oakland, Seattle, or Portland—where they'll pass through customs before being released to domestic shipping agents and beginning the journey to a brand's central distribution center. There, the shoes are warehoused before being shipped to running specialty stores, sporting goods shops, department stores, and e-commerce retailers across the United States.

"It's pretty amazing to see what a labor-intensive process it is to build a single pair of shoes," says industry veteran Fritz Taylor. "There are so many little steps that go into making this thing that runners pull out of a box and try on at their local retail store."

I return to the start of the line and watch the same woman applying the glue that temporarily secures the foam strobel board to the lasts. She has barely moved, still intently focused on her task, as is everyone else on the line. I step back a bit and watch the process from afar. There is a stated goal of 2,500 pairs of shoes to be produced today, and efficiency is key.

The woman finishes one glued-up last and reaches for new materials about every 10 seconds. Quick math tells me that she's handling about 6 pieces per minute, or 360 per hour. This is not just her pace but also the pace of the entire assembly line. Each task in the line appears to have been devised to take the same amount of time, and all are tuned to the silent metronome of the slow-moving conveyor belt. Hourly production averages are slightly less than that when mandatory stretching breaks and a 30-minute lunch break are figured into the mix, but on average, it will take a full 8-hour shift to produce 2,500 pairs of this particular shoe.

While much has been made of harsh working conditions in Asian shoe factories over the past 25 years—rightly so, given some of the reports that have come out—conditions at this family-owned factory appear to be respectable in the ways I can observe. The rooms are clean, organized for safety, well ventilated, and well lit. Most workers are well dressed and in casual clothes (not factory-regulated uniforms), most have mobile phones, and most smile congenially, especially when Phillip Chen, a well-known shoe manufacturer's representative based in Taiwan, comes by to say hello.

Chen has worked in the shoe manufacturing business for more than 30 years and has spent time with several major brands, including Nike, Adidas, Brooks, and New Balance. He tells me that conditions have improved considerably from their previous state, partially as a result of scathing media reports in the 1990s about some of the Nike and Reebok factories.

China surpassed the United States in 2011 to become the world's largest producer of manufactured goods. The country's huge manufacturing engine has boosted living standards by doubling the country's GDP per capita over the last decade. Because of China's rising economy and many new opportunities for its upwardly mobile working-class residents, factory owners have to compete for workers. Chen tells me this factory provides free lunch during a 30-minute midday break, pays a respectable wage that is higher than that earned by local agricultural workers, and follows the new government labor standards created in the mid-2000s to protect workers amid the pressure of watchdog groups such as Labour Behind the Label and China Labor Watch. The new standards include regulations for work hours, rest breaks, vacation time, holiday leave, and overtime as well as greater protections for female and juvenile workers.

"Things are much better than what they used to be," Chen says. "Production rates have become more reasonable. The pace of production was much faster in the 1980s and 1990s, and it was hard to keep up. There were more injuries, more mistakes. And back then, if someone made a mistake, the floor boss would come over and hit you on the head with a shoe. We used to call that getting 'Niked.' But that doesn't happen anymore."

At the very least, I can observe that the workers in this factory are afforded breaks, and there's no presence of a dictatorial floor boss. True,

I am an invited guest of the factory owner, but no one knows I am a journalist working on a book about running shoes. Perhaps the best indication of the mood on the floor becomes apparent when a tiny woman dressed in a bright T-shirt and a poodle skirt stops what she is doing and stands up to take my picture, creating a ripple of giggles throughout that corner of the room.

"She's never seen such a tall, fair-skinned person before," Chen says with a laugh. "She must think you're a ghost."

I observe the various segments of the day's shoe production process in awe—not just because I am watching running shoes come to life for the first time but because I am amazed at how many people are working on the assembly line. I've run in and wear-tested more than 1,200 pairs of running shoes over the past 30 years, and it only now strikes me that the construction of every single pair of shoes is a hand-curated process. I had assumed that the entire process was fully or mostly mechanized, but I was wrong. I had never considered the number of laborers handling every single pair of shoe for every single process, but I know that will be the first thought in my head the next time I try on a new pair.

From start to finish, the assembly line at this factory includes about 100 stations, which means that 100 workers will have touched all of the 2,500 pair of shoes produced, each completing a small but crucial task on the journey from singular parts to finished product. There's gluing, stitching, stretching, heat-welding, pressure-sealing, cooling, drying, and dozens of other steps along the way, including die-cutting various pieces of foam and fabric just off the line, lacing the shoes, and assembling and organizing all of the various parts—including rubber outsoles and laces— that have been shipped from other factories throughout East Asia.

While the process includes many modern machines, materials, and manufacturing techniques, much of the assembly-line process dates back to a much earlier time. Although conditions have greatly improved in this factory and thousands like it in China and other Southeast Asian countries, the system itself—the pace and timing of each task, the well-trained personnel, and the coordinated arrival of every material and prefabricated piece that goes into a shoe—has existed for decades. Some factories are more high-tech than others, but every running shoe brand in the world utilizes a similar labor-intensive process.

"It's stuff that was learned from Henry Ford," says Newton Running cofounder Danny Abshire, who recently launched his own line of Active88 shoes, which is manufactured at a similar facility in China. "It's all about having everything in place and being efficient and eliminating mistakes on the day production starts."

———

My factory tour brings me up close and personal to how a shoe is born, but how a shoe is *conceived* is another story altogether.

As with the factory assembly line, conception is a multistep process that starts years before a shoe appears at a store, in the pages of *Runner's World*, or on an online gear review site. For example, if you bought a new shoe model in the spring, it probably hit stores sometime between mid-January and late February but began as a design brief 18 to 30 months before that. By the time that model was actually available for you to purchase, the brand's product team was already finalizing next year's model as well as working ahead on future editions that will come out two years down the road.

It's part of the constant and complicated evolutionary cycle of running shoes that marches on, even if the end users—runners like you and me—don't always request, want, or like the changes.

The process highlights an awkward paradox common in many consumer goods categories, but especially for products with a relatively short lifespan, such as running shoes. If used on a regular basis—say, 10 to 20 miles per week—running shoes will typically wear out in less than a year or after about 400 to 500 miles of running, whichever comes first. That means that many runners are regularly in the market for new kicks.

The paradox comes from the notion that runners love shoes and want to find one that works for them—that matches their foot size and shape and individual dynamic movement patterns—but they don't necessarily love having to find new models as their favorite shoes alter from year to year.

Like many runners, I have found a shoe I really like only to be frustrated when the next year, that shoe is altered. Take the Nike Pegasus. I've run in more than a dozen editions of it since the mid-1980s, and each one has been different from the previous one, sometimes slightly so, sometimes drastically so. Some I loved; some I didn't like at all.

Something similar happened when I fell for the Brooks Ghost. The original model felt perfect for me, and I gave the Brooks footwear team an earful when that model changed dramatically between 2009 and 2013 from the nimble, lightweight trainer I loved to a midweight, hypercushioned model. It was a drastic alteration in just three years' time, but the bottom line was that Brooks sold considerably more shoes as the model morphed into a more comfortable shoe for a wider range of runners.

This predicament prompts some runners to buy multiple pairs of a model they really like in order to preempt the next season's changes. As a runner, I get that, although as a shoe geek, I admit that I am fascinated to observe the sometimes mystifying, always intriguing evolution in models.

Why is it that brands mess with a good thing? Does the old adage "If it ain't broke, don't fix it" simply not apply here?

To be sure, there is a lot of smart (and expensive) research and development taking place within a running shoe company as it tweaks existing models or develops new ones. Projects to learn more about how to build better running shoes involve analyzing runners through high-speed, slow-motion video, 3-D modeling techniques, and robotic leg durability tests; using cadaver parts to understand the intricacies of the human running gait; and collecting on-the-ground wear-test feedback from real runners.

While some shoe changes are copycat reactions to trends in the market or are merely aesthetic upgrades, some are genuine innovations that fuel lasting improvements and raise the bar for the fit, feel, and ride of future shoes. In the case of those Ghosts I loved, the Brooks team told me that the changes were based on three key factors: retail sales, the bigger picture of how the Ghost fit into Brooks's line, and an increasing consumer demand for more cushioning in the postminimalist era.

The bottom line, though, is that changes, updates, tweaks, and innovations are mostly about one thing: selling more shoes. And whether we like those changes or not, shoe brands seem to know what they're doing. Despite my less-than-enthusiastic input, the Brooks Ghost was put through several major changes and went on to become the brand's best-selling model and one of the top sellers across the industry, with roughly 700,000 pairs sold at running specialty stores and close to 1.5 million through all outlets combined.

Shoe manufacturers make a point of updating or changing every model every single year, says New Balance Global Marketing Manager Keith Kelly. Even models that do very well—based on robust retail sales, editor's choice awards, or high approval ratings on digital and social media platforms—are updated regularly. That's the nature of the business in the world of consumer goods, he says: "People want to see new things when they go shopping. It's the essence of retail."

It's also the essence of marketing, so whether you adored the last pair of shoes you bought—because it was comfortable, because it improved your running, or because it helped you lose weight—is irrelevant from a brand marketing point of view, he says. Ultimately, consumers as a whole prefer what's new, whether it's a shoe that's slightly updated or one that is completely overhauled, because with change comes the assumption of improvement, the notion that a new model is better than a previous one.

Unfortunately, that's not always true, as many runners have found out. Sometimes they are better, but sometimes they are much worse, in which case you scratch your head and, after a few runs, try to find a discounted pair of the previous model.

Kelly says that New Balance typically makes only minor changes to shoes that are deemed highly successful; however, there are times when new technology, new design techniques, or new materials—and, as a result, a new brand marketing campaign—can be a catalyst to completely overhauling a shoe. Those changes might be made to improve a shoe that's badly in need of an upgrade; to help a brand react to new trends in the marketplace; or to utilize modern, leading-edge materials.

New Balance's changes to its 1080 neutral-cushioned training shoe in 2016 offers an illustrative example of the peaks and valleys in the update process. The 1080 had been a modestly successful shoe, built on the brand's REVlite, N2, and Abzorb foams, which the brand had used in its shoes for several years. The 1080v4 earned a "Best Update" award from *Runner's World* in 2014 and experienced a modest boost in sales over the previous edition. But the 1080v5, updated slightly with a new lacing system and cosmetic changes to the upper, was panned in reviews, partially because it was a half ounce heavier than its predecessor, and retailers just couldn't sell it as well.

As the v5 declined in sales, the New Balance footwear team was already at work on the 1080v6, with a proprietary midsole foam they called Fresh Foam.

Fresh Foam used data-driven design cues to create concave and convex hexagonal patterns that New Balance claimed enhanced sponginess and firmness in specific areas. As part of the R&D for Fresh Foam, the brand recorded the footstrike patterns of thousands of runners to understand specifically where cushioning, flexibility, and resiliency features were most needed. Combined with an interior bootie for optimal fit and the soft, smooth ride that it served up, the Fresh Foam technology provided a new story for New Balance to sell.

Not only did consumers like the new version, but the shoe served as a successful rival to Adidas's groundbreaking Boost midsole foam that had debuted a few years earlier and represented New Balance's entry into the growing maximalist shoe movement that brand Hoka One One continued to stoke.

The 1080v6 won numerous high-profile awards, as did subsequent editions. With minor changes over the next three years, the 1080 has become not just one of New Balance's best sellers but one of the most successful shoes on the market.

"Shoe trends have changed quickly over the past several years," Kelly says. "Back when minimalism was the thing, if you made a bigger shoe, you were an idiot. But when minimalism fell off and no one wanted that kind of shoe anymore, you had to change your game plan. We got behind the 1080 and developed our own story to push the technology and our version of maximal cushioning."

═══

How new models of running shoes are conceived and come to life depends on the brand, but generally next year's new shoes emerge in one of two ways. The most common way is as an update—slightly or significantly— of a previous edition via a brand's inline footwear team.

Updating an inline shoe typically starts with a company's footwear team reviewing the shoe's historical evolution in a meeting of the departments that have a stake in that shoe: product development, retail sales, and consumer marketing. They create a design brief for how the shoe will move forward, finalizing the design, materials, and specs. The footwear crew considers how that model could or should be updated in the next two iterations based on the shoe's recent updates and current materials package, along with long-term sales analytics, market trends, and new fabrics, foams, and construction techniques that have become available.

As the existing shoe goes to market, the brand takes a hard, analytical look at interest in the current version, from retailer buy-in to wear-test reviews to early consumer sell-through. Because next year's version is already well into development, only minor or late-stage tweaks can be made from that type of input. However, feedback from the existing edition can typically lead to greater changes to the model two years down the road.

Updates to a brand's staple models usually take 18 to 24 months to identify, develop, and execute, and include a few rounds of prototypes for preproduction wear-testing. In recent years, the most common revisions to inline models have been the introduction of new types of midsole foams that provide higher levels of cushioning and energy return and new dynamic mesh uppers that offer variable stretch, comfort, and support characteristics. Saucony's inclusion of EVERUN foam, engineered mesh uppers, and its quasi-custom ISO fit system in its popular Triumph, Ride, Guide, and Kinvara models exemplifies a brand continuing to evolve its key models with new features.

Sometimes a brand will update the outsole to offer more flexibility or traction or to reduce the weight (because the rubber outsole is the heaviest piece of a shoe) by placing only segments of rubber on the outsole. At the simplest level—and sometimes as a cost-saving procedure—a shoe manufacturer might simply update a shoe's color palette. Color trends change annually, and the jewel tones that looked good a year ago (and were planned two years before that) might be obsolete amid a retro rebound of high-visibility Day-Glo colors. Brands may also produce these "color-ups" during the second half of a year in order to differentiate the look of their popular shoe models between the spring/summer season and summer/fall sales season.

Feedback about existing shoes is extremely important, especially when a particular model, such as the Nike Pegasus, ASICS GEL-Kayano, or Brooks Ghost, has been on the market for several years. A slow year in sales could indicate that something in the previous year's update—the fit, feel, ride, materials, or color—wasn't as well received as was hoped.

Traditionally, that feedback came from retailers, who tend to hear real-time commentary from customers as soon as new shoes drop. While brands still value that on-the-ground feedback from "real" customers, they've also turned to digital analytics along with a reliance on social media stars, key influencer groups, and urban run crews.

Running, technology, and the sales process have changed considerably in the past decade, and runners (and how they use shoes) can't be defined as easily as in the past, says Claire Wood, the business unit manager for global performance running footwear at New Balance.

"Running shoes are an object of desire, a product you want to be highly attached to, and they're more emotional than most products I can think of," Wood says. The strong feelings that people have for their shoes can translate into a sales win or a sales disaster. A negative change in how a popular shoe fits, feels, or rides will likely lead to complaints, bad reviews, and returns—today, more quickly and publicly than ever. While a brand could survive a mediocre model in the 1980s and 1990s with strong marketing and retail support, in the Internet age, there's nowhere to hide.

SCOTT JUREK || Brooks special makeup trail running shoe

American ultrarunner, *New York Times* bestselling author

Back in 2004, I had just signed on with Brooks as their only trail running athlete to help them design the Cascadia shoe and help them get deeper into trail running. I was going back to Western States that year to try and win it for a sixth year in a row and set a new course record, so the race was a big deal for me. At the time, Brooks's only trail shoe was the Trespass, but that wasn't going to cut it for the Western States course. I needed something superlightweight, almost like a racing flat, with a more durable trail-oriented upper.

At the time, Trip Allen was heading up the footwear development team after coming over from Nike, where he had been a shoe designer and a protégé of Bill Bowerman. Being a size 12, I never got any of the prototypes, and they couldn't crack the factory molds on the Cascadia in time to make something in my size. So I worked closely with Trip and his team, and we created a new shoe for me by mashing the outsole and midsole of a Racer ST road racing shoe together with the upper of the forthcoming Cascadia. They sent me two pairs right before I went to Western States, and it was the first time that I tried them! I had run in the Racer ST, so I knew the outsole and midsole would work, so I was just hoping the new Cascadia upper was going to wrap around my foot in a comfortable way.

To be able to put trust in that shoe, never take it off once during the 2004 Western States, and break the course record was really amazing. They will always be one of my favorite shoes of all time because I was just starting with Brooks, getting to work with Trip and his crew was really special, and it was the first time I was so involved in a shoe design project.

The other way new shoes emerge is a more complicated and impactful path born out of innovation. Those developments are typically pursued either to round out a gap in a brand's existing line—for example, adding a maximally cushioned model or a zero-drop trainer—or to create a novel model that comes from a brand's top-secret special projects team.

Nike's Vaporfly 4%, a shoe several years in development before being released at various levels of availability in 2017 and 2018, is an example of an advanced innovation project. Hoka's Carbon Rocket and Carbon X racing shoes and ASICS's MetaRide efficiency-enhancing shoe are examples of entirely unique shoe releases that debuted in 2019.

When it comes to shoe development based around new or groundbreaking concepts, those models typically have longer development timelines—24 to 48 months—and include focus-group research, internal laboratory testing, advanced materials, new construction techniques, and 3-D printed mockups in the development process.

Highly innovative models require considerably more prototyping cycles, sometimes as many as 20 or 30, to ensure that the new concepts are functionally sound.

But, as in new development in any industry, some innovative ideas never see the light of day because the concept just never became functionally realistic or cost-effective. Nike may be the industry's leading innovator, but for every Vaporfly 4% Flyknit that it brings to market, there are dozens that die on the drawing board or after several rounds of prototyping.

Launching a brand-new shoe is always a risky process with a lot at stake. "But at some point, you have to stop with the prototypes because it's a process that could go on forever," says Danny Orr, strategic business unit manager for innovation at New Balance. You can't create a perfect shoe, he says, but you can accept that you've made a groundbreaking and truly innovative shoe for that point in time. "You have to step back and look at how far you've come and just go to market with it."

Innovation doesn't come cheap. When a brand develops a new or updated model, the cost of materials, labor, manufacturing, packaging, shipping, insurance, tariffs, and taxes is negotiated down to pennies to make sure the "landed cost" (the cost of a shoe when it arrives in the United States and heads to a retail shop) is slightly more than half of the wholesale cost.

The wholesale cost of a shoe bought at running stores is typically 50 percent, or, in other words, a 100 percent markup. That means when you buy a shoe for a retail price of $120, the cost to the store is $60 and the landed cost for the brand, if built overseas, is about $34.50. That means the profit margin for the store is $60, while the net proceeds to the brand are typically about $25.50.

The $34.50 landed cost typically includes about $31 for labor and factory costs in Asia (known as the "free on board," or FOB, costs or the cost per shoe before shipping), roughly $1 for shipping to the United States, and $2.50 for tariffs. (Note: these figures were computed prior to the U.S.–China tariff war that ensued in early 2019.) Added to that is another $25.50 manufacturer's markup that includes administrative fees, marketing costs, taxes, and the shoe company's approximate 9 percent profit margin. So for every $120 pair of running shoes sold, a shoe company's take-home profit is only $10.80.

The Internet has changed this equation. The ability to buy a pair of shoes from a computer or phone, from anywhere and at any moment, day or night, has weakened running retailers, with brands selling shoes directly from their own sites, as discussed in Chapter 1. Simple math shows that cutting out the middleman, i.e., the neighborhood retail store, can boost a brand's profit margin from 9 percent to as high as 45 percent after various costs associated with e-commerce and shipping.

The increasing sophistication and continued evolution of shoes over the past 40 years have changed the equation too. Whereas the average price of a pair of running shoes sold in 1980 was about $28, today it's in the $110 to $120 range, with dozens of models priced at $150 or more. The cost of doing business in a cycle of constant evolution—plus rising materials and manufacturing costs, fuel costs, shipping fees, and tariffs—has significantly driven up prices.

"You've got to be as efficient as possible with design, manufacturing, marketing, and distribution to be able to maintain your profit margins," says Skechers' Dan Sullivan. "But it's a highly competitive business, and you've got to have great product to make that happen."

═══

In a different shoe factory, I watch the methodical wave of an assembly line churn out shoe after shoe, and that rousing "new shoe smell" of foam, fabric, rubber, and glue permeates the air. This time I'm not in China; I'm in Lawrence, Massachusetts, in one of the few running shoe factories in the United States.

I marvel at the line's smooth, systematic flow, with each of the 40 or so workers repeatedly completing small, simple tasks, all of which contribute to the completion of the small batch of running shoes at the end of the line, which is then inspected, boxed, and prepared for shipping. Runners somewhere in the United States will soon be trying these on, experiencing the unfettered joy that comes with jogging those first miles in a pair of new shoes.

Many aspects of this factory, situated in a 100-year-old brick building on the Merrimack River, are identical to those of the factory in China: modestly dressed workers quietly going about their focused tasks, good air quality, and a priority on safety. New Balance has been building shoes in Lawrence since 1982, part of a commitment to American manufacturing that company owners Jim and Anne Davis have insisted on despite the economic challenges.

While an estimated 95 percent of the world's running shoes are *manufactured* in East Asia, the lion's share of those are conceived, designed, and prototyped in the United States. Most of that work happens in and around two U.S cities: Boston, Massachusetts, and Portland, Oregon.

Historically, Beantown and the surrounding New England area has been a shoe-making hub since the 1860s. American companies such as New Balance, Saucony, and Converse all have roots in the Boston area that date back more than 100 years. The area's large talent pool and industry influence also made it a logical place for European-based brands such as Puma, Inov-8, and Reebok to open their U.S. offices. Japanese company ASICS added a U.S. base in Boston in 2017.

Portland, on the other hand, became known for athletic footwear because it's where Phil Knight lived in the 1960s when he distributed the Onitsuka running shoes that he imported from Japan; subsequently, he started Nike there in the early 1970s.

As Nike expanded in its worldwide headquarters in Beaverton, Oregon, through the 1980s and early 1990s, the Portland area became known as a modern footwear epicenter, aka Sneakertown, USA. Nike attracted a vast pool of talent in the areas of shoe design, engineering, marketing, and merchandising, and furthermore, Portland is closer than Boston to factories on the Pacific Rim.

With the aim of remaining competitive with Nike, Adidas set up its own North American headquarters in Portland in the 1990s and moved its international design center there in 2014. On Running, Keen, Columbia, and Hi-Tec are also currently headquartered in Portland, while numerous brands have research and design centers in the Rose City, including Under Armour and Mizuno.

Still, manufacturing running shoes is not an easy or inexpensive process anywhere, and especially not in the United States.

When the original running boom exploded in the 1970s, most of the American brands of the day—New Balance, Brooks, Saucony, Keds, and Nike—were manufacturing some of their shoes in the United States. At that time, the United States was among the world's leading manufacturers, and with relatively low labor and shipping costs compared to making shoes made in Europe, keeping production domestic made sense for American brands.

Until it didn't.

When Knight founded Nike in Portland in 1971, the brand was producing most of its shoes in Japanese factories, mostly because of Knight's connections from his previous role as a distributor for Onitsuka shoes and because Japan was a worldwide leader in shoe manufacturing. When a recession hit Japan in the mid-1970s, Nike shifted most of its manufacturing operations to South Korea and Taiwan. But, knowing it would be advantageous to have a domestic manufacturing center, too, the Swoosh began searching for a place to build shoes in the United States.

In 1974, it bought a century-old footwear factory in Exeter, New Hampshire, formerly inhabited by the Wise Shoe Company. It later added another factory in Maine and a distribution center in Greenland, New Hampshire. At its peak in the early 1980s, Nike employed more than 1,000 people in New England and built about 15 percent of its shoes in its New Hampshire and Maine facilities.

The Exeter operation became one of Nike's biggest and most important factories as well as its first research and development lab. Nike hired its first biomechanics and physiology experts to work there in the late 1970s, helping it advance from a traditional footwear company to an early leader as an innovative brand rooted in sport science and technology.

The Exeter operation played an important role in the development of several key Nike shoes, including the Waffle Trainer, Air Tailwind, LDV, Internationalist LD-1000, and the original Pegasus (which, with 36 models dating back to 1983, is the longest-tenured running shoe ever produced), at a time when Nike was experiencing exponential growth and skyrocketing sales.

But that domestic success didn't last. With the United States in the grip of a recession and American manufacturing becoming more expensive, the Swoosh opened its first factory in China in 1981. The United States had been one of the world's manufacturing leaders since World War II, but times were changing as rising labor, production, and fuel costs skyrocketed in the late 1970s. By then, both U.S. and European shoe brands were being lured by less expensive manufacturing alternatives in Mexico and emerging markets in Asia—Korea, Singapore, Taiwan, Indonesia, and eventually China. Nike reduced its New England manufacturing operations considerably and eventually closed its Maine and New Hampshire facilities in 1984.

It wasn't just Nike facing the challenges of expensive domestic manufacturing. By the mid-1980s, the majority of running shoes were being manufactured overseas, and numerous other industries had done the same, leaving U.S. towns such as Exeter, New Hampshire, and other once-vibrant industrial centers as depressed ghost towns dealing with unemployment, class struggles, and changing community identity.

Lawrence, a longtime industrial center less than an hour north of Boston, was struggling, too. For more than 100 years, Lawrence had thrived as a textile manufacturing hub, wool-processing hotbed, and footwear assembly center along the Merrimack River. But, like many small New England cities, it struggled in the post–World War II industrial decline, eventually bottoming out in the late 1970s.

When Jim Davis bought New Balance on Boston Marathon Monday in 1972, the tiny brand employed six people who churned out 30 pairs of shoes per day in a small Boston factory. As he grew the business into one of the world's leading brands by the mid-1970s, he, too, understood the better economies of scale that came with manufacturing overseas and New Balance eventually had no choice but to follow suit to stay competitive. But Davis, who had grown up in Boston and gone to school in New England, remained committed to building a portion of the brand's shoes in the United States to support American workers.

New Balance's Lawrence factory opened in 1982, and the brand has persisted as the only major brand to manufacture running shoes in the United States.

But it has not been easy. New Balance faced the same high labor and production costs that chased away other brands and industries. Another major challenge with manufacturing in the United States has been getting supplies. When competitors in athletic footwear went overseas, many suppliers—for example, companies that produce rubber outsoles—left as well. In order to label a pair of shoes *Made in the USA*, New Balance requires that 70 percent of the materials come from the United States.

Given the metrics, not surprisingly, the most prominent running shoe produced by the Lawrence facility is the New Balance 990, which was the first $100 running shoe in the early 1980s. To date, New Balance has produced more than 15 million pairs of the 990 series. Today, at around $175, it's still on the high end of the price spectrum—there is no way around the high labor costs—but it is also known as one of the most durable and highest-quality shoes available.

Through the years, the brand has had to work smarter and harder to make its domestic manufacturing operations successful. It continues to refine and adapt its production line with modern equipment and manufacturing techniques, knowing that efficiency is the key to success with the high hourly wages it must pay for skilled manufacturing labor. In recent years, it has used the Lawrence facility in order to quickly produce and ship the premium-priced one-off shoes ordered through the customizable footwear program it offers online—something that could not be done as expeditiously with an overseas factory.

New Balance employs about 250 workers in its Lawrence facility, which is capable of producing 3,000 pairs of shoes per day. For its more labor-intensive 990 model, it typically manufacturers about 600 pairs per day. The Lawrence facility also doubles as a research, design, and innovation center that produces prototypes for the footwear team at the New Balance world headquarters in Boston, greatly shortening the development cycle when coordinated with an Asian factory. Whether through modern techniques such as 3-D printing or more traditional manufacturing, the Lawrence facility can shorten the time it takes to create the initial models from several weeks to less than 10 days.

The company's domestic manufacturing operation has been a story of success for more than 35 years, even in the face of considerably higher labor and manufacturing costs. Ten years ago, it took the facility eight days to make the 990 start to finish, says Brendan Melly, the company's former director of manufacturing. "Nowadays it's roughly three hours," he says. "In the 1980s, the industry left the United States to chase cheap labor and drive profit, but we've stayed put and grown throughout that process."

As of 2019, New Balance employs about 1,500 people who produce four million pairs of shoes annually in its five U.S. manufacturing facilities, including one in Boston and three in Maine. In all, about 25 percent of the shoes that New Balance sells in the United States are built in New England. Most of the rest are built in China and Vietnam, although New Balance does have facilities in England that build the shoes it sells throughout Europe.

While domestic production has been successful for the brand, it's also been a boon to the local workforce. The average employee tenure at the Lawrence factory is 18 years, and a handful of employees have been working there for at least 30 years. The turnover rate is less than 1 percent, Melly says.

New Balance takes pride in supporting American workers, but it is quick to point out that many of the employees who work at the Lawrence factory originally hail from the Dominican Republic. A sizable Dominican population has been present in Lawrence since the late 1980s when immigrants arrived to work in other industries. When New Balance started hiring footwear workers, more Dominicans arrived, many of whom had worked in the footwear trade in their native country. Since then, multiple generations of families have worked for New Balance in Lawrence, with grandparents, parents, sons, daughters, and siblings on the current workforce.

Karen Coombs, plant manager at the Lawrence production facility, is proud of the high-quality workforce in Lawrence, and says that part of making the team successful is giving them the tools, skills, and climate to get the job done right. "In everything we do, we aim to be more effective and efficient," she says.

New Balance says its American-made business model has helped the company to become more efficient in a highly competitive industry. Indeed, according to Coombs, the New Balance manufacturing process is more than three times more efficient than its Asian-made counterparts.

"It takes a lot of ingenuity and guts," Coombs says. "If you had a publicly traded company and were working on a quarterly budget basis, it would make no sense to make shoes here because Asia is cheaper. For Jim and Anne to have this vision and stick with it has been bold. So bold that no other brands have followed our lead."

That dogged perseverance has helped revitalize the economy in Lawrence, which has attracted new businesses, from manufacturing operations to high-tech firms. To see indications that life is changing in Lawrence, all Coombs has to do is look out the window of her factory office to see the luxury loft condos going into a long-empty building—a former textile mill that dates back to the 1890s—across the river. It's one of many buildings that has been renovated in recent years. Some are coming back as modern industrial centers, while others are being converted to residential and retail.

"We're seeing the community come back, and the economy is growing," Coombs says. "It's cool to know that New Balance has played a part in helping to create jobs and lift the community."

Is the New Balance model an isolated example, or does it signal a change that could swing the pendulum back to domestic manufacturing? Likely the former, shoe industry observers suggest. It would be too expensive for other brands to start now, and even if a brand did begin domestic manufacturing, it would only make sense to build a modern facility.

New Balance found a way to take a late-20th-century manufacturing model and make it work in the 21st century through innovation, ingenuity, and efficiency. But there's no way a company would start a similar facility in the United States now, says Powell, because the cost to start up a domestic manufacturing facility would be astronomical. Plus, such a move would make sense only if the company built a new facility that was considerably more advanced and automated than the predominantly manual facilities that New Balance operates, he says.

But, he adds, change is possible, maybe even imminent. "Innovation and mechanization are rapidly progressing in Asian factories," Powell says, noting that advanced knitting machines can produce the entire upper of a shoe in just five minutes. "Those kinds of machines, when they become more affordable, could be a key to bringing some manufacturing back to the States."

The footwear industry left South Korea in the 1980s when Korea found more lucrative opportunities producing high-tech products. Today, the same transition is happening in China. As real estate, production, and labor costs in China increase, running shoe factories are being pushed deeper into inland China as well as into Vietnam, which has become a more affordable destination for shoe manufacturing in recent years.

While the economies of scale in Asia are tied to inexpensive labor, they're also connected to the supply chain for the modern materials that go into most shoes—engineered mesh for uppers; lightweight, adhesive rubber for outsoles; and resilient, featherweight foams that provide cushioning and energy return.

"Bring manufacturing back to the U.S.? Who wouldn't want that?" says Spencer White, vice president of human performance for Saucony. "There's a trend to see how we can make factories more automated to bring the manufacturing process closer to retail. It's going to happen; it's just a matter of when. But if jobs come back, they're not going to be assembly jobs for factory workers. They're going to be well-paying robotic manufacturing maintenance type of jobs. Instead of 300 people on the floor, you might have 16."

With the production run of a new batch of New Balance 990s humming on the factory floor—as well as some custom pairs of baseball cleats heading to the next week's Major League Baseball All-Star Game—I leave the Lawrence facility with mixed feelings. What I learned about New Balance's efforts there makes me want to go out and buy a pair of New Balance 990s just to support American labor. But looking deeper also makes it clear to me that the prospect of bringing manufacturing back to the United States might not be as rosy as politicians like to imply on the campaign trail.

While a mostly automated running shoe manufacturing facility may be imminent, the flip side is that it would curtail or eliminate much of the hands-on craft that I marveled at during my factory visits.

THE SUB-2-HOUR MARATHON QUEST AND THE RISE OF MAGIC SHOES

8

> I've worn lots of shoes. I bet if I think about it real hard, I could remember my first pair of shoes. Mama said they'd take me anywhere. She said they was my magic shoes.
>
> FORREST GUMP

I have always loved the feeling of running fast—running across the backyard, running across the playground, and eventually running races on the track, roads, and trails. It was thrilling—legs churning like pistons, self-generated wind in my face, moving fast under my own power—and, quite frankly, it still is.

From an early age, I associated the thrill of speed with the sneakers on my feet. I wasn't allowed to go out and play in my saddle shoes, so there was an early connection with lacing up my little red sneakers and having the freedom to run at will. There was plenty of outside affirmation, too. I remember my dad raving about my sneakers and cajoling me to run as fast as I could across the grass. He didn't call them magic shoes, but his encouragement was the only inspiration I needed.

I experienced modest success in running races while in school, but that thrill was never contingent on top race finishes or the time on the clock. It was mostly about how alive and free I felt running at speed. In fact, my most electrifying running moments haven't occurred in formal races at all but rather during demanding track workouts, romps down a steep trail, or hurtling across a beach with friends.

That stimulating conversation between sneakers and speed persisted into adulthood, even as I got considerably slower along the way. I've never lost my appetite for it, or the accompanying delight. In fact, in the fall of 2018, just shy of my 50th birthday, I was gearing up to boost my fitness and speed to run a 3:10 at the California International Marathon. It would be far from my 2:51 PR of yesteryear but a noble quest nonetheless, as a *fast-for-your-age* marathon goal always is.

I felt that familiar tingle of excitement when I received a FedEx package from Eastbay one early October morning. A few weeks earlier, Kenyan marathon great Eliud Kipchoge had shattered the world record, dominating the 2018 Berlin Marathon with a shocking 2:01:39 effort. He'd sliced a whopping 78 seconds off countryman Dennis Kimetto's 2014 time, marking the biggest drop in the men's world record since Australian Derek Clayton ran 2:09:36.4 in 1967 and took 2 minutes, 23.6 seconds off Japanese legend Morio Shigematsu's 2:12:00 1965 world record.

Kipchoge achieved his unfathomably speedy time wearing a pair of brilliant red magic shoes, otherwise known as Nike's Vaporfly 4% Flyknit.

He wore a second-generation model of the marathon racing flat, around which great hype had been fomenting. With a full-length curved carbon-fiber plate embedded in the shoe's featherweight and resilient "ZoomX" foam midsole, the design aimed to increase stiffness, reduce fatigue, and minimize energy loss, all while creating a momentum-boosting downhill running sensation in every stride. Judging by the performances of Kipchoge and dozens of other Nike athletes, it seemed that the mission had been accomplished.

Nike had unveiled the original version—the Zoom Vaporfly 4%—16 months earlier, after creating enormous demand with perhaps the greatest marketing event in running history: the Breaking2 Project. The venture was Nike's attempt to help Kipchoge and fellow elite runners Zersenay Tadese and Lelisa Desisa break the 2-hour barrier in a marathon for the first time in history. (More on that topic in a bit.)

During their first year on the market, the shoes were nearly impossible for runners to get. Nike sold out of the limited quantities it made available to consumers in July 2017 and then sold out again in early 2018. With hype for this hard-to-come-by shoe at an all-time high after Kipchoge's record-setting time, Nike released a wider allotment of the second generation of the shoes in early October 2018.

I was well aware of this release, and so while driving back from a morning run, unable to wait even until I got home, I pulled over and logged onto Eastbay.com on my phone. I ordered a pair of those brilliant red magic shoes in a size 10.5, not even flinching at the $250 price tag. In that moment of excitement, the price seemed well worth the rejuvenated running thrill that these shoes were going to evoke in me, as well as the marathon goal they were going to help me achieve in California.

When the box arrived two days later, I ripped through the packaging, flipped open the classic orange Nike box, pulled out the shoes, and put them on my feet—only to be grossly disappointed to find that they were uncomfortably tight.

For the previous 35 years, I'd worn size 10.5 in every one of the dozens of Nike shoes I'd owned. But the mesh upper tapered down to the front of the Vaporfly 4% Flyknit in a way that created an unusually low-volume toe box, unpleasantly crimping my toes to the point that they were protruding into the fabric.

Dang it! I immediately grabbed my phone, pointed my browser to Eastbay.com and found a size 11, which I ordered in three eager clicks. Now I just had to wait two more days and somehow justify my possession of $500 worth of the fastest running shoes ever made. (Meanwhile, I gingerly placed those 10.5s back in the box without getting a speck of dust on them so I could return them.)

Knowing that the shoes would be delivered on Friday, I put off the 8-mile downhill tempo run that I had planned for that day until Friday afternoon. Forty-eight hours later, I was dressed to run and waiting for the FedEx truck. When it drove up, I met the driver halfway down my driveway, took the package out of his hands, and tore it open to find another brilliant red pair of magic shoes. I slid them on, and *voila!*—they fit perfectly. I laced up and was ready to roll. I don't remember ever being so eager to go on a run.

To execute my planned downhill tempo, I hopped on my bike, pedaled 2.5 miles up Boulder Creek Path, parked at a friend's house, and started with a jog. At a 9-minute warm-up pace, I was surprised by the mushy sensation in my heel that made my easy effort feel a little unstable. I found that I was compressing the heel foam significantly with each stride, causing some wobbling in my rear foot before rolling forward, yet also feeling a small boost of energy. The latter sensation was a bit underwhelming, however, with only a hint of the promised levering effect of the carbon-fiber plate.

The shoe wasn't designed to run at slower paces, I concluded. So I cut my warm-up short, did some dynamic warm-up drills and light stretching, and then headed to the upper terminus of the path. It was go time. I started my watch and rolled gently into a moderately fast clip, aiming for 8 miles at a 6:15 average pace back to downtown Boulder. My training plan called for a 7:15 pace, but I knew my first 3 miles would be faster than that because of the 5 percent downhill grade through Boulder Canyon.

I had left my truck at a local microbrewery, where I would meet friends afterward for a beer, but that was more of a reward than motivation. I had all the inspiration I needed laced to my feet.

I got up to 5K race pace in the first 100 meters, and the shoes felt divine. As I ran, I paid close attention to the sensations I was experiencing. At this faster pace and performance-oriented cadence, I felt myself running with a forward-leaning posture and landing with more of a midfootstrike, thus barely engaging that soft cushioning in the heel. This created a sensation that I'd never felt in a shoe. As each foot touched the ground, it immediately and effortlessly rolled forward to the toes and then popped off the ground with ease.

I kept my cadence short and found myself running comfortably at a 5:20 mile pace, a speed that normally challenges me. It was as if I was flying, running like a cartoon character whose fast-moving legs are depicted as wheels spinning in a circular motion. On the few occasions when I took too long a stride and landed on my heels, my form became momentarily wobbly again. But, sensing the sweet spot somewhere between the front of the heel and the back of the arch, I mostly ran smoothly with a quick-turnover rhythm and footstrikes that fell just a short distance in front of my hips.

I buzzed past the 1-mile mark in 5:18 and ran the second mile in 5:35. I didn't intend to run that fast, but the downhill grade and electrifying shoes made it feel effortless and fun. *Forrest Gump never ran like this*, I thought.

I slowed in the third mile to 5:50 as the slope flattened out. The path was still angled downward, but it was closer to 1 to 2 percent as it meandered through the city. The flattening brought me back to reality, and the same effort had me clicking off the next 3 miles in a 6:15–6:25 range. Running still felt unforced, and the shoes still felt amazing, but I was working a bit harder now as I ran on a more level surface.

EIGHT EPIC SHOE FAILS

Unfortunately, shoes sometimes fail runners at the worst possible time. In some cases, runners persevere and overcome the challenge, but sometimes the shoe snafu wins out.

① Abebe Bikila, 1960 Olympic Marathon

Ethiopian Abebe Bikila is well known for winning the 1960 Olympic Marathon in Rome while running barefoot. But the only reason he ran barefoot was because the Adidas shoes he had been given in the days before the race didn't fit very well. He had trained and raced barefoot most of his life, so running as such through the streets of Rome wasn't too out of the ordinary. He returned to the 1964 Olympic Marathon in Tokyo wearing a pair of Puma shoes to protect his feet from the rough roads along the course.

② Moses Tanui, 1993 IAAF World Championships 10,000 m

With a lap to go in the 10,000-meter world track and field champion-ships, Ethiopia's Haile Gebrselassie inadvertently stepped on the back of Moses Tanui's left track spike. The frustrated Kenyan runner flung the shoe off and then tried to speed away from Gebrselassie, opening a 20-meter lead down the backstretch. But Gebrselassie remained in contact and eventually outsprinted Tanui down the homestretch to the finish in 27:46:02 to win gold by a half second.

③ Quincy Watts, 1993 IAAF World Championships 400 m

American sprinter Quincy Watts was the 1992 Olympic champion at 400 meters and was the favorite to win the event at the 1993 IAAF World Championships. But early in the race, he heard a popping sound coming from his Nike track spikes and then felt the right shoe start to come apart, opening and closing and "flapping like a banana peel" with every stride. He wasn't able to accelerate as he usually did but still managed to close strong down the homestretch to finish fourth in the race in a still-fast 45:05 seconds.

④ John Kagwe, 1997 New York City Marathon

Kenyan runner John Kagwe broke one of racing's cardinal rules by buying a pair of brand new Nike Air Vengeance at the pre-race expo and wearing them the next day in the race. As luck would have it, the right shoe came untied three times during the race, forcing him to stop each time to retie it. When it came loose a fourth time, Kagwe ran the final 4 miles with laces flapping in the wind. He still won the race by more than a minute in 2:08:12, but he missed the course record by 11 seconds. Nike later paid him the $10,000 he would have won had he set the course record.

⑤ Dejen Gebremeskel, 2011 New Balance Indoor Grand Prix

At the start of the 3,000-meter run at the New Balance Indoor Grand Prix track meet in Boston, Ethiopian Dejen Gebremeskel slipped out of his right Adidas racing shoe. Running the race with one shoe didn't stop him from running competitively, though. He stayed with the lead pack throughout the race and eventually outkicked pre-race favorite Mo Farah during the final lap to win in 7:35:37, the fastest time of the year in the world at that point.

⑥ Sherod Hardt, 2014 NCAA Division I Great Lakes Regional

At the start of this mid-November collegiate cross-country race in Madison, Wisconsin, Michigan State sophomore Sherod Hardt got tangled up with several runners, tripped, and lost one of his Nike racing shoes. With a spiked shoe on his right foot and nothing on his left, Hardt ran a strong race over the cold, partially frozen grassy 10K course, finishing 25th overall in a personal best 30:43 to help his Spartans place second and qualify for the next week's NCAA Championships.

⑦ Jenny Simpson, 2015 IAAF World Championships, 1500 m

Jenny Simpson entered the 2015 world championships having already won gold (2011) and silver (2013) medals in the 1,500-meter run. She was among the leaders in the 2015 championship race, but with a lap and a half to go, a runner clipped the back of her left New Balance track spikes. She tried to keep the shoe on by clenching her toes but eventually had to flick it off. She remained on the heels of Ethiopian Genzebe Dibaba as long as she could but eventually faded and finished 11th in the field of 12 runners with a bloodied foot.

⑧ Eliud Kipchoge, 2015 Berlin Marathon

Although he hadn't yet solidified his status as the greatest marathoner of all time, Eliud Kipchoge added to his legacy by overcoming a shoe snafu at the 2015 Berlin Marathon. The Kenyan ran most of the race with the insoles slipping partway out of a pair of Nike prototype racing shoes, a dilemma that caused painful blisters and considerable distraction over the final 10 miles of the race. A determined Kipchoge overcame the problem and ran away from the rest of the field to win the race in 2:04:00, a new personal best and the 10th-fastest time in history to that point.

After running 6:33 for the seventh mile, I was finally feeling cardiovascularly taxed, so I backed off and ran 7:05 for the final mile. In the last 50 meters, I slowed and immediately felt that wonkiness again. By the time I had jogged a 2-mile cooldown to my truck at a 10-minute pace, I felt as if I was running over melting marshmallows.

For the first half of the 20th century, running a sub-4-minute mile was perceived as impossible. The progression of the world record went from 4:14.4 to 4:02.6 over a 30-year span from 1913 to 1943, and then Sweden's Gunder Hägg lowered the record to 4:01.4 in 1945. There remained a general consensus that breaking 4:00 was impossible, that somehow it was a terminal point of human progression.

Today, we know the fallacy of that thinking. Wearing a pair of leather track spikes, British runner Roger Bannister broke through the 4-minute barrier on May 6, 1954 on a cinder track in London, a momentous achievement that shocked the world of sports. His effort not only created a swell of optimism in distance running but also changed the perception of human limitations, inspiring athletes all over the world. In the post–World War II era, when technology and mechanization were on the rise, Bannister's record was viewed as an invigorating testament to the power of the human body and spirit. Just six weeks after Bannister's record-breaking feat, Australian John Landy lowered the mark to 3:57.9, showing that when it comes to breaking through a barrier, the first time is often the hardest. Since then, the sub-4:00 "barrier" has been broken 6,000 times by more than 1,500 runners, and as of spring 2019, the world record sits at 3:43.13.

For a long time, breaking 10 seconds in the 100-meter dash seemed similarly out of reach. At the time Bannister ran his sub-4-minute mile, the 100-meter record stood at 10.2 seconds, just 0.2 seconds faster than it had been in 1921. It took 14 more years—and 23 men running between 10.2 and 10.0 seconds—before American Jim Hines broke through with a 9.95-second time at the 1968 Olympics in Mexico City. That record stood for 15 years before another American, Calvin Smith, lowered it to 9.93. Since then, the record in track's marquee sprint race has been lowered

14 more times to the still-hard-to-believe 9.72/9.69/9.58 progression that Jamaica's Usain Bolt recorded in 2008 and 2009.

The magical mark for the marathon—its seemingly unbreakable plateau—is 2 hours. The notion was once straight out of science fiction, dismissed by aficionados of the sport as a waste of time and energy. In 1896, in the first Olympic Marathon race, only one man—winner Spyridon Louis of Greece—broke 3 hours, and that race was less than 25 miles long rather than the 26.2 that became standard in 1921. But over the past century, the record has dropped at an average rate of about 5 minutes per decade, driven by the professionalization of the sport as well as advances in training and shoe technology.

In 1991, with the world record standing at 2:06:50, an American physician named Michael Joyner wrote a groundbreaking paper, published in the *Journal of Applied Physiology*, estimating the best possible time for a marathon runner. He analyzed three factors that he said limit a runner's performance—VO_2max (the maximum oxygen an athlete can consume while running), lactate threshold (the running speed above which lactic acid in the muscles accumulates prohibitively), and running economy (the efficiency with which a runner moves down the road)—and argued that the perfect time for the perfect athlete in perfect conditions was 1:57:58. In other words, the sub-2 was possible, but only just and only in theory, even if popular opinion in the running world still considered it an impossibility.

For years, Sandy Bodecker envisioned the impossible. A Nike employee for 35 years, Bodecker was regarded as one of the most creative and influential personalities at the Swoosh headquarters in Beaverton, Oregon. He began working for Nike in 1983 as a footwear wear-test coordinator, went on to lead Nike's global soccer business, helped start its action sports division, and eventually led its renegade skateboard unit.

His creativity, gumption, and leadership led to his promotion to Nike's head of global design. Ultimately, he would carve out his own niche as the brand's vice president of special projects, a position that gave him license to do what he did best: think differently and pursue goals that most thought weren't attainable.

In 2014, Bodecker was among the company's brightest minds in the Nike Sports Research Lab (NSRL). The NSRL footwear innovation team had the marathon in its sights, and the year prior, it had been working on a shoe designed to help runners of all abilities improve by a lofty 3 percent margin. That 3 percent was chosen because it was the amount of approximate improvement required for a runner to go from the then–world record of 2:03:38 (set by Kenya's Patrick Makau at the 2011 Berlin Marathon) to 1 second under the 2-hour barrier.

Team leader Matt Nurse challenged the NSRL team to direct their efforts instead toward helping Nike and its world-class runners break the 2-hour marathon barrier—a controversial concept that, like the quest for the sub-4-minute mile 60 years earlier, was widely thought to be improbable or perhaps impossible.

Bodecker took the reins of the moon-shot project. He lobbied Nike executives for funding and created a top-secret task force that was dubbed Project Able after one of the first monkeys to survive space travel in the 1950s.

The development of a supershoe was the program's key element, but Bodecker also knew that if a runner were to be in position to break 2 hours, it would take optimal everything—training, apparel, fueling, weather—and a confident, enlightened outlook that could overcome the fear and doubt associated with trying to accomplish unfathomable tasks.

"What separates the great from the good is the mental side of the equation," Bodecker said. "If they don't have an innate ability to focus all their emotion and effort on this, they won't succeed."

He spearheaded the organization of a simulated marathon that would allow a small group of handpicked athletes to compete in a time trial in near-perfect conditions at a yet-to-be-determined location. The name of the project was changed to Breaking2 when it was unveiled to the public two years later.

Although only an occasional recreational runner, Bodecker immersed himself in the project, becoming so obsessed with the idea of a runner breaking the 2-hour barrier that he had "1:59:59" tattooed on his left wrist. The same mythical time was painted in 24-inch numerals at the entrance to the NSRL in Beaverton.

Bodecker understood the magnitude of the quest and the parallels to Bannister's attempts to become the world's first sub-4-minute miler. Witnessing an athlete breaking a record or achieving a seemingly impossible goal is what fuels sport specifically and humankind in general, Bodecker said. "The sub-2-hour marathon barrier, if broken, will transform the sport," he predicted. "It will impact the way runners view distance running and human potential forever."

Lofty ideals aside, the Breaking2 Project was also Nike's quest to own and brand the world's first sub-2-hour marathon before a rival organization could lay claim to it. Like the sub-4-minute mile and the sub-10-second 100, the concept of a sub-2-hour marathon had been talked about for years, often with a doubtful or argumentative tone. But excitement grew as the marathon record was lowered twice more in Berlin by a pair of Kenyans, first Wilson Kipsang, with 2:03:23 in 2013, and then Kimetto, who took the record to 2:02:57 the following year. The growing question was not *if* the barrier would be broken but *when*.

That both Kipsang and Kimetto were Adidas athletes wearing shoes with Boost midsoles only fueled the fire of Nike's sub-2-hour task force. The German brand already owned considerable bragging rights in the men's marathon, given that the previous five world records had been set by runners wearing Adidas shoes. Although Nike claimed the women's world record of 2:15:25 that Brit Paula Radcliffe had owned since 2003 (amid skepticism owing to speculation, which has never been substantiated, that Radcliffe may have used performance-enhancing drugs), the brand hadn't held the men's record since Kenyan Paul Tergat's 2:04:55 had reigned from 2003 to 2007. Elite Nike-sponsored marathoner Eliud Kipchoge also reportedly urged the Swoosh to build an innovative marathon shoe to help him become the first runner to break 2 hours after he finished a distant second behind Kipsang's world-record effort in Berlin in 2013.

And it wasn't just Nike and Adidas in the race for the first sub-2 marathon. A 2011 paper in the *Journal of Applied Physiology* titled "The Two-Hour Marathon: Who and When?" received dozens of responses from academics interested in helping runners approach the magical barrier. Meanwhile, Yannis Pitsiladis, a physiologist from the University of Brighton in England, announced in 2014 that he was seeking $30 million in sponsorship for his own sub-2-hour marathon project.

According to a report in *Runner's World*, Nike was willing to consider anything to advance its own quest, including variations in common running form, training methods, and recovery techniques. Eventually, though, Nike put its energy into what it knew best: footwear.

Bodecker paid a visit to Alberto Salazar, famed coach of the Oregon Project, Nike's elite running program. Salazar was training his star athletes Mo Farah and Galen Rupp in St. Moritz, and soon after Bodecker's visit, the idea of making "a track spike" for the marathon started to be tossed around. Track spikes are typically featherweight shoes with an airy, "barely there" mesh upper attached to a very rigid platform to maximize energy return, efficiency, and speed. If Nike could capture those qualities in a shoe design for running long distances, it would be on to something, Bodecker surmised.

Initially, Nike constructed an ornately designed, exceptionally lightweight shoe with an airy upper and a carbon-fiber base that had a thin layer of resilient foam under the forefoot but zero heel cushioning. That choice was based on the idea that most elite distance runners were midfoot and forefoot strikers, not heel strikers, thus would not require heal cushioning. This idea was quickly tossed aside, however, when Nike's group of experienced subelite wear-testers informed the innovation and design teams that in a marathon, even the world's most efficient runners need heel cushioning over the last half of the race. "That would have been a horrible marathon shoe," one wear-tester said later. "It might have seemed like a good idea in design meetings, but it wasn't practical."

That design idea was one of many incarnations that didn't make it past the R&D phase, but the drawn-out process helped Nike focus on other variables. There had been plenty of lightweight racing flats through the years—for example, New Balance had unveiled the 3.2-ounce RC5000 in 2012 for running 5K and 10K races on roads—but subsequent research and feedback suggested that the weight of a shoe wasn't the sole factor leading to faster running. A light shoe—but not necessarily the lightest ever—that provided sufficient cushioning and maximal energy return would likely be the secret sauce.

So Nike stepped away from trying to make the lightest shoe possible and focused on other elements that it believed were necessary to create the ultimate shoe: a midsole foam with high resiliency and a carbon-fiber plate that would help propel a runner's foot forward or perhaps enable the runner to use less energy in every stride.

=====

Nike's focus on midsole foam coincided with a true innovation explosion (and competition) in that particular arena. For more than 30 years, EVA had been the primary midsole cushioning agent in running shoes, and it is still a staple in athletic footwear owing to being versatile, soft, flexible, and relatively inexpensive. However, it compacts quickly and loses its cushioning power over a few hundred miles, so shoemakers were on the hunt for lighter, more resilient alternatives.

Nike had long been a leader in innovative cushioning systems with its Air-Sole technology and its Phylon, Zoom, and Lunarlite foams, all of which had led to breakthroughs in lightweight footwear design. But that supremacy was being challenged from all sides.

Hoka One One started the commotion by featuring a blended rubber EVA foam known as RMAT in its maximally cushioned shoes. With better shock absorption and more rebound than traditional EVA foam, the RMAT compound, along with the thickness of the midsoles, helped differentiate Hoka from other brands. Had Hoka built its first shoes with traditional EVA midsoles, the shoes would have weighed 3 to 4 ounces more, but using RMAT foam meant that most of the initial Hoka shoes weighed less than 10 ounces, offering runners soft cushioning, protection, and some resiliency, too.

The biggest foam breakthrough in the first portion of the 21st century, however, came from Adidas. The German brand shunned EVA for an innovative midsole material made from extruded thermoplastic polyurethane (TPU) pellets molded together with heat and pressure. The brand called the foam Boost and unveiled its Energy Boost shoe, featuring a slab of the bouncy midsole foam, in 2013.

Boost was the first foam material that not only attenuated shock with aplomb but also returned a high percentage of the energy in every footstrike, which sent other brands scrambling for something similar. Until then, most midsole foam materials were capable of one or the other of those tasks, but not both. When a greater density of EVA was used in foam midsoles for increased responsiveness, they tended to lack cushioning. It was a frustrating inverse relationship: When cushioning value went up, responsiveness decreased.

Adidas's TPU-based wonder material also proved to be more durable and resilient than EVA, even in extremely hot and cold conditions. And initial tests showed that Boost provided a 1 percent reduction in energy cost, a significant value over the course of a long run. There were downsides, however—notably that the TPU-based material was heavier than EVA and led to an unstable ride in thicker applications. Still, the Boost foam was deemed a huge breakthrough, both because it expanded the range of what a running shoe could do and because it forced manufacturers to think outside the box, which was precisely what Nike's NSRL innovation team had been tasked with doing with its Breaking2 Project.

Nike desperately needed a new midsole material to compete with Boost and the other lightweight, resilient foams that followed, including Saucony's EVERUN and Brooks's DNA AMP. Many brands were working in partnership with chemical companies such as BASF and Dow to formulate new materials specifically for next-generation midsole compounds. Nike had plenty of those relationships as well; however, its materials science research team saw potential in a foam that was already in production, but in an entirely different industry.

Zotefoams, a London-based company, had been manufacturing an exceptionally light and responsive thermoplastic formula for use in automobile bumpers. After testing samples of the material, commonly known as Pebax, Nike's team found it to be off the charts for cushioning and responsiveness, offering a cross between the properties of foam and rubber at one-third the weight of typical midsole materials. It compressed more consistently than most foams and returned considerably more energy than EVA—up to 87 percent, according to lab tests. Standard EVA midsoles test in the 50 to 60 percent range, and some of the best modern foam midsoles chart around 70 percent, making the 87 percent rate of the Zotefoam material astounding. Nike successfully negotiated for exclusive rights to the compound in footwear applications and started calling it ZoomX foam.

Within that supersoft yet super-resilient foam midsole, Nike embedded a curved carbon-fiber plate for forward propulsion. The idea of using carbon-fiber elements in a running shoe wasn't new. Reebok had been the first to incorporate a lightweight carbon-fiber support bridge under the arch of its Graphlite Road shoe in the 1990s. In the early 2000s, Adidas used a carbon-fiber propulsion plate in the ProPlate racing flat, and Zoot Sports incorporated one into its Ultra Race triathlon racing shoes in 2007.

In 2014, a start-up brand called Ampla Running unveiled prototypes of the Ampla Fly, a running shoe with a carbon-fiber springlike flange intended to load under pressure and launch forward as a runner's foot landed and then lifted off the ground. The shoe looked like most running shoes, with a mesh upper, foam midsole, and rubber outsole. The big difference, however, was that the carbon-fiber spring was "sprung" when sitting idle, so it looked like an open hinge until a runner slipped it on, stood on it, and compressed it.

Ampla was the brainchild of David Bond and Tom Hartge, who each had more than 25 years of running shoe industry experience at Nike, Adidas, K-Swiss, Patagonia, and Quiksilver. They collaborated with Dr. Marcus Elliott, a Harvard-trained physician who specializes in performance enhancement and injury prevention of pro athletes in team sports and endurance sports at P3 Applied Sports Science in Santa Barbara, California.

"This shoe is a running tool that empowers the most efficient use of force," Bond told me when the shoe launched. "As a runner, force is your friend. Good, well-trained athletes use force. Poorly trained athletes waste force."

I understood the logic as I watched Elliott and his team collect wear-test data using a force-plate treadmill at the P3 laboratory. But after my own wear-testing of the shoes on a half-dozen runs over the next several weeks, I was unconvinced. Regardless of lab data, it seemed problematic that the carbon-fiber springs were not tuned for different-sized runners in the same-sized shoes. Even if there was an energetic sensation at the start of each new stride (and there was, albeit small), it couldn't possibly be equally effective for my 170-pound frame as for that of a 120-pound runner or a 195-pound runner.

Ampla, which was started as an innovation project under surfing and lifestyle brand Quiksilver Inc., sold several hundred pairs of its first batch of $180 Fly shoes beginning in December 2015. The company received additional funding after it was spun off during Quiksilver's bankruptcy reorganization, but it folded in 2018 after it failed to realize commercial success with a second shoe model that utilized the same technology. It was a good idea in theory but not in practice. However, the Ampla entrepreneurs were definitely on to something with their idea of using a carbon-fiber component to maximize energy return.

At the same time that Ampla was getting off the ground, Hoka was developing a shoe with a carbon-fiber propulsion plate. The brand's innovation director Jean-Luc Diard showed me some of the initial designs at the Hoka design center in Annecy, France, in June 2015. It would take four more years for the brand to bring two shoes with carbon-fiber plates to market, and during that time, Nike was fast-tracking its own project. There has been scuttlebutt within the industry that a product line manager who left Hoka to join Nike in the spring of 2015 took Hoka's carbon-fiber shoe designs with him to the Swoosh's headquarters in Beaverton, Oregon, but those within Nike insist that its NSRL team was already well along that path at the time.

Nike's push into the area was the brainchild of Geng Luo, PhD, a Chinese-born biomechanist who was well respected as a scientist and was also known to be creative, ambitious, and willing to try new things—all the ingredients for a great innovator.

Luo's theory behind embedding a rigid carbon-fiber plate in the shoe was that a runner would engage the foam midsole with a midfoot footstrike and quickly engage the plate, which would then push the foot forward toward the toe-off phase with almost no additional energy expenditure at the point where the runner's toes would bend. While studies had shown that this action would force the ankle and muscles in the rearfoot to do more work, Nike created a plate with a more exaggerated curve in the forefoot that would eliminate that energy outlay.

Nike footwear developer Chris Cook fashioned the original prototype models in 2015 with uppers borrowed from Nike's Streak LT 2 racing shoes and two thick layers of ZoomX foam sandwiched around the carbon-fiber plate. Nonplated versions were also created, and both versions of the shoes were put through endless wear-testing.

In all, more than 50 prototype variations were made, with results that were increasingly positive with each new version. The company's elite-level wear-testers raved about the shoes—with and without a plate—for long runs, treadmill tests, and during a series of 2-mile repeats on the roads through a Portland neighborhood. The thickly cushioned shoes felt fast, comfortable, and effortless, reported the testers, among whom was three-time Olympian Shalane Flanagan. And they seemed to reduce the impact, muscle fatigue, and next-day soreness typical of long runs.

Much to the dismay of some of the wear-testers, though, the non-plated version was set aside to focus on the model with the carbon-fiber plate. The plated version wasn't necessarily superior or more well liked; however, the carbon-fiber plate was the technology story that everything would be built around when Nike's quest for the 2-hour marathon and the shoes went public. The plated shoe would be the pinnacle product aimed at the top-tier runners capable of running with exceptional form.

Nike didn't drop the nonplated version, though; it kept working on it and eventually released it as the Pegasus Turbo in the summer of 2018 as a shoe with high energy return and a more palatable price point intended for subelite to middle-of-the-pack runners.

While testing the shoes with the carbon-fiber plate in the lab, Nike physiologists and researchers were getting data commensurate with the 3 percent benefit that the NSRL task force had set out to achieve. Wanting some outside verification, they invited Rodger Kram, PhD, a University of Colorado (CU) professor of integrative physiology who had conducted studies on the metabolic costs of minimalist running shoes and barefoot running, to Beaverton to view the shoes and the testing process.

At the time he visited Nike's campus, Kram was conducting a study to determine whether the weight of running shoes directly translates to altered running economy and performance. In that study, 18 male runners capable of running a sub-20-minute 5K underwent treadmill tests and 3K time trials wearing control shoes and identical test shoes with 100 g and 300 g of added mass. While that study would show that added weight would make it 3 percent more "expensive" to run from a metabolic cost point of view, Nike's research team told Kram they wanted to show him a shoe that would make it 3 percent *cheaper* to run.

When he had a chance to wear-test the prototype shoes and view test results, Kram was blown away. "I didn't foresee this shoe. I didn't see this coming," he recalled thinking after learning about the energy return of the prototypes with carbon-fiber plates.

Nike asked Kram to test the metabolic cost of the shoe in his CU lab and compare it to the Nike Zoom Streak 6 and the Adidas Adios Boost 2, which were then considered the two fastest marathon shoes on the market.

The study's research associates were experienced runners in their own right: Wouter Hoogkamer, a former sprinter turned 2:32 marathoner, and

Shalaya Kipp, an NCAA champion and 2012 U.S. Olympian in the 3,000-meter steeplechase. To conduct the study, they gathered a test group of 18 runners capable of running a 31-minute 10K and able to wear a size 10 racing flat. Each runner came to the lab on three separate testing days. Each day, they ran six 5-minute treadmill trials wearing each of three pairs of shoes twice: the prototype of the shoe that would later become known as the Nike Vaporfly 4% with the carbon-fiber plate, the Nike Zoom Streak 6, and the Adidas Adios Boost 2, which Kimetto had worn when he set the marathon world record in 2014.

On one day, participants ran at a 5:22 mile pace; on another day, they ran at a 6:02 pace; on another, they ran at a 6:54 pace. Meanwhile, they breathed into a device that measured oxygen consumption to ascertain calories burned per second during running. The study showed that wearing the prototype shoe, the energy savings was between 1.59 percent and 6.26 percent for every test subject, with an average of 4 percent.

"Every single day at every single speed, every runner used less energy with the prototype shoe," Kram said.

The researchers then calculated what that energy savings could mean for the current marathon record. A 4 percent reduction in energetic cost translated to a 3.4 percent improvement in running speed at world record marathon pace (4:41 per mile), thus reducing the finishing time to a potential 1:58:54 without consideration of variables such as weather, course variations, and wind.

"Our extrapolations suggested that with these shoes, the technology is in place to break the 2-hour marathon barrier," said Hoogkamer, a post-doctoral researcher who was the lead author for the study. "Now, it was up to the athletes to make it happen."

But, Hoogkamer noted, the shoe technology had the potential to benefit subelite and recreational runners even more. With its next-generation foam cushioning, carbon-fiber plate, and thick but soft midsole, runners at a variety of speeds would be able to significantly improve their times, he said.

"We don't know specifically what would happen for a 4-hour marathoner in these shoes because we never tested it at that pace," Hoogkamer said when we spoke in late 2018. "But because the results from the 2:20- to 3-hour range were constant, it's fair to assume it's going to be independent of speed. The other side of it is that, because of that relationship, the 4% shoes will only make Kipchoge 2.5 percent faster, but the 4% shoes could maybe make the 4-hour marathoner 4.5 percent faster."

The CU study was published in the peer-reviewed research journal *Sports Medicine* in July 2017, explaining how the shoe provided a 4 percent increase in running economy and ultimately gave the shoe its name. But there were plenty of people in the running industry and academia who were skeptical of the study, given that Kram is a paid consultant to Nike, that the Swoosh paid for the studies, and that it published only limited aspects of the science behind the tests.

With rival brands and athletes suggesting that the International Association of Athletics Federations (IAAF) look into the shoe to see if it fell within the legal guidelines of competitive footwear, Kram vehemently denied that the shoe's carbon-fiber plate acted as a spring—which would be illegal under IAAF competition rules—and insisted that it was merely a lever. A month after Kipchoge's astonishing world record, CU published a subsequent study in *Sports Medicine* that suggested that the soft and resilient ZoomX foam, not the plate, was the secret sauce. The energy stored and returned by the carbon-fiber plate is minuscule, Kram said; the plate is really just acting as a facilitator for the foam.

"This paper demonstrates that the bulk of the energy saved through this shoe comes through its softer, better foam," Kram said. "The carbon-fiber plate is just a cherry on top."

The curvature of the carbon-fiber plate helps stabilize a runner's ankle joint, thus reducing the load on the calf muscles. The stiffness of the plate helps keep a runner's toes straight and relaxed, preserving the energy that would otherwise be spent in flexing during the push-off phase of a new stride.

Subsequent high-profile victories and record-breaking perfor-mances continued to validate Nike's magic shoes, as did a July 2018 report in the *New York Times* that analyzed data from about 500,000 marathon and half-marathon running times—taken from public race reports and fitness app Strava—over the previous four years. It found that "runners in Vaporflys ran 3 to 4 percent faster than similar run-ners wearing other shoes, and more than 1 percent faster than the next-fastest racing shoe." Another independent study conducted at Grand Valley State University in Michigan and published in late 2018 also came up with a 4% edge in efficiency.

———

In early 2016, Nike had started quietly having some of its elite ath-letes wear prototypes of the yet-unnamed shoes in competition. Galen Rupp (2:11:20) and Amy Cragg (2:28:20) won the 2016 U.S. Olympic Trials Marathon in Los Angeles wearing prototypes of the shoe. Shalane Flanagan, also wearing the shoes, placed third in the same race (2:29:19) to earn her fourth Olympic berth, edging out former Nike athlete Kara Goucher, who, running for her new sponsor, Skechers, placed fourth, a disappointing 65 seconds back.

Those close to the project at Nike credited Flanagan's finish—and the ability to hold off Goucher—to the secret shoes. Goucher didn't crit-icize the shoes at the trials; however, she has since been openly skeptical of the concept.

"If technology is affecting races and what times people are running, if that is found to be an unfair advantage, then that's an issue," Goucher said later.

Kipchoge (2:08:44) won Olympic gold in Rio de Janeiro wearing a similar pair, as did silver medalist Feyisa Lilesa (2:09:54) and Rupp (2:10:05), who came home with bronze in what was the second-fastest marathon in Olympic history. On the women's side, Flanagan wound up sixth in the Olympics (2:25:26), while Cragg was ninth (2:28:25), both wearing the prototype racing flats.

Nike officially launched the Breaking2 Project, an international exhibition built around the development of the ultimate running shoe and a quest to make history, in late 2016. It announced a multipronged approach that would give three handpicked elite athletes a shot at breaking 2 hours in a highly curated time-trial setting on a motorsports race track in Monza, Italy, the following May. The venue was chosen because it was close to sea level (600 feet in elevation); protected from the wind; and historically had good weather in early May, when Nike aimed to pull this spectacle off.

The runners picked were Kenyan Kipchoge, regarded as the best marathoner in the world; Eritrean Zersenay Tadese, the half-marathon world record holder at the time; and Ethiopian Lelisa Desisa, the 2013 and 2015 Boston Marathon champion with a 2:04:45 marathon PR.

Backed by an elite group of physiologists that had monitored their training for months and wearing wind-resistant apparel and the thickly cushioned prototype shoes with carbon-fiber plates and a unique shark's-fin taper design at the back of the heel (then referred to as the Vaporfly Elite), Kipchoge, Tadese, and Desisa would run behind an exhaust-free Tesla pace car and draft off a pack of six world-class pacers in an arrowhead formation to further maximize wind resistance.

Unlike in a typical race, fresh pacers would take over throughout the time trial, one of the many tactics that made the event ineligible to be sanctioned as a world record even if any of the racers should finish under Kimetto's official 2:02:57 record mark. Among the pace group were a wide range of accomplished runners.

At 5:45 a.m. on May 6, 2017, Kipchoge, Tadese, and Desisa toed the line at the racetrack in Monza. They had been tested, poked, prodded, and analyzed for months, as had every detail surrounding the racetrack venue. The temperature was a moderate 54 degrees, and there was a bit of light rain, neither ideal nor what Nike officials had hoped for but not enough off the mark to postpone the event.

All that was left was to start running and see how history played out. Dozens of international media representatives watched trackside, while an estimated 100,000 spectators from around the world tuned in for the livestream broadcast.

In order to break 2 hours, the runners would have to average 4:34.5 per mile while running 17.5 laps around the 2,402.4-meter racetrack. The trio started off at a history-making clip, but Desisa fell off the pace just 3.5 miles into the event. Tadese held on for longer but also fell behind just after the 12-mile mark. Kipchoge remained on pace through 15.5 miles and was just 1 second off pace at 30 km, or 18.6 miles.

But even with fresh pacers joining him over the final 12 km, Kipchoge began to lose valuable seconds on each lap. His 40-km split of 1:54:04 (a 4:35 mile pace) was the fastest ever recorded for that distance, but it confirmed that it would take a huge final effort to finish within 2 hours. In the final miles, the laws of human physiology were bound to take over as lactic acid in his muscles began to tear down his ability to maintain efficiency—just as it does for every runner at some point in a long-distance race.

In the end, Kipchoge crossed the finish line in 2:00:25, shy of Nike's aim but still more than two and a half minutes faster than Kimetto's existing world record and 2:40 faster than his own personal best.

"On the last lap, I lost 10 seconds and the time escaped," Kipchoge said moments after the event. "It has been hard; it has taken seven good months of preparation and dedication. This journey has been a long challenge, but I'm a happy man to run a marathon in 2 hours."

While Kipchoge's marathon time would go down as perhaps nothing more than an asterisk in the history books, it certainly gave cues as to what is humanly possible. No longer did running a marathon under 2 hours seem an insurmountable barrier, but rather a feasible, approachable goal. "We are now just 25 seconds away," Kipchoge said. "I believe in good preparation and good planning. With that, these 25 seconds will go. I hope next time people believe it is possible."

———

After years of playing second fiddle to Adidas, Nike regained the throne as the most dominant name in marathoning, thanks to the Vaporfly Elite, although they were as yet unavailable to consumers. (They were eventually released on a limited basis in 2017 with a price tag of a whopping $425.)

A few months after the Breaking2 event, Nike athletes Geoffrey Kirui of Kenya and Rose Chelimo of Bahrain won the men's and women's marathons, respectively, at the 2017 IAAF World Championships in London, both wearing Vaporfly Elites. Later that fall, Flanagan wore a pair as she ran to victory in the 2017 New York City Marathon, the first marathon win of her career, at age 36.

Kipchoge went on to win the 2017 Berlin Marathon in 2:03:32 and the 2018 London Marathon in 2:04:17 before his record-shattering effort at the 2018 Berlin Marathon, solidifying his status as the greatest marathon runner in history. Showing that he had more left in the tank—and wearing a pair of Nike's new ZoomX Vaporfly Next%—he won the 2019 London Marathon in 2:02:37, the second-fastest time in history.

Through the spring of 2019, the 34-year-old Kipchoge had won 12 of the 13 marathons he had run. His career *average* time for a marathon in those races was 2:03:21, a time only six other runners had ever surpassed once. What's more amazing is that Kipchoge has gotten faster with age—and with the new shoes. Following his Olympic victory, the average of his five subsequent 26.2-mile efforts wearing a version of the updated Vaporflys—including the Breaking2 time trial—was 2:02:30, a time that made him 25 seconds faster than any other athlete in history.

A week after winning the 2019 London Marathon, Kipchoge announced—on the 65th anniversary of Roger Bannister's first sub-4-minute mile in London—that he would attempt to break the 2-hour marathon barrier while wearing Nike's ZoomX Vaporfly Next% shoes in London. While the plans for the October 2019 event were not fully understood as this book went to press, Kipchoge confirmed that time-saving strategies similar to those used in the Breaking2 Project, including using a pace car that acts as a giant wind shield and having a collection of pacemakers who sub in and out of the time trial, would be employed, making the effort noncompliant with IAAF record criteria.

"It's not about the IAAF, it's about history," Kipchoge said at a press conference announcing the event. "I really want to leave a big legacy. This will surpass everything I have achieved. It will be history for the human family."

Nike's Next%, which debuted on the feet of a few elites in the 2019 Boston and London Marathons, has 15 percent more ZoomX foam in the midsole, a grippier outsole, a new hydrophobic upper, and a lower heel-toe offset (8 mm, down from 11 mm), but the carbon-fiber plate remains the same as that in the Vaporfly 4%. I got a glimpse of a prototype in 2018 during testing at CU. It was originally going to be called the Vaporfly 5%, but the research apparently bore out only 4.7 percent average improvement, so Nike opted for a different name.

Say what you will about the Breaking2 Project and the Vaporfly shoes, but impressive results indicate that they work.

In sports, athletes and brands are always seeking an advantage, and that—whether through ingenuity, science, or effort—spurs performance, Kram says. Indeed, Nike's investment in helping Kipchoge and other athletes push the envelope of human performance has resulted in a flurry of shoes with carbon-fiber plate innovations from other brands, including Hoka, New Balance, Brooks, and Saucony.

Hoka launched a low-to-the-ground racing shoe with a carbon-fiber plate as a prototype in 2018, and Canadian runner Cam Levins shattered his country's national record wearing the shoe in his marathon debut, running 2:09:25 at the Toronto Waterfront Marathon. That shoe became known as the EVO Carbon Rocket when it was released in early 2019. Hoka also released the more thickly cushioned Carbon X racing shoe in the spring of 2019, and American runner Jim Walmsley set a new 50-mile world record of 4:50:07 in it the day it debuted. The difference is that the midsole foam of the Carbon X shoe is firmer than that of the Vaporfly 4% and Next% shoes, making it a little more democratic in its accessibility for a broader range of recreational runners.

New Balance used similar technology, albeit a more dynamic carbon-fiber plate and a considerably softer foam, to create a shoe designed for short-distance road racing. The FuelCell 5280, so named for the distance of a mile in feet, debuted in May 2019. It feels so soft that it's spongy, but it's designed for fast running with a forefoot gait, and three-time Olympian Jenny Simpson won the Fifth Avenue Mile for the seventh straight year in 2019 wearing a prototype pair of 5280s. Saucony and Brooks have had their elite athletes racing in yet-unnamed models that are expected to debut prior to the U.S. Olympic Trials Marathon on February 29, 2020, in Atlanta. Clearly, carbon-fiber plates have been a positive new direction for shoe designers. But they are not necessarily the answer for every runner.

Unfortunately, I never personally experienced the exhilarating benefits of the Vaporfly 4% shoe despite my considerable excitement and investment in it. A week after that downhill tempo run, with my sights still set on Cal International, I laced the shoes up for a 16-mile long run at an 8:35 pace. The decision to wear them was impulsive, given that the shoes weren't made for running that slowly—or so I painfully discovered.

I suspected soon after I started out that the shoe wasn't a good choice for that Sunday long run, but I rejected the advice of my training partner, who suggested that we turn back so that I could change into a more substantial shoe. Feeling fresh and eager to run, I waved off her well-intended input and, for the first mile or so, enjoyed a light, energetic feeling underfoot.

My exhilaration was short-lived, however, as after a few miles, I found that I was dramatically heel striking and deeply compressing that soft foam under my heel, just as I had done in my tempo warm-up jog the week prior. While I was still fresh early in the run, I could feel my running mechanics overcome the rearfoot collapse once I rolled through my midfoot and gained the benefit of the carbon-fiber plate. But by mile 5, my form was consistently lagging, and my previously tight and weak left hamstring started to rapidly fatigue. For the final 10 miles, I felt the gross imbalance in my stride as my left foot scuffed the ground repeatedly.

When I finished the run, I could barely lift my left leg over a curb, and my upper hamstring attachment ached painfully. The next day, I could barely walk. Although I continued with my marathon training in a modified way, my hamstring—and my form—never fully recovered. I managed to attain the necessary mileage through the end of the training plan, but I struggled in the faster, marathon-paced workouts, when I needed to run with full leg and hip extension.

Six weeks later, I arrived in Sacramento still hopeful—or perhaps delusional—that I could run 26.2 miles. The California International

Marathon is a marquee race for elite, subelite, and performance-oriented recreational runners to chase PRs, Boston Marathon qualifying (BQ) times, or a qualifying time for the U.S. Olympic Trials Marathon. My own hope had been to run somewhere in the neighborhood of 3:10—which was what an early-October workout had seemed to predict—but at that point, I would have settled for a 3:25 just to earn a BQ for the first time in a few years.

I made it to the starting line in Folsom, California, with my fit and energized training partner, but I was feeling neither good nor hopeful. I noted that about 75 percent of the runners in the front of the starting corral were wearing brilliant red Nike Vaporfly 4% Flyknit shoes. Not me. I was wearing a pair of well-balanced Brooks Launch 5 that had been prescribed to me by a discerning salesguy at NRC. I felt a bit out of place wearing a thickly cushioned training shoe that was 30 percent heavier and considerably less energetic than the brightly colored racing flats surrounding me, but at that point, I was just hoping for the ability to run smoothly.

I began at my intended 7:15 race pace, but my gait was wonky from the start as I favored my left side to compensate for the weakened hamstring. Because I wasn't getting full drive out of my left hamstring, I subtly altered my gait, causing my foot to land differently and my left calf to do more work. Just as I passed the 1-mile mark in 7:17, I slipped on a wet section of pavement and felt my left calf muscle tear. I stubbornly continued for 2 more painful miles but eventually hobbled to the side of the road. As I watched my training partner run out of sight, I marveled at the vision of so many bright red Vaporfly 4% shoes heading down the road with her.

After struggling through a few more painful miles at a sluggish pace, I swallowed my pride, summoned an Uber, and headed back to my hotel. I walked to the finish line and arrived in time to watch unsponsored athletes Brogan Austin (2:12:39) and Emma Bates (2:28:19) outrun several seasoned pro runners to the finish line. Both runners set new PRs and won their first national titles. Both wore brilliant red magic shoes from Nike.

In the days that followed, dozens of subelite runners who had finished among the top 10 percent raved about the Vaporfly 4% shoes on social media outlets, but I quietly relished a few comments I heard about runners with challenges similar to mine.

Ultimately, it wasn't the Nike Vaporfly 4% shoes that did me in, but I am certain they were a catalyst that led to a disappointing DNF that day. I know shoes don't cause injuries—repetitive form flaws, inherent anatomical deficiencies and areas of weakness or imbalance do. But the shoe is designed for the light midfoot footstrikes that are common to elite and subelite runners repeatedly running a 4:35 to 5:30 mile pace. While I can still run some fast miles on a downhill course, I am not a subelite runner capable of a sub-2:30 marathon, and my days of running moderately fast, sub-16-minute 5Ks are well behind me.

For me, it was a perfect storm. My body was already taxed after a summer of ultradistance races, and I should have taken a break before transitioning into a marathon-specific buildup for the Sacramento race or scrapped it entirely. Fatigued heading into the fall, I sensed that my well-honed aerobic fitness was fleeting, and even during some of my first marathon-specific workouts, I found it difficult to maintain a consistent rhythm to my gait.

I'd naively hoped the Vaporfly 4% shoes would be the magic bullet that would help me reach the finish line at or ahead of my goal time, like Eliud Kipchoge and seemingly thousands of other faster marathoners. But what really did me in was my own inner shoe geek—my fascination with running shoes—which led to me be overzealous about shoes that so many runners seemed to be benefiting from.

The journey served to remind me that it's less about the shoes than about the runner who is wearing them. In distance running, there are no magic bullets, no shortcuts, and no magic shoes. Success in distance running is obtained only through months of dedication to smart, diligent training. Mind-boggling performances in electrifying kicks certainly may leave us awestruck, but in the end, every runner has his or her own needs when it comes to the shoes on his or her feet. In my case, the Vaporfly 4% just wasn't Cinderella's glass slipper.

9 MADE **TO ORDER**

Always remember that you are absolutely unique. Just like everyone else.
MARGARET MEAD, CULTURAL ANTHROPOLOGIST

It was late one night a few years ago, and I knew I should be shutting down my laptop and getting some sleep ahead of an early-morning trail run. But I was wired from too much caffeine, and so instead of powering off, I pointed my browser to miadidas.com (since discontinued) and started designing a custom version of the Adidas Adizero Boston 6 shoes.

The only "custom" aspect of the shoes available on miadidas.com that night was the color palette. But that was OK with me. I had my pick of 8 to 16 colors to decorate various parts of the shoes, including the upper, the outsole, the laces, and the Adidas trefoil logo. I pointed and clicked my cursor in a fury, creating what I anticipated would be an ideal shoe to lace up for the upcoming Boston Marathon.

When the finished product came up on the screen, my orange-yellow-and-white color motif looked less than stunning. I clicked through to the final step of the process, entered my credit-card number, and hesitated. Should I buy these shoes for $150? *Nope*, I thought, clicking off the site. My reluctance wasn't because I already owned a pair of Adidas Adizero 6 in the standard black, blue, and white. And it wasn't because the standard version cost $120, $30 less than the personalized version I'd created. My change of heart had nothing to do with those bits of logic and everything to do with the fact that the pair I had designed was just plain ugly.

Beauty might be in the eye of the beholder, but color and appearance are two of the biggest factors influencing how runners choose their shoes—including me—and, quite frankly, I couldn't see myself running in these, let alone wearing them casually with jeans. I opened a new browser window and surfed my way over to NikeID.com to see if I could work my artistic magic on a pair of Pegasus 32s instead.

Nike was the first brand to launch a custom online shoe design service to consumers when it debuted NikeID.com in 1999. The program started with Nike's popular Air Force 1 basketball shoe, giving consumers 31 different customizable parts and materials—including the base, overlays, accent, lining, stitching, outsole, laces, and lace medallion.

The program experienced strong initial success and eventually expanded to offer a variety of running, basketball, tennis, and casual footwear silhouettes for a $10 to $20 price markup and the promise of a one-week turnaround time.

Customizing was one of the first big breakthroughs for running shoes on the Internet. While online sales of running shoes were slow in the late 1990s—the notion of buying things online was still perceived as something of a Wild West—custom orders were red-hot.

Today, industry estimates suggest that 15 to 20 percent of all online orders of athletic shoes are personalized shoes, with running models hovering at about 10 percent. That volume makes sense given the importance consumers place on color and aesthetics. And as with anything you might buy—a coffee cup, a couch, a car—statistics show that you're more likely to make a purchase if you have a hand in designing the product the way you want it.

The NIKEiD service offered runners a chance to create one-of-a-kind shoes, which meant Nike had to figure out how to develop a one-off shoe production system. As with its standard shoes, one-at-a-time online shoe orders were processed at one of Nike's factories in China, where each custom-designed shoe was built on an assembly line that included a few dozen people and work stations. However, with one-off shoes, each customizable piece was individually sourced from bins holding an array of colors for every part of the shoe.

Take the 2000 Pegasus, for example. Instead of building the standard white-and-gray upper, red-outlined black Swoosh, gray midsole, black outsole, and white laces, line workers chose the colors of the customizable pieces that matched the photo of a customer's order. Then, as with a standard version, the shoe was glued, stitched, and molded together. It was then checked for quality assurance, boxed, and shipped via air freight to its new owner.

NIKEiD wasn't initially a big moneymaker because, as cool as the concept was and as slick as the interface was, it was inefficient to produce one-off custom shoe orders, and for that reason, the program would never reach the profit margins of the standard, inline Pegasus. But the launch of the program changed the game in key ways: how shoes could look; how they were sold; the importance of customer input; and, for better or for worse, runners' realization that they didn't have to settle for what was on the shoe wall of their local running store.

In 2000, as NIKEiD was starting to gain traction and other running brands were trying to develop their own custom programs, a start-up called Customatix came on the scene with a more intricate (and cheaper) approach to creating custom running shoes. Like NIKEiD and other brands' color-custom operations, Customatix.com allowed armchair designers to create their shoes. But Customatix was able to give customers more choices, claiming there were no fewer than three million combinations of colors, graphics, logos, and materials.

Founded by former Adidas and Nike executives, Customatix created made-to-order footwear by offering consumers different component materials, colors, graphics, and text options. The company proudly proclaimed, "Shoes designed by you. Not the corporate Mafia."

For $85, you could go through 16 design steps, choose a few specific model options related to the shoe's cushioning and structure, and then pick from three different color schemes and 12 accent colors. If you wanted blue-and-orange stability shoes with silver laces or a black-and-red neutral cushioning shoe with gold laces, it was all at your fingertips.

After you made your selections, a custom model appeared as a 3-D image on your computer screen. Once you were happy with your design and entered your credit card information to make the purchase, the shoes were manufactured in China and shipped to you within two weeks.

Customatix offered nine models that could be customized—including a popular maximally cushioned model known as the N Dorf'N—and loads of visual variety. The process fed a driving consumer urge to personalize a shoe's appearance, but margins were extremely tight. It cost the company about $40 to make each pair, plus an $8 import duty and a $20 delivery fee to ship the shoes from the U.S. seaport to the consumer. Although the company reported robust sales, profits were nonexistent, and the company disappeared after five years in business.

Customatix fell somewhere between the air-pump-assisted, semicustom fit of a 1991 Reebok HXL and the personalized color choices offered by the NIKEiD program. It was successful as far as it went, but like other custom-color footwear design services offered at the time, Customatix didn't make a connection between a runner's gait patterns and foot shape and how they interacted with the fit, feel, and ride of a shoe.

In the ensuing years, Adidas, New Balance, Under Armour, and Puma all joined the personalized or quasi-custom shoe fray. They started by offering just a few silhouettes with color variations but as sales increased and manufacturing became easier, they expanded the range of shoes that could be customized. New Balance set itself apart by eventually bringing its customizable shoe manufacturing business to its New England factories, knowing it would mean quicker shipping across North America and would also boost its made-with-American-labor story.

Not to be outdone, Nike amped up its NIKEiD business from a small web-based service by employing advanced software applications to give its customers a greater range of personalization in a variety of Nike shoes and clothing. Then it went a step further, bringing the customizing process to life via NIKEiD studios in more than 100 cities around the world. You could walk into a Nike store that had a NIKEiD studio—in New York, Los Angeles, Toronto, London, Tokyo, Beijing, and other international locales—and design a custom edition of the specific shoe being made at that location. If that NIKEiD studio was making Pegasus running shoes or Air Force 1 basketball shoes or Killshot tennis shoes, you could sit at a design console and pick the colors (and in some cases materials or patterns) that suited your tastes and then watch as a Nike associate built the shoe by hand, assembling all of the parts in the colors you chose. In essence, Nike created minifactories on location and a small-scale one-off production system at the point of sale.

Nike upped the ante again in 2017 with the opening of its Nike Maker Experience at the Nike By You Studio in New York City, a temporary custom-shoe studio that merged digital design with traditional footwear making. The product highlighted at the studio was Nike's casual/fitness-oriented Presto X. For $200, consumers could choose a traditional laced version or a slip-on model. While the basic silhouette, base materials, and geometry of the shoe came standard, consumers could customize most other aspects of a shoe.

The experience began with a series of graphic options, generated from either Nike heritage or on-the-spot phrases input via a keypad, which were then customized into patterns through shifts in size and color. Eventually, Nike added dip-dyeing, shoe printing, embroidery, footwear patches, laser etching, and a full footwear accessory bar (laces, zippers, tongue tags, etc.) to the experience.

But as engaging as these cocreation processes were becoming, none actually created a truly customized shoe. While they addressed the aesthetics of shoes in increasingly new ways, the shoes were ultimately the same base silhouette of a standard model sold at thousands of stores across the world. Whether it was a Nike Presto X, a New Balance 990 or an Adidas Adizero Boston 6, the only unique aspect of a custom version was the appearance. The process didn't address customization in the deeper sense—namely, that every human being has a unique running gait, not to mention a variety of anatomical differences and idiosyncrasies.

Some runners need extra stability and specific support to balance their feet and smooth out their running mechanics, says physical therapist Plaatjes; the challenge is knowing how much stability that runner needs and where extra support should be placed. No standard off-the-shelf shoe can possibly address a single runner's gait in such a precise way; however, adding an insole—whether over-the-counter or custom-made—can help provide a semicustom fit and functionality.

"Typically, the standard insoles that come in running shoes are flimsy and wear out within a month or so because the foam materials pack down," Plaatjes says. "However, an over-the-counter insole will typically last through two or three pairs of shoes and provide a lot more support and cushion. It also makes the shoe function better based on a runner's mechanics and allows a shoe to last longer."

To get specific support and create a more direct interaction between the shape and movement patterns of a foot and the shoe while running, a custom insole is preferable, he says. Custom insoles, which are made from an imprint of the bottom of a runner's foot and then adjusted to match a runner's various anatomical and gait irregularities, can help reduce foot fatigue and plantar fascia strain while also increasing running efficiency. Insole materials range from simple foam compounds or gel (or a combination of the two) for cushioning to plastic, carbon fiber, or cork for rigidity and support to aid proper foot and lower-leg alignment, with a layer of foam for comfort.

But insoles can only accomplish so much. Brands have kicked around the idea of creating truly customized running shoes for years, but how to create a one-of-a-kind running shoe for the masses that is able to specifically address the needs of an individual runner's gait?

Surprisingly, the first story in truly custom running shoes came not from a global power brand but rather from a small husband-and-wife operation in Maine. In 1982, Bart and Jan Hersey started customizing shoes in a converted sheep barn. Bart had worked for several shoe brands, but later in his career, he wanted to stop working in a corporate setting and do something on his own. The Hersey Custom Shoe Company built shoes with the same modern materials that the big brands used at the time—dual-density die-cut EVA midsoles, nylon-and-suede uppers, and rubber outsoles—but created every pair one at a time by hand. It offered a limited color palette—just gray and beige colorways with small blue, red, green, and pink highlights—and it took a few days to design and build a single pair, especially when unique specs were requested.

The Herseys built a reputation for quality workmanship and developed a loyal following among people with different-sized feet, severe bunions, hammer toes, leg-length discrepancies, or other anatomical issues that could be accounted for in made-to-order shoes.

The novel idea might never have been more than a side-hustle hobby in a cottage industry if *Runner's World* had not named one of the Hersey models, the DPS, the number-one shoe for 1985. Suddenly the Herseys' phone rang off the hook, and orders skyrocketed from new runners and seasoned marathoners alike.

The Hersey Custom Shoe Company remained profitable into the 2000s owing to a strong customer base of repeat buyers who appreciated the Herseys' handiwork and earnestness. Still, competition from NIKEiD and other brands' online portals eventually began to erode their business. The couple prepared to shutter the doors and retire.

But in 2007, Stephen Keoseian, a footwear aficionado who had previously worked in the Keosa Brothers Shoe Repair Company started by his grandfather in 1921, bought the business, moved it to Fitchburg, Massachusetts, and infused it with new life. He continued the Herseys' custom sneaker business but added modern fabrics and materials to some of the shoe styles and spun them off into Victory Sportswear to bring them to a mass market.

Thanks to a boom in retro-style running sneakers and a handful of retail partners in the United States, United Kingdom, and Japan, his Victory sneaker business grew modestly. But when Nike, Brooks, New Balance, Saucony, and Puma jumped into the fray with their own vintage models in the early 2010s, selling an off-brand retro-looking shoe became a tall order.

Like the Herseys before him and New Balance's domestic shoe production, Keoseian represents one of the last vestiges of a dying shoe-making industry in the United States.

"It hasn't been easy," Keoseian says candidly during a long phone conversation that was tinged with sadness even as it oozed passion for footwear craftsmanship. "It's hard to keep up with changing trends and styles compared to what's out there on the Internet. But our biggest challenge is that we can't make the shoes fast enough, and as a result, our profit margin is very low."

Keoseian's businesses are decidedly low-tech and old-school; neither Victory nor Hersey utilizes digital design applications, and most Hersey customers are still mailing in hand-traced outlines and pertinent measurements of their feet. Keoseian takes the length, width, and volume measurements to determine which size last to build the shoe around. But instead of creating a three-dimensional schematic of that foot based on those specs, as designers at big shoe brands do, Keoseian manually matches the numbers to a chart detailing an array of dozens of 50-year-old lasts hanging in his workshop.

Making a custom sneaker takes about 12 steps, Keoseian says. Every part of the production cycle—material cutting, lasting, sewing, trimming, and gluing—is done by hand, one pair at a time. On the Victory side of the business, Keoseian and a couple of part-time staffers can produce 5 to 10 pairs of sneakers per day with about a six-week turnaround time from start to ship. The shoes have a $220 suggested retail price, and he produces 1,200 to 1,500 pairs every year. With low profit margins, it's barely enough to keep the business operating.

The Hersey custom business still jogs along at a pace of a pair or two per week (about 100 pair per year) with a 12- to 18-week delivery schedule from the time of ordering to the time of shipping. And with prices from $250 to $500, it's where Keoseian says he'll be shifting more of his efforts in the coming years. Given his workload with the family shoe repair business, it's the most efficient and logical way to go forward, he says.

As a kid, I saw Hersey's black-and-white classified ad in the back of *Runner's World* and wondered why someone would want a stodgy-looking, handcrafted shoe when they could get the latest and greatest from Nike, Adidas, Saucony, or New Balance. But now that more than 75,000 miles of running have taken their toll on my body, I appreciate the value of what a customized shoe can do. It works with a runner's individualized gait pattern and the asymmetrical abnormalities that come along with it.

Although I have always run with a neutral gait, I have propped up my left side to mitigate a 12-mm functional leg-length discrepancy for the past dozen or so years. Without a custom shoe, the only way to do that is by inserting a sloping, hard-foam heel lift under the sock liner of my left shoe. If I don't do that in every pair of shoes I wear, I wind up with excruciating pain in my pelvis that eventually leads to sciatica pain down my left leg.

Keoseian has heard similar stories from customers for years, not to mention from runners who have vastly different-sized shoes—including a repeat customer who wears a women's size 4 on his left foot and a man's 11 on his right. Those are the reasons that he keeps forging ahead, he says, even though he knows a storm of high-tech custom shoe concepts from Nike, Adidas, New Balance, and Brooks is on the horizon.

"Everything we produce is entirely handmade, and every single pair of shoes passes through my hands, sometimes 10 to 15 times during the manufacturing process," he says. "It's a struggle, trust me. It's passion that's keeping me going. I love what I do, and people that wear our shoes love them, and that's why I keep doing it."

———

The most potent way to approach truly customized shoes has been via advanced technology and digital analytics, a goal that almost every big shoe company has been racing toward for the past five years.

Adidas has been on the leading edge of that trend. In 2015, it unveiled a 3-D-printed midsole that could be tailored to the individual cushioning needs of a runner's foot. The 3-D concept is part of Adidas's Futurecraft Series, a next-gen initiative that combines open-source collaboration and cutting-edge craftsmanship to drive innovation across all elements of production. The Futurecraft 3D series midsole project was launched as a prototype and a statement of Adidas's intent to push toward individually customized shoes.

JENNY SIMPSON || New Balance MD800 spikes
Three-time U.S. Olympian

For most of my career, I didn't let New Balance create custom-sized racing shoes for me. That's rare among pro athletes because having spikes fit precisely to the shape of your feet is important. But for me, the New Balance MD800 spikes already worked very well. I started wearing them when I turned pro in 2010, and they worked. I didn't want to come in and demand a bunch of special changes, but I never needed any, either. I've won four medals with that shoe, and it has taken me around so many laps of the track in so many stadiums around the world. I'm so proud of the craftsmanship New Balance put into them that I've always worn just the standard model of that shoe right off the shelf. Until recently, the only difference between my spikes and the ones available at running stores was that New Balance made mine with cool color patterns on the upper and my name printed on the tongue. To me, that's a testament of the quality of the shoe and a perfect endorsement without me ever saying a word about it.

I can't even describe how much joy it brings me to go to high school track meets and see young girls racing in those shoes. They don't know and maybe can't appreciate the fact that it's an identical shoe to what I wore in the Olympic Games, but it makes me so happy to know that they're out there running and racing in it, too.

How might this 3-D experience come to life for you, the runner? Imagine walking into a store and running briefly on a treadmill to get individualized specs for a 3-D-printed running shoe. Flexible and fully breathable, the midsoles created from those specs match the exact contours and pressure points of your left and right footstrikes. Where your foot exudes high force, you see more support from the 3-D web structure, and in low-force areas, you see that the links in the web are broken.

That data will be collected and stored in the Adidas data center at an Adidas Futurecraft location in New York, Los Angeles, London, or Tokyo (or potentially your local running store) and then printed remotely from a modified thermoplastic polyurethane at the Adidas production center in Scheinfeld, Germany, where it will then be assembled with the upper portion of the shoe and a rubber outsole.

Adidas has also been working on custom concepts through its automated Speedfactory laboratories in Atlanta and Ansbach, Germany. These R&D centers are advanced technology proving grounds where Adidas produces customized shoes for individual customers in specific cities across the world. The custom shoe line is called Adidas Made For—AM4 for short—and it's based on the individual specs of a runner's foot and gait grounded by analytical data from thousands of other runners in the same region. Adidas started by designing shoes for runners in Germany and then expanded the program with pop-up labs in London, Paris, New York, Tokyo, and Shanghai to specifically develop shoes for runners in those cities.

Why do runners in different cities need different shoes? An analysis of runner data in different cities revealed some intriguing running gait anomalies. For example, Adidas discovered that runners in the Big Apple tend to make sharper turns at higher speeds than runners in London or Paris. So it made subtle tweaks to the upper of the AM4NYC shoe to help improve stability and agility.

The brand showed off its data-driven technology in 2018 at a pop-up Speedfactory Lab Experience in Brooklyn, New York. Inside the temporary facility, designers scanned participants' feet to determine their exact length, width, volume, and shape, and high-speed cameras recorded their stride, speed, and gait patterns. The program interpolated all of an individual's data, incorporated data acquired by tracking a wide range of runners' gaits in New York City, and used the combination to design and make shoes specifically for that runner. Using 3-D printing and an automated manufacturing system, it produced a singular pair of the AM4NYC model that it claimed was "digitally perfected" for precision, fit, comfort, and support while running the streets of New York.

_____

While Adidas has taken a unique approach to customizing shoes, it has yet to solve the challenge of how to mass-produce one-off shoes in an expedient and cost-effective manner. That's something that Brooks has been on the road to figuring out.

At a trade show in Austin, Texas, in December 2017, I find myself standing barefoot on the glass bed of a high-tech scanner. As the blue light of a laser beam measures the size and shape of each of my feet, a data set appears on the computer screen in front of me and shows how my feet differ just slightly. I have high arches in both, but my right foot is slightly longer and narrower, and my left big toe is straighter than its decidedly crooked counterpart.

I'm instructed by Brooks staff to do a few run-bys along a rubber runway mat and strike my foot on a force plate to determine my specific gait characteristics. After the impact data of each foot is recorded twice, my stride data appears on the screen in the form of a series of pressure-mapping diagrams. They reveal that my left foot lands with a heavier heel strike and then dramatically rolls inward before straightening as it approaches the toe-off phase of a new stride. Meanwhile, the 3-D scans—done via the leading-edge technology of a system known as FitStation by HP—show that my right foot lands considerably more softly at the midfoot and rolls to the lateral side before rolling back toward the big toe and launching off the ground.

My grossly asymmetrical gait is the result of numerous injuries and irregularities up my kinematic chain—from the bottom of my feet to my hips—that have occurred over nearly 40 years of running. The most stride-altering impact came from a severed Achilles tendon 10 years earlier. It didn't stop me from running, but the post-surgery atrophy of the muscles in my left foot, ankle, and lower leg took its toll, and my body has been compensating ever since, even though aided by the heel lift under my left foot. Truth be told, my right leg has long been considerably stronger after more than a decade of running on the track, where left turns make many runners right-leg dominant.

That's just my story; every runner has his or her own foot and gait irregularities. While that probably doesn't come as much of a surprise to a runner, it has only recently become a key point of understanding in the running shoe industry, especially as chatter about developing customized footwear has become more prevalent.

"A runner's foot is like a fingerprint," says Jean-Yves Couput, the innovation director at Amer Sports Corp., the parent company of Salomon. "How a runner moves across the ground, and the type of shoe they'll perform best in, is based on the unique characteristics of their feet," he told me in 2017 as Salomon was about to launch its own custom shoe project.

Salomon's ME:sh project allows customers to design shoes that match their personal gait patterns and comfort preferences by giving them choices for heel-toe offset, outsole features, and cushioning firmness and flexibility once their feet have been scanned during a treadmill run. The upper is made of a socklike fabric called Twinskin, which is knit in the 3-D shape based on the individual's foot size and volume and fused to the chassis with heat. With high-tech pulling so much of the weight, shoe assembly uses 50 percent less labor than that needed for a standard shoe made on an assembly line in an Asian shoe factory.

The challenge for Salomon's custom project—as for the one-off models built in Adidas's pop-up lab—is the limited number of venues where a runner can go through the process. The program debuted in nine European cities in 2017–2018 and has yet to debut in the United States.

Meanwhile, Brooks is en route to figuring out that aspect with its personalized shoe program. Which is precisely the reason I'm getting my biometrics recorded at this trade show.

In 2017, Brooks announced a partnership with Hewlett-Packard and Superfeet to pursue the production of "truly made-to-measure footwear" utilizing HP's FitStation scanning technology, Brooks's footwear expertise, and Superfeet's Flowbuilt factory in Ferndale, Washington. Once up and running in mid-2018, the process was expected to take two weeks from scans to a finished product that would then be shipped straight to the consumer.

The undertaking is the next step in Brooks's Run Signature research program, which follows the notion that enhancing comfort and improving performance are not about fixing a runner's flaws but instead about working with the natural preferred motion path of a runner's muscles, bones, and joints. The ultimate aim is to create one-of-a-kind shoes tuned to an individual runner's specific biometric data. The midsole of each shoe will have to have unique dimensions—width, length, thickness—as well as unique density, flexibility, and rebound characteristics.

"Through [our] beta research program, we will gain valuable insights about what runners want from their personalized running products, which can then be used to create a personalized product for all runners, by runners," said Pete Humphrey, Brooks's vice president of research and development, when I talked to him later. "We believe the future of performance running is personalization, and [this] is the first step in delivering this experience to runners."

Brooks, Superfeet, and HP have assembled a mini–shoe factory on Austin's trade-show floor, where they are scanning the feet of retailers and media representatives and demonstrating how a personalized shoe will come to life. Using the Brooks Levitate shoe as a model, the partners show that the midsole shape and midsole density can be varied to match a runner's specific running gait data.

I'm stoked to try out a pair of running shoes made specifically for me. The dozen or so members of the Brooks/Superfeet/HP crew wear white lab coats and hard hats for dramatic effect as they press a handful of new shoes using a few variable components and an individually formulated midsole compound. But my hope and excitement fade as the machinery and demonstration process encounter more challenges than successes. I am advised to come back later to pick up my shoes, but when I do, I'm told that I won't be getting my prototype pair. The mini–production facility broke down, they say, and my specs will be saved for when the prototype factory is up and running in Ferndale.

The program was set to launch to consumers in June 2018. But as the year progressed, that date was pushed back as the research team realized they needed more time to nail down the process and manufacturing. The company eventually put the program on hold and reorganized. Finally, in December 2018, Brooks officially launched the Genesys program with 500 initial wear-testers via a beta research program.

The plan is to create a personalized version of the Genesys shoe by combining a runner's digital profile (captured with foot scanning and gait analysis) with Brooks's Run Signature principles, which suggest that the best way to enhance comfort and improve performance is to create shoes that work with a runner's natural motion path and incorporate that runner's comfort preferences. The resulting data is then translated into specific fit and feel requirements for each shoe and assembled using custom-sized materials and a specifically designed midsole unit constructed with a state-of-the-art foam injection molding machine.

Although the process hadn't come to fruition as this book went to press, Brooks is confident that it is well on its way to the mass production of personalized shoes. Whenever it happens, it will be the first semblance of a truly customized running shoe available to the masses.

"We have a long history of bringing innovations to runners that help them get more out of their run, ranging from the Varus Wedge in 1977 to the DNA AMP (midsole foam) in 2017," Humphrey says. "The next evolution is leveraging a runner's biometrics to deliver a personalized running shoe that works even better with a runner's natural preferred motion path."

With each midsole having a unique width, length, thickness, and density pattern, manufacturing and pricing are the biggest challenges that Brooks will have to solve before it can bring the program to market. Another obstacle is the speed of production and the ability to quickly deliver products to consumers, says footwear industry analyst Powell.

"Today's consumer wants it now," he says. "It used to be that the standard was two-day shipping; now everybody expects same-day shipping. So custom products will be a growing part of the business, but it will never be a major part of the business."

Although Brooks isn't saying how much the personalized shoes would cost, the price tag is likely to be high—in the $250 to $400 range at the start. Made-to-order Salomons in the ME:sh program started at $300, partially because the production process is so inefficient. At full capacity, a Salomon ME:sh facility might produce 10 pairs of shoes per day, considerably less than the 2,500 to 3,500 that might be built in an eight-hour shift at a Chinese factory.

But consumers looking for these high-end products don't seem to be troubled by price. In 2018, Adidas sold its first Futurecraft 4D model—the initial commercial release of a shoe with a 3-D printed midsole—for $350 per pair, and it immediately sold out. The shoes were neither customized nor personalized, but they did raise the bar for small-batch production of running shoes. And with Nike's Vaporfly 4% shoes selling out at $250 and ZoomX Vaporfly Next% following suit at the same price, it seems clear that shoe consumers aren't afraid of a hefty price tag. Add customization to the shoe, and it's likely that certain runners still won't flinch at the price, especially if it mirrors how other customized sports equipment (skis, snowboards, golf clubs, bikes) has been priced.

Brooks's endeavor is certainly an innovative push into the future. But will it lead to a majority of shoes becoming personalized or semicustomized? Probably not, says senior director Caprara.

"You'll see a lot of premium product become personalized, but I think your price point models will still follow a mass-produced process," Caprara says. "I do think there will become a deflection point where even mass-produced stuff will become a little more personalized. But it's well in the future, because the manufacturing needs a lot of work."

In the summer of 2019, Tecnica launched a new semi-custom trail running shoe called The Origin using heat-moldable components and a choice of midsole foams. The shoes are being constructed at a handful of U.S. retail shops on a while-you-wait basis for $170.

As for me, I'm still waiting for my one-of-a-kind personalized shoes, and I hope it's not in the same way that I wanted a futuristic personal jet-propulsion pack when I was a kid. The shoe delay hasn't stopped me from logging many miles in the same off-the-rack models that everyone else wears. But I am secretly hoping for an anatomy-enhancing fountain-of-youth moment once I lace up my personalized shoes and go for a run.

10 <u>WHAT'S NEXT?</u>

The human foot is a masterpiece of engineering and a work of art.
LEONARDO DA VINCI

Running shoes are constantly evolving. And thanks to the continual ebb and flow of creative innovations, bizarre fads, and leaps in science and our understanding of the human body, they will continue to do so as long as humans are lacing up shoes and running for competition and recreation.

Landmark athletic events such as the Olympic gold-medal marathon of Joan Benoit Samuelson, the record-setting double-gold medal performances of Michael Johnson, Usain Bolt's outrageous speed, and Eliud Kipchoge's boundary-pushing world record inspire us to want more—from ourselves and from our shoes.

At the same time, fitness and cultural trends come and go, and these too have a powerful influence on shoes. The original running boom—and the performance-oriented shoes that accompanied it—eventually morphed into a more relaxed approach to running. That generation of "look at me" recreational runners led to the development of visible technology in running shoes. By the 1990s, how shoes looked and the range of what you did in them became more important than how they performed or how fast you could run. By the 2000s, however, running shoes were trending back toward their primal roots of functional performance. They took a sharp turn toward minimalism before reverting to comfort and casual appeal. It's been a wild ride.

So where are we going next?

Powell sees the growing separation between traditional runners and the athleisure market as something that the running industry will need to grapple with. That gap, along with the convenience and ease of online sales, will continue to change how shoes are sold and how people identify with wearing running shoes. Already, running brands have started to develop $100 athleisure models for a more casual wearer.

"The athleisure market's biggest contribution might be that it steered people away from buying a $150 running shoe when all they really wanted was a $90 sneaker that looked athletic, fit well, and was fashionable," Powell says. "Prior to that, there were a lot of people buying expensive running shoes for reasons other than running. Now there are athleisure alternatives that suit their needs for a lot less money."

Coinciding with the rise of athleisure shoes and a trend toward less-sophisticated fitness running, there has been a decline in race participation for the past several years, according to the "State of Running" report released in spring 2019. Despite big growth in Asia, ebbing participation in running events in North America, Europe, and Australia has led to a worldwide decline of 13 percent since 2016, when a peak of 9.1 million runners finished a race. By 2018, participation had fallen to 7.9 million, a significant reduction (although that total is still 58 percent higher than 2008 when there were 5 million). Those declines may eventually mean more competition and more consolidation among shoe brands.

Dicharry believes the future of running shoes will continue to involve personalization and customization, which he insists are possible even for the masses. Right now when you go into a running store, whether you're a 110-pound woman who runs marathons or a 205-pound man just trying to get in shape, you could wind up with the same model. Most shoes aren't commensurately tuned to match the body mass, gait, and running economy of an individual. If you're prescribing the same model to each person, Dicharry says, there's a good chance you're fitting one person with the equivalent of a bedroom slipper and the other with the equivalent of a brick. Could running shoes instead be tuned to a runner's individual mass, gait style, and comfort preferences, allowing the right amount of cushion, firmness, protection, and stability based on that runner's stride?

Dicharry suggests that instead of offering simply a neutral cushioned shoe or a stability shoe, a brand could instead offer a range of shoes with varying degrees of those qualities. If that brand created a base model with three different layers of cushioning foam—thin, medium, and thick—with known rebound characteristics, several dozen runners could be put into these models for wear-tests that measure the flex and foam deformity rate of each runner in each shoe and plot them on a regression curve that shows three speeds of runners in three weight ranges and where each runner fits on that curve.

For example, if you had baseline values for women runners who weigh 105 pounds, 125 pounds, and 145 pounds and who run a 7:30 mile pace, 8:45 mile pace, and 10:00 mile pace, you could check the chart and figure out which shoe they should be in.

"It's a math problem, and it's simple to do," Dicharry says. "There is a way to tune a certain model of a shoe within ranges and eliminate a lot of the misinformation out there now. I don't know why shoe companies aren't doing it." (A likely answer is that it would force a shoe brand to ditch its legacy models and years of marketing investment for what might seem like a homogenized product.)

Continued investment in developing "magic" shoes that reduce the metabolic cost of running may also be a fixture on the horizon. Nike, Hoka, New Balance, Saucony, and Brooks are all building shoes with carbon-fiber plates and superlight foams with the aim of improving efficiency—perhaps as much as 4 to 5 percent improvement. Significant for the average runner? Absolutely.

Hoka's Diard thinks that looking at innovation differently is the way of the future. "If you look at the evolution of running shoes compared to other products out there, not much has really changed over the past 30 years," he says. "A running shoe from 1980 and one from 2010 look very similar if you consider they both have layers of foam and rubber and textile. If you look at other sports equipment or cell phones or cars, the spectrum of variations is much greater. That suggests there is much more innovation ahead in running shoes."

One of the constants, Diard says, is that human anatomy won't evolve anytime soon, meaning our feet won't suddenly develop an opposable big toe to change how they interact with the ground.

"The foot is what it is; we can't change it," Diard says. "But we can change the interface between the foot and the ground, and that's what's important. If you look at a shoe purely as an extension of the foot, you limit yourself in your thinking. But when you look at it as a piece of equipment that can offer a dynamic blend of attributes—how it provides comfort, how it contributes to performance, how it interacts with terrain—then you start to push the boundaries of how shoes can be designed."

To extend Diard's point, what if shoe design were thought about in more radical terms? Is there a way to make running inherently more efficient, couple that with modern running shoes, and make humans exponentially faster and less prone to losing energy in every step?

A few brands have incorporated electronic sensors in shoes—notably the Adidas 1; the Nike+ system; and, most recently, the Altra Torin IQ and Under Armour's Connected line of shoes. The Torin IQ and Under Armour's HOVR Velociti 2 track numerous data points of a runner's stride (pace, distance, stride length, and cadence) that are relayed back to the runner via wearable technology (a smartwatch or a smartphone app) to cue form improvements in real time. Next, Under Armour hopes to incorporate the ability to monitor runners' blood pressure via their shoes. At the same time, new wearable technology products such as Stryd and RunScribe have emerged to track numerous gait efficiency data points no matter what shoe a runner is wearing.

Brands have also been tinkering with mechanical propulsion concepts. In 2013, Adidas debuted the Springblade, a shoe it said was six years in the making. In place of a foam midsole, the Springblade had 16 individually tuned, elastic polymer "blades" engineered to compress and release energy upon impact with the ground and during the push-off phase of a new stride—in a motion specific to the runner's footstrike and the surface below—with the intent of helping propel the runner forward. It was an interesting concept but an incomplete and flawed one. While springy, the shoes were also heavy, unstable, and clunky to run in.

Christian Freschi, an avid runner who owns an aeronautical design and production company in Toulouse, France, has taken mechanical propulsion even further. A few years ago, his start-up brand, ENKO Running, designed a mechanical running shoe with a twin shock-absorbing system designed to store energy upon impact and return it at the start of a new stride.

Like a traditional running shoe, the G4.1 has a mesh upper, standard lacing system, rubber toe bumper, and reinforced heel. But set off from the bottom of the shoe is a hinged mechanism that acts as midsole and outsole as the runner goes through a gait cycle. The company claims that the shoe reduces impact by 70 to 80 percent and lasts three to four times longer than a standard running shoe. And it's the world's first production-model running shoe that can be tuned to a runner's weight. The price? A cool $372. Although no validating science has been revealed, the shoes have been favorably reviewed by several media outlets and bloggers.

Another possible avenue takes cues from the vast changes in adaptive equipment used by Paralympic athletes. Dr. Alena Grabowski, a physiologist at the University of Colorado, studies the interaction of physiology and biomechanics during human locomotion—specifically how assistive mechanical devices, such as adaptive prostheses and exoskeleton systems, influence walking, running, hopping, and sprinting.

One of only a half-dozen researchers on the planet who specializes in studying lower-limb prostheses for runners, Grabowski, director of CU's Applied Biomechanics Laboratory, has dedicated her career to helping elite amputee athletes such as former South African sprinter Oscar Pistorius, aka the "Blade Runner," and German long jumper Marcus Rehm, aka the "Blade Jumper," address a controversial question with the potential to make or break athletic dreams: Should runners with prosthetic legs be able to compete against nonamputees?

Her research was instrumental in the case to allow Pistorius to be the first double-amputee runner to compete in the 2012 Olympics against able-bodied runners. Grabowski's efforts showed that Pistorius's "blade" prosthetics did not give him an unfair advantage over able-bodied runners because his prostheses pushed off with less force than a biological limb would (although many still argue that athletes such as Pistorius don't have to contend with lower-leg muscle fatigue, don't have to pump blood quite as far to their lower extremities, and carry less weight below the knee). While Pistorius didn't earn a medal in 2012, he helped South Africa earn a silver medal in the 4 × 400-meter relay at the 2011 IAAF World Championships and ran a double-amputee record of 45.07 for 400 meters while competing against able-bodied runners.

The next blade-enabled runner who could make Olympic headlines is American Blake Leeper, a 29-year-old sprinter who was born without legs below the knee.

The promising sprinter finished second to Pistorius in the 400 at the 2012 Paralympics in London and is currently training to become the second double amputee to run in the Olympics in 2020. But he, too, has needed to plead his case to the IAAF to show that his blades would not provide him with a competitive advantage.

I bumped into Leeper in 2018 at Grabowski's lab while I was sniffing around for Nike's top-secret ZoomX Vaporfly Next% shoes, which were quietly being tested at Kram and Hoogkamer's lab next door and would in 2019 supplant the Vaporfly 4% as the world's most efficient marathon shoe. Two months earlier, Leeper had run the fastest 400-meter dash ever run by a double amputee—clocking an eye-popping 44.42, a time that would have won the 2018 U.S. outdoor track championships and placed seventh at the 2016 Rio Olympics—with the aid of Ossur Flex-Foot Cheetah running blades.

As I watched him run on a treadmill at more than 25 miles per hour, his mechanics were fluid, efficient, and flowing. I captured it on slow-motion video, and when I watched the replay, I was amazed to see that his blades appeared to barely impact the treadmill deck while still producing a propulsive forward drive. In contrast to runners in shoes, there was no sloppiness or inefficient lateral rolling or settling to the deck in the way that Leeper's foot blades impacted the surface. Instead, it was a pure smoothness that continued up through the rest of his kinematic chain as his knees, thighs, hips, shoulders, and arms moved in perfect harmony. Because he was so efficient, he could run with more power and thus much faster.

I felt as though I were watching poetry in motion and wondered aloud whether what Leeper could do on blades could ever possibly be mimicked by a runner wearing shoes. That's the goal, Grabowski offered, but so far it's been rare to find a runner who moves with so little energy loss while wearing running shoes because a runner's foot interacts with the treadmill surface based on how it interacts first with the materials of the shoe. Leeper's interface was much simpler, which led me to suspect that his blades didn't give him an advantage as much as running shoes put most runners at a disadvantage.

It was a heady moment, especially watching as Leeper took off the blades after the workout in much the same way that a runner unlaces his or her shoes after a hard session. It all begged some fundamental questions: What *is* a running shoe? Isn't it something that we wear on our feet to provide cushion, support, traction, and propulsion to ultimately promote running efficiency? And isn't that the definition of giving ourselves a competitive advantage every time we lace up our shoes?

Along those lines, Grabowski is developing a new generation of prostheses—a type of blade—for the purpose of allowing able-bodied athletes to run significantly more efficiently. The contraptions are affixed to a runner's legs and feet like a mechanical boot, in much the way that a prosthesis fits over the stump of an amputee. They have springy blades on the bottom to help propel the runner forward and allow greater efficiency via a standard, albeit modified, running gait.

Grabowski admits that the initial prototype has many limitations— not the least of which is its weight. Each leg extension weighs about 38 ounces, more than four times the weight of a lightweight running shoe. Furthermore, it reduces the body's ability to move dynamically and eliminates one of its primary propulsion-accentuating movements: plantar flexion in the foot. But, at least hypothetically, it starts to create a scenario for understanding how running might become more efficient, even if is light years from being practical and even though the IAAF, the sanctioning body for competitive running, would likely never allow it.

"I'm not convinced that it's an advantage or that it's better," Grabowski says. "You lose sensory capability when you have something springy under your feet that you can't totally control or has stiffness. It's challenging to move in it, and balance is all over the place."

And comfort is a challenge, she says. For now, building prototypes, even if they are not realistic for running, is easier than designing a springy treadmill that could potentially return energy. Ultimately, she's interested in how runners can improve efficiency in various types of footwear, whether shod in traditional running shoes or in a newfangled prosthetic device.

"I never take for granted the fact that I can get up in the morning and go for a run without even thinking about it," says Grabowski, 45, who runs about 60 miles a week on the trails near Boulder. "I just want everyone to be able to move like I can."

Grabowski isn't the only one who has thought about that concept in a laboratory setting. A few years ago, Rezvan Nasiri, a graduate student at the Cognitive Systems Laboratory at the University of Tehran in Iran, was out on a training run when he realized how much energy he wasted each time one of his feet hit the ground. He began considering ways to harness the energy before it was lost.

He and fellow researchers began tinkering in the lab with ways to couple a runner's hips so that the energy created as one leg swings backward at the end of a stride could somehow be transferred to the other leg as it moves forward. Ultimately, the goal was to find a way to decrease the metabolic cost of running and a runner's muscular output.

The team developed a lightweight harness for a runner to wear around the waist. The device includes metal straps affixed to the runner's thighs just above the knee that are connected to a metal loop arching out of his or her lower back, creating a spring effect that gathers and transfers energy from one hip to the other while running.

They tested male runners on a treadmill, having them run 10 minutes at about 9 minutes per mile both with the device and without it. Running with the device proved to be much more efficient, decreasing a runner's energy cost by an average of 8 percent. That's a huge change, especially when compared to the 4 percent gains from the Nike Vaporfly 4% shoes that Eliud Kipchoge used to smash the marathon world record.

If nothing else, the experiment proves that it is possible to make runners more efficient through scientifically advanced accessories. But, just as with Grabowski's device, it begs the question of where to draw the line when it comes to running shoes. Where do the limits of human propulsion end and man-made technological advances—whether midsole foams, energy-saving carbon-fiber plates, or springs—take over?

"It's interesting, for sure," says Kram, who studied Nike's Vaporfly 4% and ZoomX Vaporfly Next% shoes and reviewed the University of Tehran study that was published in *IEEE Transactions on Neural Systems and Rehabilitation Engineering* in October 2018. "At a basic level, it's something that allows a runner to use their own muscular energy more effectively to run more efficiently. And that's one of the challenges that every running shoe manufacturer is looking at as it develops new models of performance-oriented shoes, too."

———

Running shoes have gone through a whirlwind of change, and there's no sign of it letting up. New materials, new construction techniques, new design paradigms, new brands, new sciences, and new trends have all played a role in shaping the shoes we're running in this year and make the shoes we ran in a decade ago—or even a year ago—seem antiquated and out-of-date. It's an ongoing cycle that won't cease as long as we're still running and brands are competing for sales.

While some long-standing industry stalwarts—Nike, Adidas, New Balance, Saucony, and Brooks—remain vibrant, other top brands—ASICS, Mizuno, and Newton, to name a few—have stumbled in recent years, and some—Pearl Izumi and Patagonia—have stopped making running shoes entirely. Meanwhile Arc'teryx, Hoka, On, Altra, 361° USA, Salming, Skechers, and Topo have burst on the scene with new ideas, while Reebok and Diadora are back with a vengeance. Along the way, Nike purchased Converse, Adidas acquired Reebok, Columbia bought Montrail, Deckers acquired Hoka, and Descente bought Inov-8.

Amid industry consolidation, advances in technology, and changes in the running population, one thing has remained the same: Innovation for both fashion and function continues to drive excitement among performance-oriented athletes and recreational runners alike.

In 2018, Inov-8 unveiled two models with outsole rubber made from graphene, a strong and lightweight derivative of graphite. Lab tests have shown that the new Graphene Grip outsole rubber on the Mudclaw G 260 and the Terraultra G 260 is more than 50 percent stronger, 50 percent more elastic, and 50 percent harder-wearing than Inov-8's previous outsole materials. In practical terms, that means lighter, more flexible, more adhesive, and more durable outsoles—and potentially trail running shoes that will hold up considerably longer.

Adidas continues to push innovative "woke" concepts with its FutureCraft Loop, a model it calls the world's first 100 percent recyclable performance running shoe. In 2019, Adidas plans to produce 11 million pairs of shoes containing recycled ocean plastic from plastic waste collected on beaches, remote islands, and coastal communities.

"What happens to your shoes after you've worn them out? You throw them away—except there is no away," says Eric Liedtke, executive board member at Adidas responsible for global brands. "There are only landfills and incinerators and ultimately an atmosphere choked with excess carbon, or oceans filled with plastic waste. The next step is to end the concept of 'waste' entirely. Our dream is that you can keep wearing the same shoes over and over again."

Meanwhile, Nike is developing a shoe that it claims will greatly reduce the rate of common overuse injuries. "For forty years, a high percentage of runners have gotten hurt. We think we can help change that," said Scott Gravatt, Nike's specialty running sales director, explaining Project Fearless, as the project has been known internally, to a gathering of retailers in June 2019. "We believe through innovation and technology and science, we can completely solve for injuries. And yes, it's a big, ambitious goal."

The shoe, which is expected to debut in January 2020, will be called the Epic React Pro Infinity and will have 33 percent more cushioning than previous editions of the Epic React Pro. The shoe has been constructed with a very lightweight and resilient foam and what's known as *generative design technology*—which utilizes artificial intelligence to mimic nature's evolutionary approach to design—to create an outsole pattern that can better facilitate a wider range of footstrike patterns. While details were still sketchy at the time this book went to press, it sounds as though the model offers a whole new way to think about stability shoe design.

The project is ambitious, to be sure, but it is not without a scientific foundation. Over the past several years, the University of British Columbia in Vancouver has put hundreds of runners through prototype versions of the shoe and compared the results to those of other stability shoes, helping Nike refine a shoe that will help keep runners aligned with the natural movements of their own running gait.

If you're skeptical, it's understandable. The injury rate has remained the same for more than 40 years—with no brand, shoe, or common design understanding making a difference in reducing it—yet now Nike has figured it out? My first inclination is to roll my eyes, wait to read the reports, run in the shoe, and see how it works after dozens of runs. But, as Gravatt reminded the group of retailers, Nike was greeted with plenty of doubters and skeptics when it unveiled the original Vaporfly Elite—that is, until all of the records were broken.

Whether this shoe lives up to its promise of drastically reducing injuries remains to be seen. But if nothing else, it's a sign that the more things change, the more they remain the same. Nike's earnest endeavors and continuing push for innovation, mixed with a swirl of marketing pixie dust, is what the running shoe industry has always been built upon.

═══

One of the world's newest running shoe brands, Enda, has emerged in an unlikely place in perhaps the most modern way possible. Founded in 2015 on the heels of a Kickstarter crowd-funding campaign, the brand was started by Kenyan Navalayo Osembo and American Weldon Kennedy as a social change enterprise organized on the premise of sharing Kenyan running culture with runners around the world while also creating sustainable jobs and social benefits for Kenyans. Its first model, the Iten, a trainer/racer named after Kenya's distance-running capital, was designed and manufactured in Nairobi and eschewed fancy technology in favor of a back-to-basics, lightweight, low-to-the-ground design that embraces a runner's natural movements. Its second model, a lightweight, softly cushioned high-mileage trainer called the Lapatet, debuted in the spring of 2019, and the majority have been sold to runners in Kenya and the United States.

Enda's story is a reminder that running shoes aren't what set us apart; rather, they're what bring us together. Running is a primal act that people in all cultures all around the world engage in, even if in different ways for different reasons. And while nearly everything about running shoes may have changed through the years—how they look, what they're made of, how we buy them—the way they inspire us has remained the same.

For years, Brooks has promoted "Run Happy!" as part of its messaging, which has less to do with its shoes than with the emotional experiences they provide, says Brooks president Jim Weber. "A running shoe is a tool that enables you to get the best experience from your run. And because of that, for many runners their favorite shoes carry the glow of their favorite runs. Running makes you feel good. Running makes you feel happy. That's where the emotional connection we have with running shoes comes in because they're connected to your run and your experiences and the meaning that carries in your life."

Certainly running shoes have been the tool that has helped some exceptional individuals—Bannister, Samuelson, Bolt, Flannagan, and Kipchoge, to name a few—do amazing things by running fast and, in doing so, uplifting and inspiring the world. But running shoes have also helped average Joes and Janes accomplish their own amazing feats and uplift themselves and others in the process. For some, that might mean achieving a faster PR; for others, it's a first-time finish. Or it's a journey to regain a healthy lifestyle, lose weight, or raise money to fight cancer.

Running shoes are no longer about the singular pursuit of just running—they are a vehicle for self-expression, footwear that is meant to feel good and make you feel good. While performance-oriented innovations will continue to help push the limits of human achievement, equally important are advancements that improve the fit, feel, ride, and yes, even the look of shoes for everyday runners and keep us on the move.

So is it more important to be inspired to run fast or to run inspired? Maybe it doesn't matter as long as you're lacing up your shoes and running with passion. Your kicks are simply the vehicle, taking you wherever and however you choose to go.

APPENDIX A
Getting the Most out of Your Running Shoes

1. Get the right size.

The most important aspect of picking out a new pair of running shoes is getting a pair that matches the relative size of your foot. But understand that not all size 9s are the same for every brand. Shoes vary in size and shape based on the "last" that was used to make the shoe. Some are longer, some are shorter, and all have a different interior shape.

2. Get the right shape.

Once you've found a shoe that is the right length, the next key is ensuring that the shoe matches the shape and volume of your foot. A shoe mismatched to your foot's volume could fit too loosely or too tightly in the heel, arch, or toe box, especially when your foot is in motion during a run.

3. Understand your gait.

How a shoe fits and feels when you try it on is only part of the process. How it fits and feels when your foot is in motion might be an entirely different situation, depending on how your foot moves and flexes when it runs. It's likely that your gait pattern varies between your left and right side based on how each foot hits the ground, rotates, and flexes. Those changes lead to differences in how your ankle, knee, and hip joints move as you're running. Many running specialty stores offer basic gait analyses, and in-depth examinations are available from sports medicine clinics and physical therapy facilities. If you need help in a pinch, the Stride Lab app is a useful resource.

4. Get stronger.

Whether you're a longtime runner or just getting started, you should always be working on your form-specific strength. Doing form and strength drills and exercises to bolster your foot, lower leg, and core strength helps reduce the chance of repetitive overuse injuries. Every runner has a stronger and weaker side, so it's important to work on weaknesses to approach equilibrium. Good exercises for runners include box jumps and walking lunges for leg power and hip extension; burpees and planks for core strength; clam shells for hip strength; and single-leg squats, one-legged heel raises, pistol squats, and pedestal poses for developing balance and agility.

5. Heel drop matters.

The minimalism movement stressed having a low heel-to-toe height offset (or heel drop). While only a few brands offer "zero-drop," or level, platforms, heel heights are generally lower than they were in the past. While the standard heel-toe offset of 12 mm still exists in a few models, most modern running shoes fall into the 4 mm to 10 mm offset range. Wearing a shoe with a significantly different offset will change how your feet connect to the ground and alter your gait, so transition wisely and slowly. If you can't find the heel-drop figure printed on the shoe's insole or hang tag at a retailer, look for it on the brand's website.

6. Develop a quiver of shoes.

Don't run in the same pair of shoes every day; instead, rotate between different models depending on the type of running you're doing and the surface you're running on. For example, you might wear a cushier pair of shoes for longer runs or recovery runs and a lighter, firmer shoe for faster workouts such as tempo runs, fartlek runs, and intervals. Rotating shoes during the week will not only extend the life of each pair but also engage the micromuscles in your feet and lower legs differently and help you avoid overuse injuries.

7. Wear your running shoes only for running.

You might be tempted to wear your running shoes as casual wear. Don't do it. Wearing your running shoes as everyday shoes or for walking the dog or mowing the lawn will soon change the wear patterns of your shoes, reduce the life of the shoes, and ultimately alter your gait.

8. Untie and retie your shoes.

Don't take off your running shoes by stepping on the back of one shoe with the other and pulling your foot out without untying the shoe. Not only does it strain muscles in your feet, but it stretches aspects of the shoe. The only thing worse than removing your shoes without untying them is putting them back on without untying them. It may seem like a time-saver, but if you put them on with the laces still tied, you'll strain your foot to squeeze it back in and impair the shoe's shape.

9. Care for your shoes.

Running shoes are only as good as you treat them. Keep your shoes indoors but not in your car or garage, where extreme hot or cold temperatures can have a temporary or permanent effect on how the shoe performs. Cleaning your shoes by hand after running through mud will ensure that the shoe's traction and flex pattern are optimal the next time you wear them. Speed the process of drying wet shoes by stuffing them with newspapers or dry washcloths or briefly setting them in the sun, but never put shoes in a dryer.

10. Retire your shoes.

Most running shoes will hold up for 300 to 500 miles of running before they need to be retired. But the foam midsoles, synthetic fabrics, and rubber outsoles can start to break down after about 200 miles, which can create problems. Running too long in a pair of shoes can lead to changes in your gait, less protection for your feet, and general discomfort or overuse injuries.

APPENDIX B
Donate Your Old Running Shoes

I wear-test hundreds of pairs of running shoes every year, which means I am lucky enough to have an extensive quiver of shoes in my garage. Unfortunately, it also means I have to discard a lot of shoes. Some are badly worn out, but some have less than 100 miles on them.

I never throw old shoes in the trash. That would be disrespectful to the experiences I have had in them and to the hundreds of workers who helped build each pair. More importantly, it would be wasteful because there's someone somewhere who could benefit from getting them. I typically donate them to One World Running, a Boulder, Colorado, organization that collects used shoes and distributes them to people in need in the United States, Central America, Africa, and the Caribbean.

The volunteer organization was started in 1986 by running journalist Mike Sandrock after he returned from a trip to Cameroon, West Africa. He had noticed that many of the runners from Cameroon ran barefoot, and so Sandrock convinced a group of Boulder's elite runners—including Lorraine Moller, Steve Jones, and Arturo Barrios—to donate shoes that he could ship to West Africa.

For more than 30 years, a group of volunteers in Boulder has collected, washed, and sent more than 50,000 pairs of shoes, as well as T-shirts and shorts, to athletes and children around the world. The project has grown, with shoes and athletic equipment now being sent from all around the United States.

A few years ago, I joined One World Running on a service trip to help deliver shoes to runners in Baracoa, Cuba. Watching an appreciative runner lace up a pair of my old shoes before going out for a run with him was one of the most gratifying things I've ever experienced.

"Sharing, giving back, and helping others are vital elements of any community, and especially within the running community," Sandrock says. "Donating shoes offers the chance for people—especially young children and teens—to experience the same freedom, joy, and community we get when we are fortunate enough to buy new running shoes from a running store."

Do you have shoes you are ready to give up? Worn-out sneakers can be put to good use resurfacing tracks and playgrounds, while like-new shoes could be life-changing to those without. Here are organizations that will give your shoes a new life so they don't have to wind up in a landfill.

One World Running

This nonprofit was one of the first organizations to collect shoes and athletic clothing for people in need in Africa, Central America, and the Caribbean. **oneworldrunning.com**

Give Your Sole

Give Your Sole collects used athletic shoes at races and distributes them to those in need around the United States. **giveyoursole.org**

Soles4Souls

Soles4Souls says it has delivered more than 19 million pairs of shoes in 125 countries since 2004. It collects new and gently used shoes for relief efforts and microenterprise business efforts in Haiti, Central and South America, and Africa. **soles4souls.org**

Share Your Soles

With 1.8 million pairs of shoes delivered to date, this Chicago-based organization collects gently worn shoes in Illinois, Indiana, New York, Pennsylvania, and Arizona for worldwide redistribution. **shareyoursoles.org**

Shoe4Africa

In addition to collecting used shoes for distribution in Africa, this New York nonprofit raised money to help build the first public children's hospital in Kenya, a modern, 200-bed facility in Eldoret. **shoe4africa.org**

Nike Reuse-a-Shoe

Worn-out shoes are recycled into a material called Nike Grind and used to surface running tracks, playgrounds, and indoor and outdoor athletic courts, with nearly 30 million pairs repurposed since 1990. **nike.com/help/a/recycle-shoes**

Acknowledgments

My passion for running shoes started when I was a kid and since then has seemingly woven its way through the fabric of my entire life. There are thousands of runners, shoe geeks, running retailers, shoe designers, scientists, and academics, as well as various marketing and PR people and executives, who have influenced my understanding of and zeal for running shoes. I would like to thank and acknowledge every one of them, but the list would be too long to print here. I have taken much from their individual expertise, passion, and interest in running shoes and am grateful for the time, patience, and miles they have afforded me.

I would like to thank the immensely talented staff at VeloPress for their belief, direction, and diligent work on all aspects of this book. Specifically, I am grateful to editor Casey Blaine for championing this book from the start and then deploying her considerable smarts, clever wit, and exceptional wordsmithery to find coherence in what began as an impassioned but disorderly jumble of ideas.

I am greatly appreciative of the copyediting work of Connie Oehring and the production prowess of Sarah Gorecki for cleaning up my fat-fingered typos and prepping this book for launch. A big thanks goes to creative director Vicki Hopewell and photographer Scott Clark for the art direction of the cover, which I love as much as the day the photo shoot happened. I am thankful for the design work of Karen Matthes and the additional photography of Scott Draper; the marketing, publicity, and distribution expertise of Kara Mannix and Dave Trendler; and the publishing leadership of both Renee Jardine and Ted Costantino. Having formerly shared part of an office with VeloPress as editor-in-chief of *Competitor* magazine, I have to say thank you again for putting up with the massive, teetering piles of running shoe boxes that turned the office into my personal warehouse. The essence of all that mess has been adroitly recycled into the pages of this book.

I would like to thank former cross-country and track teammates John Byrne, Mark Ruscin, Rich Kolasa, Cully Welter, Chris Inch, and Brian Haas for keeping me inspired, especially when I was starting to slow down. Big props go to friends, professional colleagues, and frequent running partners Jason Smith, Mario Fraioli, Adam Chase, Jonathan Beverly, and Mike Sandrock for sharing their zest for running and shoes and putting up with my crazy caffeine binges.

I would have never been here without the love and support of my late parents, who appreciated and enjoyed my passion for running and continually being on the move in my formative years. Mom, thanks for driving me to Competitive Foot that rainy day to get those Adidas Oregons; Dad, thanks for going out of your way to make every one of my races that you possibly could. And things probably would have never come to this if it weren't for my older brother, who was the first to help me understand the thrill of running fast in a good pair of sneakers—and to this day, I've never beaten him in a race. It might all have started as I watched him run down Hillside Drive wearing those black-and-gray Nike Yankees.

Index

Rodgers, Bill, 23, 37
Rudy, Frank, 34, 41
Runner's Corner, 87, 116, 118, 121, 123
Runners Roost, 45–46
Runner's World, 37–39, 207
running
    booms, 5, 32, 40, 49
    industry, 4–5, 13, 44, 50, 229
    race participation, 5, 56, 98, 220
    world records, 170, 177–178
Running Insight, 3
Running Rewired (Dicharry), 91
Running Times, 23, 128

Salazar, Alberto, 26–27, 181
sales. *See* retail
Salomon, 108, 128–129, 214–215, 217
Samuelson, Joan Benoit, 26, 56
Saucony, 80, 154
science
    advancements in, 81, 93, 108
    biomechanics, 106, 107, 110, 161, 224
    versus marketing claims, 94, 95
    published studies, 78, 100, 103, 178,
        181, 190, 191, 228
    truths about running shoes, 125
shoe factories,
    Asian, 143–147, 161, 162, 166–167
    automation, 167
    New Balance, 162–167
    New England area, 160, 161, 162
    Nike, 161–162
    in Oregon, 160
shoes. *See also* minimalism
    aesthetics *versus* performance, 57–59,
        61, 63, 72, 96, 202
    articulated toes, 43
    brand popularity, 44, 61, 80, 229
    carbon-fiber designs, 170, 182,
        185–191, 196
    caring for, 235–236
    casual wear, 50–51, 54, 220, 235
    collections, 22–24, 40

comfort, 10, 27, 31, 57, 106, 110
conception, 149, 153–155, 157
cross-trainers, 54–55
cushioning, 27, 30–34, 41, 51, 91,
    117, 125, 183–185
custom, 95, 108, 201–210, 212–218
decoupled outsoles, 43
development, 157
donating, 237–239
electronic sensors in, 222–223
emotional connection with, 25, 155,
    232
energy cost, 184, 188, 189, 227
energy return, 73–75, 182, 183–185,
    186
epic fails, 174–176
evolution, 22, 25–29, 44, 219–220
feedback on, 155
fitting, 8–11, 20, 106–107, 233
future directions, 220–222
handmade, 207, 209–210
heel counters, 27
heel-toe drop, 75, 81–82, 126, 234
and injuries, 90, 91–92, 95, 97
innovations, 31–37, 58–59, 92–93,
    105, 141, 157, 222
launching new models, 157
lifespan, 150, 236
midsoles, 30, 31, 32, 33, 42
model changes, 150–155
motion-control, 34, 58, 92, 103, 122,
    125
neutral, 92, 103, 123, 125
old models, 3, 14, 17, 19
outsoles, 34, 41, 43, 229
personalized, 95, 108, 201–210,
    212–218
prices, 3, 37, 158–159, 217, 218
prototypes, 55, 95, 157, 185, 187, 191
racing flats, 26, 27, 99, 170, 182
rankings, 38–40
recyclable, 229
retiring, 150, 236

About the Author

Brian Metzler has run more than 75,000 miles in his life, competing in every distance from 50 meters to 100 miles. He's raced to the top of the Willis (Sears) Tower in Chicago, run a marathon on the Great Wall of China, crisscrossed the Grand Canyon on several Rim-to-Rim-to-Rim runs, competed in ultradistance trail runs and Ironman triathlons, and regularly raced with donkeys in Colorado. He has run in more than 1,500 pairs of running shoes while conducting wear-test reviews and reports for *Trail Runner, Men's Journal, Runner's World, Competitor, Running Times, Outside,* and *GearJunkie.* During that time, he's developed a critical outlook, utilized discerning feet, and suffered numerous injuries—all in the name of trying out the latest and greatest shoes that come to market. Metzler was the founding editor and associate publisher of *Trail Runner* and *Adventure Sports* magazines and editor-in-chief of *Competitor* magazine and Competitor.com. He is the author of *Running Colorado's Front Range* and the coauthor of *Natural Running* and *Run Like a Champion.* For more, visit BrianMetzler.com.

VISIT
VELOPRESS.COM

for more on running, cycling, triathlon,
swimming, ultrarunning,
yoga, recovery, mental training,
health and fitness, nutrition, and diet.

SAVE $10
ON YOUR FIRST ORDER

Shop with us and use coupon code
VPFIRST during checkout.